WINNING YOUR PERSONAL INJURY CLAIM

Third Edition

Evan K. Aidman
Attorney at Law

SPHINX® PUBLISHING
AN IMPRINT OF SOURCEBOOKS, INC.®
NAPERVILLE, ILLINOIS

Third Edition: 2005
Second Printing: February, 2005

Published by: **Sphinx® Publishing, An Imprint of Sourcebooks, Inc.®**

<u>Naperville Office</u>
P.O. Box 4410
Naperville, Illinois 60567-4410
630-961-3900
Fax: 630-961-2168
www.sourcebooks.com
www.SphinxLegal.com

This publication is designed to provide accurate and authoritative information in regard to the subject matter covered. It is sold with the understanding that the publisher is not engaged in rendering legal, accounting, or other professional service. If legal advice or other expert assistance is required, the services of a competent professional person should be sought.

From a Declaration of Principles Jointly Adopted by a Committee of the
American Bar Association and a Committee of Publishers and Associations

This product is not a substitute for legal advice.

Disclaimer required by Texas statutes.

Library of Congress Cataloging-in-Publication Data
Aidman, Evan K., 1958-
  Winning your personal injury claim / by Evan Aidman.-- 3rd ed.
    p. cm.
  Includes index.
  ISBN 1-57248-473-X (alk. paper)
  1. Personal injuries--United States--Popular works. I. Title.
KF1257.Z9A38 2004
346.7303'23--dc22
                                    2005004847

Printed and bound in the United States of America.

VP — 10 9 8 7 6 5 4 3 2

Dedication

To Mom, Jeanne Whitehouse Aidman,
and to Ayala, Ilana, and Chana Baila, with love.

Acknowledgements

Thanks to Frances Aidman Conaway for her skillful editing of my writing. Thanks to Michael P. Boyle, Esquire, for his input on the section on Social Security Disability. (Mr. Boyle's email address is mpboyle@infi.net.) Thanks to Robert N. Hunn, Esquire, for helping me with the Medical Malpractice section. (Mr. Hunn's email address is rnh@kgrs.com.)

Contents

Preface . . . . **xi**

Personal Injury Litigation—Then and Now
The Law is Dynamic
Sample Forms and Worksheets
Litigation Savvy

Introduction . . . . **xvii**

The Attorney
Injury Classification and Treatment
Damages
Demand Letter and Settlement
The Lawsuit
Discovery and Trial

Chapter 1: At the Scene of an Accident **1**

After an Accident
Car Accident Checklist
Fall-Down Accident Checklist
Emergency Room Treatment
Medical Treatment Worksheet
Beware of the Friendly Insurance Adjuster
Do Not Sign Anything
Remember the Deadline

Chapter 2: Handling Your Case Without a Lawyer **17**
    Handling Your Claim
    Sample Opening Letter to Insurance Company by Attorney
    Sample Opening Letter to Defendant
    Questions for Depositions, Statements, and Trial
    Sample Medical Records Requests
    Handling Your Lawsuit

Chapter 3: The Personal Injury Attorney and You **45**
    Finding a Personal Injury Attorney
    The Initial Consultation
    Sample New Client Letter
    The Attorney's Fee Agreement
    Beware of Costs
    Dissatisfaction with Attorneys
    Changing Lawyers
    Keeping Your Case Active

Chapter 4: Various Kinds of Injury Cases **63**
    Injuries to Children
    Fall-Down Accidents (Slip-and-Falls)
    Dog Bites
    Legal Malpractice
    Food Poisoning Cases
    Workers' Compensation
    Social Security Disability
    Products Liability
    Intentional Injuries
    Psychological Injuries

Chapter 5: Medical Malpractice **83**
    Determining Whether You Have a Case
    Hiring an Attorney
    The Nuts and Bolts of a Medical Malpractice Case
    The Fee Agreement
    Getting Started

Expert Witnesses
Nuisance Value
Valuing the Claim
Settling the Claim
How to Help Your Attorney
The Medical Malpractice Crisis

Chapter 6: Special Medical Concerns **97**
Choosing Your Health-Care Provider
Physical Therapy
Good Injuries
Keeping Track of Your Treatment

Chapter 7: Damages **101**
Placing a Monetary Value on an Injury
Issues Affecting the Monetary Value
Injury Severity
Monetary Assessment

Chapter 8: The Settlement Process **113**
Settlement Demand Letter
Sample Settlement Demand Letters—Represented by Attorney
Settlement Offer
Settlement Strategy
Finalizing Settlement
Sample General Release
Alternate Dispute Resolution

Chapter 9: The Lawsuit Process **133**
Statutes of Limitations
Choice of Trials
Choice of Venue
Post-Filing Battles

Chapter 10: The Discovery Process **141**
Interrogatories and the Request for Production of Documents
Depositions

The Defense Medical Examination
Sample Client Letter: Defense Medical Examination

Chapter 11: The Trial. 151
Selecting the Jury
Opening Statements
Your Testimony
Medical Testimony
Damages
Causation
The Defense Case
Objections
Closing Argument
Jury Instructions and Deliberations
The Verdict
Posttrial Motions
The Appeal
Collecting from an Uninsured Defendant
Online Personal Injury Settlements

Chapter 12: Insurance Fraud and Other Problems 181
Improper Insurance Practices
Ambulance Chasers

Glossary 185

Appendix A: Sample Forms 195

Appendix B: Checklists and Worksheets 265

Index 279

About the Author 283

Preface

The most common complaint against personal injury attorneys is that they do not communicate with their clients. Again and again individuals complain that their lawyer will not return their telephone calls. When this starts to occur, you become anxious as your questions go unanswered. The personal injury litigation process is an extremely complicated and emotionally charged affair. You need accurate information and clarification on the myriad of issues determining if it is legitimate and real. I hope this book answers many of those questions and puts to rest many of the anxieties associated with this process. If your lawyer fails to answer your questions or clarify your case, this book may help you get his or her attention.

PERSONAL INJURY LITIGATION— THEN AND NOW

Everyone these days has an opinion about personal injury litigation. Many people feel that the right to sue for injuries should be severely limited in hopes that insurance costs will be brought down. Others feel that this right should not be so limited. They fear that legislation enacted to restrict the right to sue will make big business, the insurance industry, and medical practitioners less accountable to the public. They also fear the loss of financial compensation for injuries caused by a negligent or careless act. The only constants seem to be an interest in the debate and an interest in trials.

The insurance companies and their allies—big business and medical associations—have very skillfully manipulated public opinion in the last decade. Who has not heard the anecdotes about runaway jury awards? The results of this well-orchestrated campaign have been dramatic. The average plaintiff can now expect lower settlement offers, lower arbitration awards and jury verdicts, longer delays before resolution of the claim, and more extensive investigations into the claim by the insurance company and its lawyers.

There was a time when the garden-variety car accident or slip-and-fall case generally settled within two months after the plaintiff completed medical treatment. The insurance company multiplied the number of months of treatment by some dollar figure and made a very generous settlement offer.

A gradual shift away from quick and easy settlements of personal injury cases began to occur in the mid-90's. In the last few years, it has only gotten worse for plaintiffs and their lawyers.

It is true that some claims have been exaggerated, and should be dealt with appropriately. Unfortunately, those who pursue their claims legitimately often get tarred with the same brush. It is as if a personal injury plaintiff walks into court with a presumption that the claim is not legitimate in some way, and then has to rebut this presumption.

In almost every case, skillful defense lawyers can find a way to make the plaintiff look bad. No case is perfect. Perhaps the plaintiff has had prior accidents or has an underlying degenerative physical condition that might be at least a partial cause of his or her pain. Many jurors and arbitrators are simply looking for *anything* to use to return a very low award or to find in favor of the defendant outright.

Because of this, plaintiff's lawyers have to be much more careful about the cases they accept. The plaintiff's lawyer generally pays the legal costs of the case up front and only gets paid at the successful conclusion of the case. Because of this, it is hard to find a lawyer to take on cases that are not strong, both in terms of liability and damages.

Only relatively small cases are settled these days prior to suit being filed. The only way an insurance company can do a complete investigation of a case is by subpoenaing records from the plaintiff's past and by taking the plaintiff's deposition. Since subpoenas and depositions are not available before a suit is filed, insurance companies make only *low ball* offers in all but smaller cases.

The companies assume that the subpoenas and depositions will turn up information that can be used to diminish the value of the case. Very frequently they are correct in this assumption.

For example, if a subpoena produces records showing a related preexisting medical condition, this drives down the settlement value of the case. It makes business sense to assume the worst about a plaintiff until an exhaustive investigation satisfies the insurer of the relative merit of the claim.

It is important to understand these new realities so that you will have a realistic view of your case. You cannot expect a quick settlement and you cannot expect your lawyer to work miracles.

As the plaintiff, you have a target drawn on your back. It is almost as if you are going on trial when you become a plaintiff in a personal injury claim. Juries, arbitration panels, judges, and insurance companies intensely scrutinize a plaintiff's behaviors and words. This is true on issues involving both liability and damages.

Unless you and your case are squeaky clean, you can expect a long and possibly difficult legal battle. That is the new reality, and I do not expect it to change for the better any time soon.

THE LAW IS DYNAMIC

In this book, I examine every aspect of personal injury litigation, from car insurance choices to jury trials, and beyond. The personal injury laws vary from state to state. Much of the information presented involves *general principles of law*. The law in your state may be different. Nevertheless, there is much uniformity throughout the states regarding personal injury litigation. Most of the information in this book can be used by personal injury litigants in any state. You may have to refer to local sources for the law or practice that applies to your particular situation.

One of the beauties of of the law is that it is dynamic and ever-changing. The law is flexible enough to accommodate a changing world. When the first automobile accident lawsuit was filed, the judge was not deterred by the fact that there were no automobile laws—the legal logic of horse-and-buggy cases was used. Similarly, when new technologies cause injuries in the future, the law will be flexible enough to accommodate them.

The federal and state legislatures are constantly passing new laws that apply to personal injury litigation. The courts rule every day on disputes that require interpretation of new laws, as well as laws that have been on the books for many years. When a court decides a dispute, the court's ruling becomes precedent for the future. In other words, the interpretations that the judges dispense become the laws by which future litigants can be guided. Because the law is ever-changing and growing, you should keep in mind that you may have legal rights of which you are unaware, but that an attorney could point out to you. Therefore, in all but the simplest cases, you would be well-advised to consult with a lawyer concerning the law applicable to your case. (I do not recommend that you rely on this book alone. My words to you are here as a guide and a starting point only.)

SAMPLE FORMS AND WORKSHEETS

The next thing to remember is that a book that covers the law for the entire nation, or even for an entire state, cannot possibly include every procedural difference of every jurisdiction. The sample forms provided are general in nature, but are designed to give a good idea of the type of form that will be needed in most locations. Nonetheless, keep in mind that your state, county, or judge may have a requirement, or use a form, that is not included in this book.

You should not necessarily expect to be able to get all of the information and resources you need solely from within the pages of this book. This book will serve as your guide, giving you specific information whenever possible and helping you find out what you will need to know.

Before using the forms in a book like this, you should check with your court clerk to see if there are any local rules of which you should be aware, or local forms you will need to use. Often, such forms will require the same information as the forms in the book, and are merely laid out differently or use slightly different language. They will sometimes require additional information.

LITIGATION SAVVY

Americans crave insight into trials, trial lawyers, and legal conflict. Personal injury litigation, however, encompasses much more, and the term "litigation" creates some degree of confusion. Litigation involves far more than just the trial of a legal conflict. It also extends beyond pretrial activities, such as depositions and the discovery process. Personal injury litigation begins the moment the accident occurs. Every word that is exchanged and every thought that is processed thereafter plays a part in the ultimate event—the settlement or trial of a personal injury case. The skillful trial lawyer begins litigating, that is, crafting ideas that will work toward a successful resolution of the case, from the very first contact with the client. Anything less is lazy lawyering (perhaps even malpractice).

The litigation savvy you acquire from this book will enable you to ask your lawyer sophisticated questions about your case. This may well trigger interest in you and your case. It is inexcusable for your lawyer to ignore your calls or to back-burner your case. However, today's overworked, burnt-out personal injury lawyer may do just that unless you can set yourself apart from his or her other clients.

If you would like to contact me about this book or your personal injury case, you may reach me at:

Evan K. Aidman

326 W. Lancaster Avenue
Suite 200
Ardmore, PA 19003
610-642-7676
610-642-7707 (fax)
info@legalaidman.com
www.legalaidman.com

Introduction

If you have read this book before the occurrence of an accident, you are prepared to handle the all-important events that occur at the scene of the accident. For this overview, assume that you have been in a car accident—your claim begins at the very moment the accident occurs, and in some cases, long before that. If the accident was caused by faulty design, manufacture, or maintenance of the vehicle, this would have been a condition that existed before the accident.

However, if you are simply dealing with the average fender-bender, the first event of significance will be the accident itself. What you should look for, what you should and should not say, what you should ask the other driver, how you should deal with eyewitnesses and the police, and so on, are discussed in detail in Chapter 1.

You may want to keep the checklist of what to do after an auto accident in your glove compartment. (see p.266.) Checklist 1 is a worksheet that you can photocopy for this purpose. You should try to fill it out once you have collected your thoughts. This assumes that you were not rendered unconscious by the accident. If that happens, obviously many of the *do's* and *do not do's* mentioned in Chapter 1 will be difficult to control. Finally, keep a disposable camera in the car so that you can take scene-of-the-accident photographs. (Beware that heat can affect the film.)

THE ATTORNEY

Chapters 2 and 3 address issues concerning the hiring of a personal injury attorney. They should also help with several, very crucial decisions. First, you will have to decide whether to hire a lawyer—at all. Second, you will have to decide which lawyer to hire. Third, you will have to decide how to negotiate a fee agreement with the lawyer you hire. In Chapter 3, you will find a description of the information you should bring with you to the first meeting. (The issues involved in firing your lawyer, hiring a new one, and how to keep your lawyer on top of your case are also addressed in Chapter 3.)

This book will not give the unrepresented individual all of the legal expertise needed to go up against an experienced insurance defense lawyer. If you want to fight on a truly even playing field, you will need to hire an experienced plaintiff's *personal injury (PI) lawyer.* Even so, this book can help you whether you wish to go at it alone or if you decide to hire a lawyer.

The confidence you gain from reading this book can make the difference in your case. Outward confidence is always crucial in litigation. The insurance claims representative and their lawyers can sense desperation, fear, and naïveté. They will not hesitate to exploit their advantages over the unprepared litigant.

INJURY CLASSIFICATION AND TREATMENT
Chapter 4 describes the various kinds of injury cases. Chapter 5 looks specifically at medical malpractice cases. If you have been injured in a car accident or a fall down accident, by a defective product, a negligent doctor, vicious dog, or tainted food, or on the job, you will want to check out Chapters 4 and 5.

The doctor you select to treat your injuries is vitally important—both for your physical health and for the viability of your personal injury case. See Chapter 6 for a detailed discussion of medical treatment.

DAMAGES
If you decide to pursue a claim against the other person's insurance company without a lawyer, you will need to know a great deal about the concept of *damages.* Damages is a legal term encompassing the losses you suffered because of the accident. Damages include the amount of your property damage, medical bills, lost wages, lost earning capacity, pain and suffering, emotional trauma, and any other losses that are directly related to the accident. Damages are discussed in Chapters 4, 7, and 11.

DEMAND LETTER AND SETTLEMENT

When you have finished your medical treatment, you will need to gather all of the documentation relating to your damages. This includes:

◆ photographs of your injuries and property damage;

◆ the property damage appraisal;

◆ all of your medical bills and reports;

◆ a wage loss statement from your employer;

◆ a disability statement from your doctor with regard to your lost time from work; and,

◆ any other proof of your losses and damages.

You will need to prepare a letter to the person from whom you are seeking to recover damages, in which you fully describe your losses and damages. This is most often the other person's insurance company. You must forward all of the documentary proof mentioned with that letter. The settlement process is discussed in great detail in Chapter 8.

THE LAWSUIT

If you are not satisfied with the insurance company's settlement negotiations, the next step is to actually file a lawsuit. In almost every case it is in the best interest of a plaintiff to hire an attorney at this point. If you wish to continue to litigate your personal injury claim on your own, Chapter 9 will help you become familiar with the process of actually filing a lawsuit.

DISCOVERY AND TRIAL

Chapter 10 explores the all-important discovery process. In this chapter, you will find most of what you need in order to handle interrogatories, request for production of documents, depositions, and the independent medical examination. Chapter 11 takes you through the trial itself. It is during the discovery stage of litigation and trial where unrepresented individuals are at their biggest disadvantage. Please be sure to read Chapters 10 and 11 very carefully if you are unrepresented. These chapters are also good reading for those who have retained counsel. The knowledge you gain will help you ascertain whether your lawyer is doing the job he or she should be doing. The text concludes with Chapter 12, which addresses the problem of insurance fraud and ambulance chasers.

chapter one:
At the Scene of an Accident

The actions you take at the scene of any accident and in the time frame shortly thereafter are of utmost importance in determining the course of your personal injury litigation. Whether you have been injured in a car collision, a slip-and-fall accident, as the result of equipment failure, by a doctor's negligence, or in any other way, you must, during the very earliest stages, take great care in everything you say and do. Never again will your memory of the key events be as fresh as they are on the day of injury, nor will the most crucial bits of evidence be as available. Thus, you must concentrate totally on what has happened to you and all aspects of the accident scene. You must act quickly to insure that the information you gather at the scene of the injury is preserved for your use throughout the litigation.

AFTER AN ACCIDENT

The events that occur right after an accident can determine whether the injured victim receives fair and prompt compensation. Extreme care must be taken to avoid saying anything that could later be interpreted as an *admission of fault*. An insurance company lawyer can even turn an apology uttered during this stressful time into an admission. By the same token, if you are involved in, for example, a motor vehicle accident, listen carefully to what the occupants of the other vehicle say. Write down key admissions as soon as possible. Often, people make statements at accident scenes during the heat of the moment that, given time for reflection, they would not make. The key is to *avoid discussing the cause of the accident.*

It is always a good idea to call the police to the scene. Failure to do so can lead an insurance company to deny that an accident ever happened. Photographs of your car, before it is repaired, also help to defeat this argument. Do not leave the scene until you are sure you or the police have all of the other driver's identifying information. This includes the vehicle tag (license plate) number, name, address, driver's license number, the name of his or her insurance company, and the policy number. Ask if the driver is *on the clock* for his or her employer. If so, the employer may be liable for the damages. Ask the police officer for a copy of the police report. Be aware of any circumstances or conditions relating in any way to the cause of the accident. For example, check for skid marks, accident debris, and so on. If you hire an attorney, be sure to let him or her know what you have found.

It is also vital that you get the name, address, and phone number of any eyewitnesses to the accident. People are often reluctant to get involved. However, most people will respond if you appeal to their sense of justice and fair play. Without the assistance of a witness, it may be impossible for you to obtain fair compensation for your injuries. Most people can put themselves in the shoes of an accident victim who needs the help of a witness.

You may think that fault for the accident is absolutely clear. Unfortunately, insurance companies deny claims for practically any reason at all. If the other motorist does not admit fault, your claim can be tied up for years in litigation. A solid eyewitness statement, especially by someone you have never met before, is easily the most effective way to convince an insurance company to honor your claim. Insurance companies are particularly persuaded by statements made by truly independent witnesses.

Witnesses are perhaps even more important in fall down accident (slip-and-fall) cases. Insurance companies are often suspicious of this kind of accident since property damage, which substantiates auto accidents, is not present. Thus, a prompt investigation that includes witness statements and photographs of the accident scene will go a long way towards convincing the insurance company that it should pay fair and prompt compensation.

On the following pages are checklists that should be used as worksheets for recording important car accident information and for fall down accidents. The checklists are repeated in Appendix B to copy and use. Keep **Checklist 1** in your car. You should complete this form as soon after the accident as possible.

Car Accident Checklist

Description of the Accident

Description of the accident:

Date of accident:

Time of day:

Day of week:

Location:

Direction in which each car was traveling:

Parties Involved

Names, addresses, and phone numbers of driver of each car:

Names, addresses, and phone numbers of owner of each car:

Names, addresses, and phone numbers of passengers in each car:

Names, addresses, and phone numbers of all witnesses:

Area Around the Accident

Number of lanes of each street:

One way or two way:

Condition of roadways:

Slope of each street:

Photographs of the scene:

Amount of traffic:

Traffic controls (lights, stop signs, etc.):

Vehicle Descriptions

Speed of each vehicle at the time of impact and just before impact:

Length of any skid marks:

Use of brakes by each vehicle:

Use of horn by each vehicle:

Use of turn signals by each vehicle:

Point of impact on each car:

Movement of each car upon impact:

Final position of each vehicle:

License plate number of each vehicle:

Location of your car now:

Date the car was purchased:

Photographs of damage to each car:

Damage done to the vehicles:

Years, makes, and models:

Drivers' license numbers:

Trip

Place where the trip began:

Destination:

Purpose of the trip:

Scheduled arrival time:

Conditions

Lighting conditions:

Weather:

Use of sunglasses:

Position of the sun:

Use of alcohol/drugs by any passenger or driver:

Use of car phones:

Use of radio/car stereo:

Use of windshield wipers:

Windows open or closed:

Use of defroster:

Use of glasses/contact lenses:

Driver smoking, eating, or drinking at the time of the accident:

Seat belt:

Stick shift or automatic transmission:

Date of last eye examination:

Name and address of eye doctor:

<u>Injuries</u>

Movement of your body at the moment of impact:

What part of your body came into contact with the vehicle:

Pain at the moment of impact:

Name of your auto insurance company: Policy number:

Coverages:

Name of other auto insurance in your household:

Name of health insurance company: Policy number:

Coverages:

Fall-Down Accident Checklist

Description of Accident

Description of the accident:

Names, addresses, and phone numbers of all witnesses:

Date of the accident: Time of day: Day of week:

Location of the accident:

Condition of the accident area (*e.g.*, sidewalk):

Photographs of the scene:

Place where the trip began:

Destination:

Purpose of the trip:

Scheduled arrival time:

Conditions Surrounding the Accident

Smoking, eating, or drinking at the time of the accident:

Date of last eye examination:

Name and address of eye doctor:

Use of headphones:

Lighting conditions:

Weather:

Position of the sun:

Use of sunglasses:

Use of alcohol/drugs:

Objects carried at time of accident:

Type and condition of shoes:

All conversation at the scene:

Police Involvement

Police district involved:

Name and badge number of attending officer:

Injury

What happened to your body as you fell:

What parts of your body came into contact with the ground:

How did you feel immediately after you fell:

Name of health insurance company: Policy number:

Coverages:

EMERGENCY ROOM TREATMENT

If you have been injured in an accident, the first place you should go is to a hospital emergency room (ER). Regardless of how you feel, go to the ER to get yourself checked out. You may be in shock and not even realize the severity of the trauma. Many people feel no pain until the next morning, when they often report feeling like they have just been beaten up. Going to the ER is not only a good idea from a health standpoint, but it also helps to convince the insurance company that you were injured.

Insurance companies give special credence to the ER report, since the hospital's description of the accident and injuries is generally made before much, if any, consideration has been given to litigation and lawyers. You, therefore, need to be extra careful that everything you say to the medical providers is accurate. Emergency room doctors and nurses often are extremely busy and may have little interest in accurately documenting the details of the accident. Unfortunately, the mistakes they make can come back to haunt you. The insurance company may feel that the version noted in the ER is accurate, even if it is not. While your family doctor may be willing to correct a mistake in a report, the ER doctor probably will not. So, again, be clear and accurate when describing your injuries to the emergency room staff.

Checklist 3 is a worksheet for keeping track of all the treatment you receive after an accident. You should use this to keep an accurate record throughout your recovery. The checklist is repeated in Appendix B.

Medical Treatment Worksheet

Injury

Injuries as a result of the accident:

Type of pain (sharp or dull, constant or intermittent):

Hospital

Name and address of ambulance company:

Name and address of emergency room:

Mode of transportation to the emergency room:

Treatment at emergency room:

Medication:

Orthopedic appliances:

Arrival and departure times:

Mode of transportation home:

Condition for the rest of the day/night:

Ability to sleep:

Condition the next morning:

Continued Treatment

Name, address, phone number, and specialty of your family doctor:

Names, addresses, phone numbers, and specialties of all doctors/therapists seen for your injuries:

Mode of transportation:

Purpose of visits:

Referral source for each doctor:

Results of first doctor visit:

Results of subsequent visits:

Description of treatments/therapy:

Exercises:

Whirlpool:

Orthopedic appliances:

Dates of treatment for each doctor/therapist:

Medication:

Date of last medical treatment:

Continuing Effects

Pain when discharged:

Medical instructions upon discharge:

Pain since discharge:

Pain today:

Surgery:

Effect of accident on your normal daily activities:

Effect on household duties:

Effect on exercise/sports:

Effect on driving:

Effect on sleeping:

Effect on social activities:

Marital difficulties:

Emotional reaction to your injuries:

Your physical/emotional condition before the accident:

Prior/subsequent accidents:

Prior/subsequent injuries:

Prior/subsequent doctors:

Effect on Work

Next scheduled day of work after the accident:

Time missed because of the accident:

Reason for missing time:

Effect of accident on ability to work after return to your job:

Work schedule:

Average weekly wage:

Name, phone number, and address of supervisor:

BEWARE OF THE FRIENDLY INSURANCE ADJUSTER

During the period immediately after an accident, the insurance companies involved with the case will likely try to engage you in discussions concerning your accident. You simply cannot be too careful when dealing with an insurance company, especially if you are not represented by a lawyer. This is true whether you are contacted by your company or by the company of the person who injured you. The following horror story illustrates this point.

Example: Mark signed a release with an insurance company and accepted a small sum of money in exchange. On the very day he signed the release, he went to see his psychologist in an extremely distraught state of mind. His thoughts were racing and jumbled, his heartbeat was elevated, and he was sweating and trembling. He had experienced multiple blows to his head in the accident and sustained a concussion. Even though releases typically discharge a company from any further liability, just before the trial was to begin, the insurance company agreed to provide adequate compensation for the injuries suffered. The company feared the anger a jury would feel at this company for taking advantage of an unrepresented and emotionally vulnerable person.

Your Insurance Company

Mark was fortunate because it is very difficult to *void* a signed release. The lesson here is to watch out for *friendly* insurance adjusters bearing legal documents.

You must also beware of your own insurance company. Your interests and those of your insurance company will conflict, especially when you are injured by an *uninsured* or *underinsured motorist.* In this situation, you will seek compensation for your pain and suffering from your own insurance company. (See Chapter 11 for a discussion of uninsured and underinsured motorist benefits.) Also, in every auto accident case, it is your own insurer who pays your medical bills and lost wages. This insurer's investigation of the accident is centered around avoiding any financial payout. It is vital that you contact a legal advocate whose only interest is to obtain maximum compensation for you.

Your insurance company may also send you *tips* about what you should do after an accident. A review of this information will be helpful to you.

Many insurance companies advise that there are some easy steps that should be followed at the scene of an accident. Many of these hints are quite helpful. They include:

◆ calling the police;
◆ not admitting fault at the scene of the accident;
◆ exchanging insurance information with the other driver; and,
◆ obtaining the other driver's name, address, phone number, license plate number, etc.

Consult an Attorney First

The final suggestion is to notify your insurance agent promptly. Indeed, your policy obligates you to notify your insurance company of an accident. (However, this should be done only by your attorney if anyone was injured!)

If you submit to a tape-recorded statement for your insurer or fill out claim forms without the aid of counsel, you may make mistakes that will compromise your claim. Do not underestimate the devious nature of some employees at some insurance companies. They are well-trained to investigate accident cases to defend against fraudulent and exaggerated claims. That is obviously appropriate and to the greater good of the insurance company and society as a whole. However, the unsuspecting and uncounseled individual frequently falls prey to the trickster insurance agent who seeks to protect the insurance company's pocketbook at the expense of the legitimate claimant.

Sometimes insurance companies misrepresent the amount of their policy limits in order to settle cases for far less than justified by the nature of the injuries. In some cases, insurance adjusters might advise claimants to avoid getting an attorney because the lawyer would supposedly take all of the money. Some insurance representatives place settlement agreements before unrepresented claimants, advising them that the papers applied to property damage only, when in reality, the document is a general release discharging all liability for any type of insurance claim arising out of the accident.

While there are many hardworking and honest insurance representatives, bad apples exist. You lose nothing by calling your lawyer first for a free consultation after an accident. It is just the wise and safe road to travel.

DO NOT SIGN ANYTHING

Besides the insurance adjuster, you may get phone calls from attorneys, private investigators, and others offering to *help* you and asking you to sign a contract for their services. Do not sign anything until you have time to recover from the injury, think clearly, and perhaps discuss the situation with someone who can give you an unbiased opinion.

Some states have laws forbidding lawyers from contacting victims until thirty days after an accident has passed. However, that does not always stop them. With the possibility of millions of dollars in legal fees, lawyers have been known to fly to accident scenes, and to solicit business from hospital waiting rooms and airports. Those not as bold send their employees and agents to *give solace* to victims and pass out their cards. One man even dressed like a priest while consoling the victims and suggested they consult the attorney he worked for.

Almost all personal injury attorneys will give you an initial consultation at no charge to evaluate your case. Such an appointment gives the attorney a chance to decide if your case is worth his or her time. It can also be your chance to find out if you have a case and if the attorney is someone you feel comfortable with.

There is no harm in making an appointment with such an attorney as soon as you feel well enough to do so. However, you should not feel pressured to sign any agreement with the first attorney you visit. Tell him or her that you do not feel ready to sign anything, but that you will call when you are ready.

If you do not feel comfortable with the first attorney you meet, you should see at least one or two others. As long as they agree to consult without charge, you have nothing to lose but a little of your time.

REMEMBER THE DEADLINE

While people are generally attentive to their case right after the accident, as time goes on, and weeks turn into months, it is easy to lose track of deadlines. If the other side takes weeks to answer your letter, and it takes you months to gather all the medical information requested, a year can pass before you realize it.

It is important to keep track of time because each state has a law, called the *statute of limitations*, regarding how long you can wait before filing suit. It is in the best interest of the other side or their insurance company to delay the case until the deadline has passed. Do not let this happen to you or you will lose your claim.

The shortest limit of any state to file a claim is one year. In other states, it is as long as six years. This limit is from the time of the accident until the day a lawsuit is filed. Sometimes, if the deadline is approaching and settlement is near, an insurance adjuster will try to delay past the limitation. In such a case, a lawsuit must be filed to keep the case alive.

(Further discussion of statutes of limitations is in Chapter 9.)

chapter two:
Handling Your Case Without a Lawyer

There are some types of cases that should not be settled without using the services of an attorney. Others you may be able to handle yourself. The advantage of using an attorney is that he or she is experienced at obtaining a full settlement from an insurance company or defendant, and evaluating how much your claim is worth. The disadvantage is that the attorney's fee can be as much as half of your award after costs and other fees are deducted.

Simple cases, in which the injury is minor and the fault is clear, can often be settled quickly with the insurance company without hiring an attorney. Even if the company balks at paying, you can often get a good settlement by filing a small claims case, since the insurance company's expense of going to court is often higher than the cost of settling. Complicated cases, such as those with serious medical malpractice or an accident causing death, should always be handled by an attorney who can analyze the value of the case and let the other side know that you are serious about your claim.

Many people make the mistake of settling their case without adequate legal advice. Almost all personal injury litigants should seek counsel. Achieving your desired outcome may not be the only reason for hiring an attorney. The emotional strain of doing it yourself may cost more than the attorney fees you would pay.

Example: Anne is an employee of an insurance company. Her familiarity with insurance practice tempted her to forego using an attorney to handle her injury case. She consulted an attorney but believed she could do better financially by herself. She was worried that an attorney's percentage of the settlement would leave her with less money than if she handled the case herself.

About two months later, she contacted the attorney again in a highly emotional state of mind. The combined stress of being injured and dealing one-on-one with the insurance company had left her psychologically scarred and physically drained. Her physical and emotional condition improved immediately upon retaining the services of an attorney. By relinquishing control of her case, she was also able to let go of pressures that were hindering her healing process.

It is an illusion to think that an insurance company will offer an unrepresented person the same kind of settlement money it would offer a person represented by a capable personal injury lawyer. There is virtually no way for you to know the value of a personal injury case. These values are based upon years of jury verdicts and insurance settlements. Only an experienced personal injury attorney can accurately assess the maximum amount an insurance company is likely to pay for a particular injury.

The company knows very well that it possesses superior knowledge and bargaining power. It will not hesitate to use this knowledge and power to its advantage and your disadvantage. Insurance companies pay only what they feel they will be compelled to pay by a jury. A strong personal injury lawyer on your side acts like a hammer over the head of the insurance company. The company pays far more when it fears the outcome that an experienced personal injury attorney can secure for the client. Insurance companies do not fear unrepresented individuals because such individuals lack knowledge about how to inflict pain upon the company if it does not settle the case. It is like fighting a war without modern weapons. The other side is not likely to listen seriously to your terms of surrender, if you have no ability to effectively wage the battle.

The insurance company will also know that, even if the facts and justice are on your side, your unfamiliarity with the legal procedures involved may cause you to lose the case on a legal technicality. Although the courts generally relax the rules of procedure for unrepresented parties, you cannot count on this. The rules are made by lawyers for use by lawyers. It is extremely hard to dot all the i's and cross all the t's in just the right way when it comes to a personal injury lawsuit. Again, the best advice is to retain an honest, energetic, personal injury specialist at the first possible opportunity.

Cases involving property damage alone can be settled fairly without the assistance of an attorney. It may be better here to handle the case yourself and spare yourself the expense of an attorney. There are books available that set forth the value of cars. These accepted values establish guidelines that the insurance company should follow. There are no such clear-cut guidelines concerning the *value* of pain and suffering in a serious injury case. That is why you need a lawyer for more complex cases. However, it may be possible to find a solution that falls somewhere between doing it alone and hiring a lawyer. Take the following example.

> **Example:** Kurt managed to obtain an offer of $50,000 to settle his son's case. However, he wanted to know if it was safe to take the money without retaining a lawyer. He was afraid that, if a lawyer were brought into the case, the lawyer might settle the case for $55,000 and take one-third of the proceeds. So he decided to meet with several lawyers in order to work out the best possible arrangement. He insisted that the first $50,000 was for his son and that the lawyer's fee would come out of any amount the lawyer could negotiate above and beyond that amount.

This is a creative solution to a seemingly difficult problem. You need to think your situation through carefully so you can come up with these kinds of solutions. There are plenty of unscrupulous lawyers who will rob you blind if you do not act with care. These kinds of creative solutions will win you the respect of the lawyer you finally retain.

HANDLING YOUR CLAIM

Keep in mind that *you* are the only nonlawyer who is permitted to handle your case. Even though your cousin Bernie thinks he can represent you as well as any real lawyer, it is not allowed by the law. It is called *the unauthorized practice of law*. Bernie can give you all the *off the record* helpful hints he wants, but if you do not retain a licensed attorney, you must sign all of the official court documents yourself and you must appear in court yourself. In addition, if you are handling the claim yourself, you are responsible for gathering all the information you will need to reach a settlement. There are several things you need to do to get organized.

The Accident Events

Review Chapter 1. The advice about the events that occur immediately after an accident apply whether you intend to retain a lawyer or not.

Police Report

In auto accident cases, always obtain the police report. Here you have an advantage over people who are represented by attorneys. The police, especially big city police, often will more readily and more rapidly turn over their information to you, the accident victim, than they will to a lawyer. The police report is crucial because it contains the names, addresses, and phone numbers of witnesses, insurance information for the person who injured you, license numbers, a diagram of the accident, and many other important items.

Photographs

The police may even have photographs of the accident scene and the cars. Get copies of any photographs. Be sure to take your own if the damage to the cars was more than minimal. Photographs of the accident scene should always be taken if there is any doubt as to who caused the accident. If you were rear-ended, you probably do not need photos of the scene of the accident. If you were injured in a slip-and-fall accident, photos of the area where you fell are absolutely essential. These should be taken as soon after the accident as possible. Once the ice you slipped on melts, your testimony may be the only proof that ice existed.

Rescue Report

If you were taken from the accident scene by an ambulance or other paratransit vehicle, obtain the rescue report. This report may contain useful information prepared by the rescue workers. The rescue report may document your distress at the accident scene. It may also provide data regarding the condition of the scene itself (although generally, the police report is far more helpful in that respect).

Witnesses

Contact witnesses as soon as possible after the accident. Memories fade rapidly, so speed is important.

Your adversary's insurance company will probably try to contact witnesses as well. It is always better for you to reach an important witness first. A crafty insurance investigator may be able to convince an otherwise favorable witness that perhaps his or her view of the accident was not so favorable to you. Do not wait—speed is of great importance.

If the witness is favorable to you, prepare a written statement for him or her to sign. This statement should be an accurate recitation of his or her view of the events of the accident. Some people are reluctant to be witnesses. If you sense reluctance, let the witness know that you do not plan to retain a lawyer. This may increase the sympathy the witness has for you since he or she may feel that you really need his or her help. The witness may also appreciate being able to deal directly with you rather than having to work through a lawyer. A lot of people simply do not like dealing with lawyers, so again, your being unrepresented can be an advantage here.

Private Investigation

You may want to consider hiring your own private investigator. Every good personal injury attorney has one or more private investigators who he or she relies on heavily. Among other things, the investigator may take written statements of witnesses and take professional quality photographs of the accident scene, property damage, and your scars and bruises.

First Contact

Once you have completed your investigation of the accident, contact the insurer for the person or company you are making your claim against. A sample letter to the insurance company follows.

Opening Letter to Insurance Company by Attorney

JOHN DOUGH
6265 SW 8th STREET
MIAMI, FL 33165

VOICE: (305) 274-0408
FAX: (305) 274-0706

February 28, 2005

ACME INSURANCE COMPANY
1300 INSURANCE DRIVE
COMPANYTOWN, FL 33143
ATTN: NEW CLAIMS

RE: Your Insured: Benny Fitz
                1234 Market Street
                Anytown, FL 33168
        Date of Accident: 01/10/05
        Location of Accident: Broad and Market Streets, Anytown, PA

Dear Sir/Madam:

    I am writng with regard to a claim for personal injuries suffered in an
accident involving your insured, the particulars of which are set forth above.

    Please confirm your receipt of this letter and direct all future inquiries
to me.

                            Very truly yours,

                            JOHN DOUGH

    If you do not know who the insurer is, the first letter should go to the per-
son or business you are suing. The sample letter that follows can be used as
a guide to writing your own letter.

Opening Letter to Defendant

JOHN DOUGH
6265 SW 8th STREET
MIAMI, FL 33165

VOICE: (305) 274-0408
FAX: (305) 274-0706

February 28, 2005

RICH BANKS
123 MARKET STREET
FT. LAUDERDALE, FL 33144

RE: Location of Accident: West & Main Streets, Ft. Lauderdale, FL
       Date of Accident: 11/16/03

Dear Mr. Banks:

I am writng with regard to a claim for personal injuries suffered in an accident in which you were involved, the particulars of which are set forth above. It is in your best interest to immediately refer this letter to your insurance company. Failure to do so will result in the institution of suit against you without further notice.

Please confirm your receipt of this letter and direct all future inquiries to me.

Very truly yours,

JOHN DOUGH

Use certified mail. It tends to increase the attention the recipient pays to your letter. Certainly if you get no response to this first contact letter, the follow-up letter should be sent by certified mail.

By all means have the letter prepared in a professional way and be sure there are no typos. You are trying to create an image of competence and seriousness. A handwritten or poorly typed letter with mistakes will reduce the value of your case in the eyes of the insurance company.

Recorded Statements

When you are contacted by the insurance company, be on your guard. The claim representative or insurance investigator will salivate at the idea that you are unrepresented. He or she has all the advantages of experience and litigation savvy. He or she may try, right off the bat, to take a written or tape-recorded statement from you. Do not permit this under any circumstance. The claim representative or insurance adjustor is looking to pin you down in order to trap you into a position that later you may wish you were not in. Do not get into too many details. There will be plenty of time for that if a lawsuit is required.

If you feel that you simply must give a recorded statement to the insurance company, insist on the right to take a recorded statement from the person who injured you. That is only fair. If the insurance company refuses, then you know they do not intend to fight fair.

You should probably get a lawyer in any case where recorded statements are going to be taken. However, if you are set on representing yourself, and you are willing to give a recorded statement to the insurance company, then take care. This statement can come back to haunt you.

You will be asked numerous detailed questions about the accident and your medical care. An outline of the types of questions you can expect follows. Think through how you will answer these questions before you give the statement.

Questions for Depositions, Statements, and Trial

Full name:

Current residence:

How long:

Residence on date of accident:

Age:

Marital status (then and now):

Children:

Employment on date of accident:

Where:

How long:

What capacity:

Duties:

Employed now:

Do you recall being involved in an accident on...:

Time of day:

Where:

Day of week:

Who was driving:

Passengers:

Where were you seated:

What happened (narrative):

What did you see:

Did you know you were going to be hit:

Lanes of street:

Amount of traffic:

Divided highway:

Parking on sides of street:

Which way do the streets run:

How fast were you traveling:

How fast was the other car traveling:

Which direction each traveling:

Turn signals:

Traffic controls:

Which part of the vehicles impacted each other:

What happened to your car upon impact:

Which way did vehicle spin:

Where did each stop:

What did you do after it stopped:

Where did your journey begin:

Where were you going:

Purpose of trip:

When due to arrive:

Lighting:

Weather:

Slope of street:

Alcohol/Drugs:

All conversation at the scene:

Used horn or other warning device:

Skid marks:

When did police arrive:

Conversation with police:

Who called:

Radio:

Windshield wipers:

Windows:

Defroster:

Children in car:

Date of last eye examination:

Do you wear glasses or contacts:

Car phone:

Smoking/eating (hands on wheel) (stick shift):

Where was the sun:

Wearing sunglasses:

Witnesses:

Who owned the car:

When was the car purchased:

Borrowed from owner:

Type of vehicle:

Where licensed to drive:

Since when:

Restrictions:

License ever suspended or revoked:

Describe other car:

Mechanical condition of your car:

Where and when was it last inspected:

What, if anything, happened to your body at the moment of impact:

What part of your body came into contact with the vehicle:

How did you feel at the moment of impact:

Seat belt:

Were you injured as a result of the accident:

What portion of your body came to your attention at the scene:

Investigation of accident:

What did you do about your injuries:

Emergency Room:

How did you get there:

Type of pain (sharp or dull, constant, or intermittent):

What was done for you at ER:

Medication:

Orthopedic appliances:

When did you arrive at and leave the hospital:

How did you get home:

How did you feel the rest of day:

How did you feel the next morning:

Did you go back to work that day:

Did you go anywhere else for treatment:

Why:

How did you get there:

Purpose of visits:

Used ER equipment until first doctor's visit:

Family doctor:

Who referred:

Result of first doctor's visit:

What was complained of:

What was done on subsequent visits:

Describe treatments/therapy:

Exercises:

Whirlpool:

Orthopedic appliances:

Where were exercises performed:

Did they bring relief:

For how long did you see this doctor:

How many times (total):

How many times per week:

What other doctors saw you:

Why:

Who referred you:

Specialists seen:

Purpose of visits:

Medication—side effects:

When was the last medical treatment:

How did you feel then:

How have you felt since then:

How do you feel today:

How many days a week do you feel pain—what do you do for it:

Did pain lessen at any point in treatment:

When (for each injury):

Were you ever able to resume normal daily activities:

When:

Household duties:

Sports:

Driving:

Sleeping:

Social activities:

Marital difficulties:

How did you feel before accident:

Prior accidents:

How long were you treated:

Injuries:

How long before accident had you recovered:

Later accidents:

Next scheduled work after date of accident:

Did you go to work:

Work schedule:

Date that you returned to work:

Average weekly wage:

Why did you not stay home from work:

After you went back to work, was there any limitation because of the accident:

Inability to do job:

Were you carrying anything:

Describe your shoes:

Describe your clothing:

Which foot slipped:

Describe your fall:

What parts of your body hit the ground:

What caused you to fall:

Where were you looking:

When had you last been to the scene of the accident:

Were you aware of the defect that caused your fall:

Did you have an alternate route:

Be sure to see the section on "Depositions" in Chapter 10. A deposition is a question-and-answer session that takes place after a lawsuit is filed. The suggestions in Chapter 10 apply equally to pre-lawsuit statements. If you have a tape recorder, record the statement so that you can review what you said at a later date. If you later hire an attorney, he or she will want to know what you said.

WASHINGTON, D.C. 44444
ATTENTION: MEDICAL RECORDS DEPARTMENT
RE: PATIENT: A. KEN KNECK
          Date of Birth: 5/19/66
          Dates of Service: 5/14/03
          Date of Accident: 5/14/03

Dear Sir/Madam:

I am writing with regard to a claim for personal injuries arising out of an accident that occurred on the above date. I received treatment in your hospital. Please forward a report, as well as your bill for services rendered to this patient. I am enclosing a fully completed HIPAA medical authorization that permits the release of this information.

Thank you for your cooperation.

Very truly yours,

JOHN DOUGH

Determining what to settle your case for is one of the most difficult problems you will face. Chapter 8 discusses the settlement process. The methods professionals use to evaluate cases are discussed in both Chapters 7 and 8. Review these chapters carefully. You most likely will not be able to negotiate a settlement as large as a lawyer might. The insurance company fears the jury verdict an experienced personal injury attorney is capable of getting far more than one an unrepresented plaintiff can get. In addition, the company knows that it can take advantage of your inexperience throughout the litigation process. Your lack of familiarity with court procedures can be fatal to your case. Thus, you should not expect to negotiate as successfully as a lawyer.

It is still possible for you to do better financially *without* a lawyer. If you have made it this far without a lawyer, you can use that fact to your advantage. You can negotiate with the insurance company as an unrepresented party with the knowledge that, at any time, you can hire a lawyer to take over the case. For example, if the company offers you $5,000 to settle the case, you can advise the company that you will be retaining the services of an experienced personal injury (PI) attorney if it will not increase its offer. That may get the offer up to the point where you are comfortable settling the case.

Once you have obtained the *absolute top offer* from the insurance company, you can then go out shopping for a lawyer. Tell the lawyers you interview about the status of your settlement negotiations. Offer to pay them a percentage of any amount they can negotiate *above and beyond* the best offer you got from the company yourself. You keep 100% of whatever you alone negotiated. This will be irresistible to many lawyers. Often, with a very small amount of work, the lawyer can substantially increase the offer. If the lawyer is known in the community as a competent PI specialist, his or her involvement in the case will immediately increase its settlement value.

HANDLING YOUR LAWSUIT

If the liability for the accident is disputed, it is unlikely that you will be able to negotiate a good settlement without filing lawsuit papers with the court. In most cases you should get a lawyer to do this. But if your case can be handled in small claims court, you cannot find a lawyer to handle your case, or you insist on doing it yourself, this section will provide some guidance.

Small Claims Court

In every state there is a special court for handling small claims. Typically, the limit on awards in such a court is between $1,000 and $5,000. These courts usually have rules that allow a non-lawyer to present a case easily, without the usual court formalities.

If your damages are within the limit of your small claims court, you can have a judge decide the merits of your claim. If your claim is above the limits of small claims court, you can still file if you are willing to accept the limit. For example, if your damages are $4,000 and your court's limit is $3,000, you can sue in small claims court if you will be happy with $3,000.

On the following page is a list of small claims court limits as of the time of the writing of this book. Since these limits can change, you should call your court for information.

Alabama	$3,000	Missouri	$3,000
Alaska	$10,000	Montana	$3,000
Arizona	$2,500*	Nebraska	$2,400
Arkansas	$5,000	Nevada	$5,000
California	$5,000*	New Hampshire	$5,000
Colorado	$7,500	New Jersey	$3,000
Connecticut	$3,500*	New Mexico	$10,000
Delaware	$15,000	New York	$5,000
District of	$5,000	North Carolina	$5,000
Columbia		North Dakota	$5,000
Florida	$5,000	Ohio	$3,000
Georgia	$15,000	Oklahoma	$6,000
Hawaii	$3,500	Oregon	$5,000
Idaho	$4,000	Pennsylvania	$8,000*
Illinois	$5,000*	Rhode Island	$2,500
Indiana	$3,000*	South Carolina	$7,500
Iowa	$4,000	South Dakota	$8,000
Kansas	$1,800	Tennessee	$15,000*
Kentucky	$1,500	Texas	$5,000
Louisiana	$3,000	Utah	$7,500
Maine	$4,500	Vermont	$3,500
Maryland	$5,000	Virginia	$15,000*
Massachusetts	$2,000	Washington	$4,000
Michigan	$3,000	West Virginia	$5,000
Minnesota	$7,500	Wisconsin	$5,000
Mississippi	$2,500	Wyoming	$3,000*

Arizona—$5,000 in Regular Justice Court; California—$4,000 if suit involves surety company or licensed contractor; Connecticut—no limit for landlord-tenant security deposit claims; Illinois—$1,500 in Cook County Pro Se Court; Indiana—$6,000 in Marion and Allen Counties; Louisiana—$2,000 for movable property; Pennsylvania—$10,000 in Philadelphia; Tennessee—$25,000 if county has over 700,000 residents; Virginia—up to $15,000 varies by county; Wyoming—$7,000 for County Court.

One danger of filing a suit in small claims court is that the other side may hire a lawyer and countersue you for more than the limit in small claims court. Then you will have to hire a lawyer to defend you in a higher court. In a medical malpractice suit, it is unlikely that the doctor could countersue (unless you did not pay the bill). But in an auto accident in which the fault is disputed, you could easily end up being liable for more than the amount for which you sued. Consider getting a lawyer to review your case before filing such a suit.

(The procedures and options in small claims court can take an entire book to explain. There are many good books on the subject that you can find in public libraries, law libraries, and bookstores. You should read one before going to court.)

Formal Court

If your claim is much greater than the limit in small claims court, you might want to consider filing suit without a lawyer in your regular court system. Unless you have some legal training or can devote considerable time to learning all the court procedures, this is not a good idea. Court rules are strict and your case can be lost because of a minor mistake. If the other side has a lawyer, he or she will be looking at your every move for an error that will doom your case. If you feel you cannot afford to give a third of your claim to an attorney, try to get a good offer from the other side and then seek out an attorney who will only take a percentage of what he or she gains for you over the last offer.

If you still insist upon going to formal court by yourself, go to a law library and read a good book on civil procedure in your state. The best books are often put out by bar association continuing legal education (CLE) offices and are used by lawyers who want to learn procedure. Most law libraries do not allow books to circulate, so plan to spend some time there. Bring plenty of change for the copy machine, too. If you are really serious, you might be able to buy a copy of the CLE book from the state bar association. If they will not sell it to you, try a law school bookstore.

Chapters 9 through 11 of this book provide an outline of how a personal injury case progresses through court. It will guide you through the aspects of civil procedure that are most important to your case.

Appendix A contains two sample forms for lawsuit complaints. The correct form for your court may be somewhat different. But something similar should work wherever you file. To find a more exact version of what is proper in your state, you can locate a file of a similar lawsuit filed by a lawyer in your local court. You should have no trouble viewing someone else's file since they are public records. The important thing is to find the right type of case. This is easiest to do if your court clerk has an index of cases that lists the type of case.

Look for personal injury cases and then find one similar to your own. Form 1 is a sample complaint for use for a car accident. (see form 1, p.196.) Form 2 is a sample complaint for fall down accidents. (see form 2, p.199.)

It is important that your lawsuit papers be properly filed and properly delivered to the defendant. Contact the court clerk to find out the cost for filing the lawsuit, the number of copies that have to be filed, etc.

Service of Process

You need to be very careful with service of process. *Service of process* is the legal terminology for delivering the lawsuit papers to the defendant. In some jurisdictions, only service by a sheriff is proper. If you make a mistake here, it can be fatal to your case. Do not be afraid to ask lots of questions. If one person at the court will not help you, find someone who will. While court personnel cannot give legal advice, they can usually provide *procedural guidance*. Court employees in some areas are notorious for not caring how helpful they are, so take extra care to ensure that you get good advice. You might also go to your local law library for forms and books on filing and serving papers. Alternatively, you can retain an attorney on an hourly basis to consult with about these technical, but important, legal matters. Just an hour or so of skilled legal help may be all you need.

Typically, the courts require that you retain the services of a process server to make formal service of process of the lawsuit papers. This may be the local sheriff or other qualified person. You simply supply the documents to be served, the defendant's last known address, and pay the fee for service. If the defendant has moved or is otherwise not found, the process server typically will do a brief investigation to try to locate him or her. If this is unsuccessful, the burden will fall back on you.

It is essential that you act without delay in your attempts to locate the defendant. This is especially true if you file the complaint just prior to the statute of limitations deadline. The law in your state may require that service be made either before the statute of limitations deadline or that you show a good faith and continuous effort to locate and serve the defendant. If you do not, your case may be subject to dismissal because of the expiration of the statute of limitations.

If you are having difficulty in locating the defendant, a *Google* search may be helpful. Just go to **www.google.com** and search the defendant's name. In seconds, you may find not only the defendant's current location, but also a great deal of useful information. If you still are unable to locate the defendant, you may need to file a motion for *alternative service of process*. This motion would detail the good faith efforts you have made to locate the defendant. The motion would request that the court permit you to serve the defendant by leaving a copy of the lawsuit papers at the defendant's last known address, whether he or she is there or not.

Once you have successfully filed and served the suit papers, one of many things can happen. The insurance company may then be ready to settle the case. Your skills thus far may have impressed the company enough to make them want to buy their peace. Or perhaps the company will turn its lawyers loose on you. These lawyers may file motions with the court regarding some supposed legal problem with the complaint. If this happens, it really may be time to throw in the towel and hire a lawyer. It would be very hard to fight off these legal motions without proper advice.

Discovery

Once the motions are decided, the case moves into the *discovery* phase. (See Chapter 10 for a detailed discussion of that important process.) Form 3 is a sample set of **Interrogatories** for a typical car accident case. (see form 3, p.203.) *Interrogatories* are simply questions that pertain to your lawsuit. Another form is included for fall down accidents. (see form 4, p.219.) A sample **Request for Production of Documents** is also in Appendix A. (see form 5, p.236.) These items should help you prepare your own **Interrogatories** and **Request for Production**. Unless you submit these discovery requests to the insurance company attorney, he or she will not have to turn over the information in his or her file. You need to get this information, so do not wait.

Send **Interrogatories** and a **Request for Production of Documents** to the opposing lawyer on the very day that he or she enters his or her appearance on behalf of the insurance company. If the attorney will not voluntarily turn this information over, you will have to file a discovery motion in order to get the court's assistance. The form that discovery motions take varies from court to court, so you will have to do some research. Form 6 is a sample **Motion to Compel Discovery** (see form 6, p.238.) and form 7 is a sample **Order for Discovery**. (see form 7, p.239.)

Depositions

After the documents have been exchanged and all the **Interrogatories** answered, the case will move into the most important part of the discovery phase—*depositions*. In a deposition, a *party* or other witness is put under oath and asked a series of questions by one of the attorneys. A list of questions you can expect at your deposition was presented on p.24. Chapter 10 gives you a detailed list of rules for your deposition. If you are representing yourself, you have an additional task. You need to take the defendant's deposition. (In a car accident case, this is the person who hit you. In a fall down case, this is the owner of the home where you fell or the store manager of the business where you were hurt.)

You also need to take the depositions of any witnesses who the insurance company has scheduled to testify on its behalf at the trial. You need to know what these people will say at trial. You are at a severe disadvantage if you submit to a deposition without taking one or more yourself.

It is during depositions that your inexperience may be most damaging. The insurance company's lawyer may try to take advantage of you. In fact, you can pretty much count on that. You need to be as familiar as possible with the rules for taking depositions in your jurisdiction. Once you are familiar with those rules, stick to your guns. Do not let the attorney intimidate you. This attorney will try things he would not dream of doing in court, since no judge or jury is present at depositions.

During the trial, your opponent's lawyer will try to appear to be fair. Juries hate lawyers who try to take advantage of unrepresented litigants. But in the deposition room, the action takes place in relative privacy. You will probably be in the opposing lawyer's conference room with only his or her stenographer present to record the testimony. This attorney will be on his or her home ground and you will be in unfamiliar territory. This can be very intimidating, but there is hope. Find out, in advance, which judge is in charge of discovery disputes. Then, if a problem arises during the deposition, you can threaten to call the judge. This will impress the defense lawyer greatly. He or she will very much fear having a judge come down on him or her for having tried to take advantage of an unrepresented plaintiff.

Once the depositions are done, there is nothing left to do but prepare for trial. The better your preparation and the more the insurance company understands that you are prepared, the easier it will be settle the case for a fair amount of money. Many cases settle on the day of trial or shortly before. You should prepare as if the case will not settle, and then be delighted if by chance it does. You cannot count on a last-minute settlement—preparation is the key.

Watch a trial or two before your case goes to court. You will need to find a case that is similar to yours to get the maximum benefit from watching. Ask if you can see the court *docket*. This lists cases and the courtrooms in which they will be heard. Hopefully the docket will also list the type of case. You will learn many helpful things by watching experienced attorneys try a personal injury case. Also, review Chapter 11 carefully. You will find a step-by-step analysis of the trial of a personal injury lawsuit.

Proving Your Case

You must prove every aspect of a negligence case to be entitled to an award in your favor. *Negligence* is a lack of reasonable care when an ordinary person would have taken care. The aspects you need to prove include *negligence* (carelessness), *causation*, and *damages*. Thus, you must prove that the defendant's behavior was careless or in some way unreasonable, that his or her behavior caused you to be injured, and of course, you must prove the extent of your damages. With regard to negligence, if the defendant rear-ended you, negligence is clear. Or if you trip over the defendant's broken and deteriorated sidewalk, the defendant's negligence should be no problem to prove. In the latter case, however, your own carelessness (*comparative negligence*) in tripping over an obvious defect may limit your claim. (See Chapter 11 for a discussion of comparative negligence.)

You must always prove that the defendant's behavior caused your injury. If you had a preexisting injury or were injured again shortly after the accident, the defense lawyer will try to prove that his or her client's negligence was not the primary cause of your injuries. If x-rays show arthritis, he or she may argue that your pain and suffering is simply due to old age rather than to the accident. The method for proving a personal injury case varies from court to court. Whether your case is heard by a judge, jury, or some other less formal panel will affect how you have to prove your case. For example, if your case is a jury or judge trial, you probably will have to offer your doctor's spoken testimony into evidence. If your case is an *arbitration*, it may be possible to prove your damages simply by offering the medical reports. (See Chapter 9 for a discussion of the types of trials.)

Acting as your own lawyer during the trial has certain advantages. You will be viewed by both the jury and the judge with special sympathy because you are unrepresented. The technical rules of court will probably be relaxed for you, since you cannot fairly be expected to have the sophistication of a trial lawyer. Yet the rules can only be bent so far.

For example, everyone has heard of *hearsay*. The *hearsay doctrine* prevents a witness from testifying about what another person said. There are exceptions to this rule that are too numerous and complicated to discuss here. If your case hinges on *inadmissible* hearsay and you are unaware of the rule against its admission, you will lose your case no matter how much sympathy the judge has for you. At the very least, before you go to court, hire a lawyer on an hourly basis or for some percentage of the final award to go through the evidence with you to be sure you do not make any fatal mistakes.

chapter three:
The Personal Injury Attorney and You

This chapter explores the various ways of finding a personal injury lawyer. This may be the most important decision you make throughout the entire process of winning your personal injury claim. Some of the areas covered in this important topic include the initial consultation with a personal injury lawyer, the attorney's fee agreement, dissatisfaction with and changing lawyers, and the crucial role you play during the litigation of your case.

FINDING A PERSONAL INJURY ATTORNEY

If you decide to hire a personal injury attorney, you must find an attorney you can trust. You should also be sure that he or she has some experience.

Recommendations

The very best way to find a good personal injury lawyer is by asking close friends or family members for recommendations. Be sure that the recommendation is for an attorney who specializes in personal injury litigation. The days when one lawyer was able to help you with all of your legal problems are over. Most lawyers today specialize in one or two areas and refer all other cases to other attorneys. There are so many competent personal injury attorneys out there; it is an absolute mistake to retain anyone but a specialist.

The worst way to pick a lawyer is by the recommendation of someone you first meet at the accident scene. This nation's big cities are filled with *ambulance chasers* who magically appear at accident scenes—ready to advise the vulnerable, accident victim. Do not trust your important rights to someone who practices the profession of law in this way.

Bar Association

You can also check with your local bar association to find out if the lawyer you are considering has a good reputation. (However, some bar associations are not permitted to recommend attorneys—they must be neutral.)

If you cannot find the right lawyer through the recommendation of a friend, a family member, or through a bar association, you might get really creative and do your own research. You must be willing to take some time and make a considerable effort if you wish to take this route, but it is well worth it.

Legal Journals

You can consult a legal journal in your area that reviews the results of personal injury cases. You can find these publications in your local law library or through the bar association. This review will provide you with the facts of many cases, the names of the lawyers, and the outcome. Perhaps you will find a case similar to yours that turned out favorably for the plaintiff. If so, you can contact the plaintiff's lawyer. One of the first questions he or she will ask you is how you found him or her. You can bet he or she will be quite impressed with your ingenuity in locating him or her through a journal. (One such journal is called *Jury Verdict Review*. You can obtain a copy by calling 973-376-9002.)

Internet

If the lawyer you are thinking about hiring has a website, check it out. The lawyer's website may tell you a lot about his or her personality, and it certainly should give you insight in to his or her areas of specialization. If there is something in the website that rubs you the wrong way, you can raise the issue with the lawyer if you choose to go ahead and interview him or her.

Also do a *Google* search on any lawyer or law firm you consider hiring. Just go to **www.Google.com** and do a name search. You can also use any other search engine with which you feel comfortable.

Google has a feature that allows you to find recent newspaper articles involving the lawyer or law firm. Just click on "News" and then insert the name you want to search. You may find a wealth of information right at your fingertips. If the lawyer has had recently newsworthy cases, you will be able to read about them. If the lawyer has had disciplinary problems, you need to know this, and the Internet is a great way to access this kind of information.

For example, if you do a Google search on "Evan Aidman," you will find my website, websites that will help you order this book, other publications I have authored, my synagogue's website, my high school's website, and other references. In about five minutes, you will know more about me than I would probably want you to know. (It is important to arm yourself with information when you set about hiring an attorney.)

Google News only maintains articles for a certain number of days, so it is a current, not historic record. Older articles, however, should show up in a regular Google search.

Referrals

Even if he or she cannot represent you, the first lawyer you call may be able to refer you to someone who can. A referring attorney is ethically bound to refer you to someone who will zealously pursue your case. In addition, lawyers generally receive referral fees when they send clients to one another. A referred attorney may want to work less on your case if part of the settlement goes to the first attorney for referring you. This is why it is important to exercise your right to know where your money goes and to whom. If the referring attorney and the referred attorney know that you are informed about referral fees, they will be less likely to try to take advantage of you financially or work any less zealously on your case.

In some states, the referring attorney cannot receive a referral fee unless he or she actually works on the case. The referral fee cannot exceed the proportionate amount of work he or she does. The rules of ethics for attorneys vary from state to state. You can call the bar association in your state if you have a concern about a referral fee.

> **NOTE:** *It is illegal for lawyers to pay referral fees to nonlawyers. If an attorney offers you money for sending him or her cases—find a new lawyer.*

Advertisements

A questionable way to find an attorney is through an advertisement. The Yellow Pages are filled with the ads of PI lawyers, some of whom are extremely competent. If you must choose a lawyer from an ad, interview several and then investigate the credentials of those you like. Your state or city bar association maintains disciplinary files that can help you to steer clear of unethical practitioners. These files are not always open to the public.

Treat your selection of a personal injury lawyer the way you would any matter of importance in your life. Your choice of a lawyer may make the difference between years of uncertainty and stress, and a rapid, successful, and pleasant experience. Some people actually even enjoy their exposure to this legal process.

THE INITIAL CONSULTATION

The initial consultation is similar to meeting for the first time with a doctor. The doctor takes your medical history; the lawyer reviews your legal history. The two-way communication between lawyer and client is the crucial first step in achieving a successful outcome.

Before the appointment, try to write down the details of the accident. Your notes and **Checklists 1** or **2** and **3** from this book will help you to provide your lawyer with complete and thorough information. Bring your notes, all of your insurance papers, your doctor's name and address, as well as any discharge forms you received from the hospital. If you have photographs of your car, the accident scene, or your injuries, bring them as well. Your attorney will very much appreciate your interest in the case. If the photographs are of good quality, it may not be necessary for your lawyer to go to the expense of having professional photos taken. This will save you a significant amount of money, since litigation costs are ultimately the client's responsibility.

The attorney will ask you to sign medical authorizations and a fee agreement if he wants to pursue the case. The medical authorization allows the lawyer to collect your medical records. Form 8 in Appendix A is a sample medical authorization. (see form 8, p.240.) The fee agreement is the contract for the attorney's fees. Immediately after the initial meeting, an attorney will often send a *new client letter*. A new client letter may resemble the one on p.50.

Personal injury lawyers almost never charge for the initial consultation. You can interview as many as you like before you sign a fee agreement. However, it is a bad idea to wait too long before selecting one. A prompt investigation by your lawyer may be crucial to your case. So if you are comfortable with the first lawyer you meet, you can sign a fee agreement and let him or her begin the investigation. If you sign a fee agreement, but then change your mind, you can still fire the first lawyer and hire a new one. The first lawyer is required to

turn your file over to the new lawyer. The lawyers will divide one attorney's fee. You should not have to pay extra for changing lawyers.

Many of your questions about the process can be answered during the initial consultation. However, not all questions can be answered at that time with any degree of certainty. For example, there is no way for the lawyer to know at the initial meeting what the case is *worth*, how long before it will settle, or whether you will have to go to court. More questions will arise in your mind in the weeks and months to come. Do not hesitate to call your lawyer for answers—that is why he or she is there.

During the initial consultation, tell the lawyer that you want to receive copies of all letters sent out on your behalf. Many lawyers make this a practice for several reasons. First of all, they feel they have an ethical obligation to keep their clients informed about their cases. But further, an informed client is often a very helpful client. Clients who take an active interest in their case provide important details that might otherwise be overlooked. They can also correct mistakes made by the lawyer or his or her staff. While the lawyer has the legal expertise, no one is more aware of the factual background of the case than the client. The team approach helps the client feel involved and respected, and it helps the lawyer do a good job for the client.

Ask the lawyer who interviews you if he or she will be the one who will actually handle your file. If the lawyer you meet is one of the firm's senior partners, it is likely that your case will be handed off to an associate. This is information you are entitled to receive before you sign a fee agreement. You should insist that the lawyer who interviews you will handle the file, if that is the lawyer with whom you are most comfortable.

Also ask the lawyer who interviews you about his or her credentials as a trial attorney. Ask him or her how many jury trials he or she has taken all the way to verdict. Many trial lawyers are afraid to actually try cases in front of juries and will ultimately settle for whatever they can get. You need a lawyer who is willing to take your case all the way—if necessary. The law firm you hire should not be afraid to spend thousands of dollars getting your case ready for trial, if necessary. If medical testimony is necessary, ask for an estimate of what it is going to cost to bring the case properly before the jury. You should confirm clearly at the initial interview that the firm will be willing to spend the money that needs to be spent.

New Client Letter

Dear New Client:

I have begun processing your claim and I intend to protect your interests and achieve the maximum possible recovery. You can help assure our success by doing the following:

1. Read this letter carefully and save it for future reference.
2. DO NOT DISCUSS THIS CASE WITH ANYONE, EXCEPT FOR ME OR SOMEONE FROM MY OFFICE. REFER ALL OTHER PERSONS TO ME AND ASK YOUR FAMILY, WITNESSES, AND DOCTOR TO FOLLOW THE SAME PRECAUTIONS.
3. Notify me of any change in address or telephone number.
4. Record all expenses you incur as a result of this accident and collect the bills.
5. Keep a journal of your daily pain and suffering and the effect your injury has on everyday activities and relationships. Also, inform your doctor of all symptoms so that he has accurate and complete records of your treatment.
6. Follow your doctor's advice precisely and tell me when he has finally discharged you.
7. Make a copy of your prescriptions and forward them with receipts to me.
8. Do not sign any papers concerning your claim for any insurance company, investigator, or attorney.

The normal processing of a personal injury claim involves the following steps: a) the accident is investigated and necessary witness statements are secured; b) when your doctor discharges you, I collect and review all medical reports and bills, along with any record of lost earnings; c) after I carefully evaluate your case, I will attempt to negotiate an out-of-court settlement; d) I will promptly advise you of the results of the negotiations with my recommendations; and, e) if no settlement can be achieved, I will institute a lawsuit on your behalf.

It is a pleasure representing you. Rest assured that your legal rights will be well-protected.

Sincerely,

YOUR ATTORNEY

THE ATTORNEY'S FEE AGREEMENT

Personal injury lawyers usually use what are known as *contingency fee agreements*. These are agreements that base the attorney's fee on a percentage of the overall settlement. The lawyer's fee is contingent upon settlement of the case. These agreements have been called *the key to the courthouse* for many people, since the client usually does not have to pay any money *up-front* to the lawyer.

Some feel that contingent fee agreements promote litigation. There is no doubt that more people sue because of these agreements. Many countries do not allow such agreements and have much less litigation. However, others feel the empowerment they provide to the average citizen and the accountability they force upon big business justifies their use. Contingent fee agreements are the great equalizer. They allow both the indigent and the middle class to engage in expensive litigation to recover for losses.

The typical contingent fee agreement calls for the client to receive two-thirds of the settlement, with the balance of one-third going to the lawyer. These agreements give the attorney a stake or ownership interest in the litigation. The lawyer gambles that the outcome of the case justifies the time expenditure, monetary investment, and stress involved.

Do not hesitate to try to negotiate a better deal with your lawyer. Especially if you have a good case, your lawyer will be willing to reduce the fee if he or she thinks you will shop for a more favorable arrangement. For example, you could offer 20% if the case settles before a suit is filed; 25% if a suit must be filed; and, 33% if a trial is necessary.

This country is filled with lawyers. There are many dishonest, unscrupulous PI lawyers. But there are also many skilled, honest, and energetic personal injury attorneys to choose from. It is a client's market and you should take advantage of that fact. If you feel that the fee your lawyer wants to charge to handle your case is too high, let him or her know that you would like to negotiate a fee arrangement that will result in you receiving a larger part of the settlement proceeds.

You are free to take your case and leave if you are not satisfied with the terms the lawyer offers. You will be amazed at how willing a lawyer will be to renegotiate if he or she senses that you are ready to head for the door.

At the same time, the fee agreement the lawyer is willing to offer you is not the most important factor in choosing a lawyer. It is more important that you choose a lawyer who is honest, hard working, and experienced in personal injury work. If you shop around for the best possible fee agreement, you may find a bad lawyer who will outbid the rest. Be sure you know what you are getting into before you sign on the dotted line. Again, speak to friends you trust or consult your local bar association before retaining a lawyer.

There is an element of uncertainty for the lawyer with contingent fee cases. The lawyer assumes the risk that there may be no or little recovery after years of work and thousands of dollars of the attorney's own money invested in the costs of litigation. Because of this risk, it is fair that personal injury lawyers sometimes earn more on a contingent fee case, than if they were paid hourly.

Lawyers usually bill on an hourly basis for cases that do not involve personal injuries. The insurance company's lawyer, in defending against the personal injury claim, generally bills the company in this manner. Hourly rates of $150 or more are commonplace. Lawyers who work on an hourly basis are often criticized for putting in unnecessary time on the case. This is called *padding* the time sheet. Attorneys who work with contingency fees are not subject to this criticism, since more time spent on the case does not necessarily translate into higher attorney fees. In fact, the criticism is just the opposite. The clients of PI lawyers frequently complain that they cannot reach their attorney. The lawyer may avoid the client because the lawyer cannot bill the time and may feel that client contact is unnecessary or a nuisance.

Contingency fee agreements motivate the lawyer to work efficiently. Since the lawyer cannot bill hourly, he or she hopes to settle the case for as much as possible, as soon as possible. The lawyer does not get paid until the conclusion of the case. This arrangement, at least theoretically, rewards diligence and hard work. It works for trial lawyers and it works for their clients. When big business and the insurance industry complain about contingent fee agreements, they are thinking only of their self-interest.

One of the most attractive aspects of contingent fee agreements is that the client owes no attorney's fees if the case is not won. This should provide the lawyer with strong motivation to aggressively handle the case in order to obtain a large and prompt settlement.

Insist on receiving a copy of the fee agreement for your records. There is a sample contingent fee agreement in Appendix A. (see form 9, p.241.)

BEWARE OF COSTS

In addition to the lawyer's fee, there will be other costs involved in pursuing your case. These include court filing fees, court reporter fees, expert witness fees, and many things you would never imagine. In major litigation cases, the costs can amount to hundreds of thousands, or even millions of dollars.

Unless the case is extremely difficult, the PI lawyer puts up the costs required to investigate the case, file the legal papers, etc. These are repaid to the lawyer at the successful conclusion of the case. In auto accidents and fall down cases, the lawyer almost always pays for these costs up front. (In medical malpractice cases, unless the liability seems clear and the injuries are severe, the client may be asked to pay the cost of gathering the medical records and having them reviewed. This varies from case to case and from lawyer to lawyer.)

How these fees are paid should be spelled out clearly in the fee agreement. One major issue is whether the costs come out of the client's share of the proceeds or if they are taken out before the proceeds are split. Because the costs can be extremely high, how this is calculated can make a big difference in the outcome.

> **Example:** Consider a $100,000 award in which the costs are $20,000 and the lawyer gets a fee of 33.3%. If the costs come out before the lawyer takes his or her share, the balance is $80,000. Of that $80,000, the lawyer will get $26,666 and the client $53,334. If the lawyer takes his or her 33.3% before costs are taken out, the lawyer will get $33,333. The client will have to pay the costs from his or her share, so he or she will be left with $46,667 ($66,667 - $20,000). This is a difference of $6,667 between the two calculations.

> **NOTE:** *Insist that the costs be taken out of any award first, before the attorney takes his or her percentage. Otherwise you will end up with a much smaller percentage of the net proceeds than you thought.*

DISSATISFACTION WITH ATTORNEYS

The first thing we do, let's kill all the lawyers. Those words, first uttered hundreds of years ago by one of Shakespeare's characters, still reflect the feelings of a large segment of the population. The complaint that is most commonly heard is that the lawyer does not communicate properly with the client or telephone messages are not returned promptly, if ever. The lawyer may well be doing a satisfactory job for the client, but if communications break down, the client can be left feeling powerless, irritated, and dissatisfied.

While you should not stand for being ignored by your lawyer, keep in mind that he or she cannot make progress on your case or those of other clients if he or she is on the phone all day answering clients' questions. If you have a question about your case, consider asking your lawyer's secretary or paralegal. Often he or she can provide the right answer just as easily as the lawyer.

If a communication problem persists, the solution lies in letting your lawyer know in clear and certain terms that you are unhappy. A strongly worded letter, sent by certified mail, will get the lawyer's attention and probably assure a prompt phone call. The letter should express your specific complaints and your desire to hire a new attorney if the necessary steps are not promptly taken. If a satisfactory response is not forthcoming, it may be time to seek out the assistance of another attorney.

CHANGING LAWYERS

Most clients are reluctant to fire one attorney and hire another one. You might be afraid to hurt the lawyer's feelings by rejecting him or her in this way. You may believe that a double attorney's fee will have to be paid if a second lawyer is brought into the picture. This is not the way it works in personal injury cases. You should not be charged one extra dime when you fire one lawyer and hire another. The two lawyers will work out an arrangement in which they split one attorney's fee.

Lawyers are often hesitant about taking another lawyer's case. There are many valid reasons for this. The client may simply have unreasonable expectations about the case and the second lawyer may end up having to deal with the first lawyer's headaches. The second lawyer may fear that some day the first lawyer may take revenge for losing the client. The second lawyer may simply feel that the case cannot be profitably handled since the fee has to be split with the first lawyer. Nevertheless, it is worth checking into changing attorneys if, after expressing your concerns, you are still dissatisfied with your lawyer's performance.

Expressing Your Concerns

Lawyers frequently receive telephone calls from individuals complaining about the lawyer currently handling their personal injury case. Many of these calls involve requests to evaluate the strategy, or lack thereof, of the caller's current attorney. When a lawyer receives this type of call, he or she may respond in a way that is somewhat unsatisfactory to the caller. The lawyer does not mean to be evasive, but the request for this kind of information places him or her in a very bad position. He or she does not have access to the caller's file and is in no position at all to evaluate the other attorney's strategy.

Requests for information about your file should be directed to your present attorney. Your attorney has the obligation to communicate with you in a timely and courteous fashion and to respond to all reasonable requests for information. Again, if your attorney is not responsive, send a certified letter requesting the information you seek. This is sure to get your attorney's attention.

Further, you can be sure that your attorney will very much resent being second-guessed by an outside attorney who has only one side of the story. Most attorneys prefer not to advise a client at this stage that the first attorney is handling the case improperly. If they were to provide such advice, they would open themselves up to lawsuits or complaints to the disciplinary board by the first attorney.

Worse yet, because the second lawyer is operating with only one side of the story and very incomplete information, any advice given would likely be unsatisfactory, and perhaps completely erroneous. This might subject the second lawyer to a later lawsuit by the client for legal malpractice. Thus, if an attorney politely refuses your request for an evaluation of a case another attorney is handling, there may be sound reasons for the refusal.

Occasionally, you can find an attorney who will inform your attorney that you are concerned and need clarification regarding the case. If you do not mind paying this other attorney to act as a buffer for you, a simple phone call may help alleviate your fears that your case is being mishandled. If you have a friend or relative who is an attorney, but not a personal injury attorney, he or she may be able to talk lawyer-to-lawyer with your attorney and express your concerns without making the attorney fear he or she will lose the case.

Seek a New Attorney

If all attempts at resolving the problem with your lawyer fail, you should seek out a new attorney. You have the right to expect competent representation and courteous treatment. You deserve the same level of representation that the insurance company expects from its lawyers.

If you decide to change attorneys, you must take certain steps to assure a smooth transition. First, the new lawyer tells the old lawyer that you desire the change. The new lawyer may ask you to write to the old lawyer to advise him or her to turn your file over. The lawyers then must work out financial arrangements so that everyone's interests are protected. The old lawyer is entitled to be reimbursed for the costs he or she has spent on the case and for the time spent—although that payment generally comes at the end of the case.

The second lawyer hopes to review the file as soon as possible in order to determine if he or she indeed wishes to represent the client. If it looks like the case can profitably be pursued, the second lawyer will take the case over. The case needs to be quite attractive since the lawyers have to split the fee. If there is *not enough to go around*, the second lawyer may make a business judgment that he or she is not interested in taking the case. That leaves the client with an upset first lawyer and a case in legal limbo. The client could be left with no choice but to go lawyer shopping. That is the risk you run when you fire your lawyer, and that is why it pays to select a good one in the first place.

Understand the Insurance Company's Reaction

Insurance companies react in various ways to a change in lawyers. They may view the switch as a sign that the case or the client is a problem from your lawyer's perspective. This can result in increased reluctance to settle and a stepped-up investigation into the merits of the case. Another possibility is that the new lawyer will breathe needed energy into the case, causing the insurance company to start thinking seriously of settlement. The reputation and ability of the new lawyer are key to the insurance company's reaction to a switch in representation.

There is one thing you must avoid doing if you are dissatisfied with your lawyer. Under no circumstances may you contact the insurance company yourself. Whether you distrust your lawyer, believe that by contacting the insurance firm you will find out *what was actually going on*, or you simply do not believe your lawyer's explanation concerning a delay in the settlement of the case, this is a big mistake.

Insurance companies operate out of a *where there is smoke there is fire* mindset. If you contact the insurance company yourself, this will signify to the insurance company that something is wrong either with you, your lawyer, or both. Once the insurance company smells smoke, the chances for a quick settlement will immediately fly out the window.

Then, instead of securing a quick settlement, your lawyer will probably have to file the lawsuit and prepare to engage in extended and expensive discovery. (See Chapter 9 for more on discovery.) The insurance company will not only demand your deposition, but it will also undoubtedly subpoena every record that conceivably can provide it with information to use against you. It may subpoena your doctor's records, your employment records, and maybe even your school records. Only after all this discovery, if it turns out that despite the *smoke*, there was no *fire*, will settlement discussions resume. Even worse, the insurance company's lawyers often find something during discovery that can severely damage your case. If that happens, the settlement value of your case drops and the case may have to go to trial. The bottom line: never contact the insurance company directly. You should let your lawyer handle *all* contacts with that company.

KEEPING YOUR CASE ACTIVE

It is your job to be actively involved with your case, from the day of the accident until the check clears the bank. That is the best way to ensure that your lawyer does his or her job properly. Many personal injury attorneys are overworked or are simply too lazy to do the job right without some prompting. Everyone has heard that *the squeaky wheel gets the grease*. Nowhere is this more important than in personal injury litigation.

Firms

If you have entrusted your case to one of the larger personal injury firms, your situation may be pushed onto an associate who has nothing financially to gain by handling your case aggressively. The famous partner who is known for several multi-million dollar jury verdicts may simply not have the time for your case. Many young lawyers are filled with energy for effective battle with the insurance companies. But many are handling a hundred or more other files, and yours may be placed on a very slow assembly line. They may be inexperienced, stressed out, and unprepared to handle your case properly.

Worse, the associate may have no financial stake in your case. The arrangements vary from firm to firm, but with the vast majority, the only lawyer who has a financial interest in your case is the one who brought the case into the firm. The lowly associate who actually ends up processing the case is undoubtedly on straight salary. His or her financial incentive is to turn over his or her cases with the least personal bother, even if this means settling the case for less than it is worth.

If, however, you retain a solo practitioner or small partnership, the lawyer who handles your case will actually receive the attorney's fees earned on the case. Nothing motivates like a financial incentive. Even though lawyers are ethically bound to zealously represent the interests of all their clients, human nature should tell you that you will do best if your lawyer has something to gain by prosecuting your case aggressively and forcefully.

On the other hand, hiring an attorney from a larger, personal injury firm may have some very important advantages. A large firm typically has resources that the solo practitioner or small partnership does not. A large firm typically has a larger support staff than a smaller firm. Further, the attorney or attorneys handling your case should have access to the expertise of all the firm's personal injury lawyers. In a large firm, one lawyer may have expertise in products liability cases. Another lawyer may be the medical malpractice specialist. A third lawyer may be a star in front of the jury. The large firm practitioner has the luxury of being able to call on these other lawyers for help with the cases he or she is handling. A solo practitioner may have to rely on outside attorneys for help with novel or difficult issues or with complex jury trials.

These days, however, the playing field is much more level. The resources available on the Internet provide the solo or small firm practitioner with access to materials and experts that were previously unavailable. For example, many trial lawyers associations now have *listservs*—computer-based sounding boards used by professionals of all kinds, as well as individuals with a special interest in a particular subject. Trial lawyers have listservs that allow them to share information in a dynamic format concerning the battlefront issues in personal injury litigation.

In years past, finding the answer to a complex legal question usually required a trip to the law library. Now, this type of question can be answered in mere minutes through a listserv. It gives almost instant access to the top personal injury lawyers in the area.

Legal research materials are also readily available on the Internet. It used to be that a big firm with a large law library had the advantage over the solo attorney. These days, the material is all available on the Internet. For the price of belonging to a local bar association, an attorney now has instant access to virtually all of the relevant case law and legal digests.

For the same reasons, the playing field is much more level between the small plaintiff's firms and the insurance defense firms. The latter typically have many more lawyers and larger support staffs. With the easy access to listservs and legal databases via the Internet, the small plaintiff is on more equal footing with the big defense firm.

When it comes to selecting a lawyer, the bottom line, regardless of the size of the firm, is the competence and professionalism of the lawyer or lawyers who will actually handle your case. Whichever type of firm you interview, make sure you ask if the firm's lawyers use the Internet and belong to and participate regularly in trial lawyer's listserv.

Your Part

Staying active throughout the process is important regardless of the lawyer you retain. If your case has been shuffled off to an associate, your involvement is especially critical. You should insist on receiving copies of all correspondences your lawyer sends out on your behalf. You can even ask for copies of all letters from the insurance company and its lawyers.

The only way you can know for sure that your lawyer is being straight with you is if you have access to the file. Since the lawyer knows you are keeping a watchful eye, he or she will be sure not to *back burner* your case. In other words, he or she will know that unless he or she stays very active, you will be calling with difficult questions. It is your right to know what is going on at all times with your case. It is also your right to have a lawyer who will aggressively pursue a rapid and fair settlement of your case. Do not accept anything less.

After the initial interview with the lawyer, wait a week or so before you call to find out how things are going. You will want to know if witnesses have been contacted, if a request for the police report has been made, and so on. Follow up a couple weeks later and then perhaps once a month after that. Of course, if specific questions come up, you should feel free to call anytime.

The Problem Client

In keeping your case active, you do not want to turn into a *problem client*. Problem clients call every other day, often just to talk. Problem clients may call to complain about everything that is wrong in their life. Your lawyer is not there to hold your hand or to become your social companion. Most lawyers are simply too busy for that. Organize your thoughts before you make the call so that you can make your points and ask your questions clearly and concisely.

Lawyers are used to processing information quickly and directly. If you chatter endlessly in a disorganized fashion, your lawyer may wish to terminate the conversation as soon as possible.

Trial lawyering can be a very stressful way to make a living. If your phone calls add to this stress, your lawyer may dread your calls. If prematurely terminated calls cause your attorney to miss out on useful information, your case will suffer. Your lawyer will resent the fact that he or she has to waste a lot of time on activities that do nothing to further your case. Human nature may cause your lawyer to recommend settlement of your case for less than it is worth so that he or she can close your file and get rid of a problem client.

Settlement Package

When your medical treatment is completed, let your lawyer know. Insist that he or she immediately finish the process of gathering your records and organizing them into a *settlement package*. A settlement package is a collection of your medical bills and reports, photographs, and expert witness reports. Expert witnesses can be economists retained to determine your economic losses or vocational specialists who help determine the jobs available for injured plaintiffs. Assuming the cooperation of your doctors and experts, the settlement package should be on its way to the insurance company within a month after you finish your treatment. If it is not, find out why. The first offer of settlement should be made within three weeks after the settlement package is sent. If it is not, find out why. If the case is not settled within six weeks after the package is sent, find out why.

If the case does not settle, insist that your lawyer immediately prepare the lawsuit papers. This should take no more than an hour to complete. These papers should be in your hands within a week. The suit should be filed by the time another week passes.

These things will happen only if your lawyer is on his or her toes. Most lawyers need prompting from their clients to stay there. Keeping tabs on the progress of your case does not make you a problem client, just actively concerned. Your lawyer should appreciate your interest.

Discovery

Even after the suit is filed, you need to stay active. Be sure your lawyer is aggressively pursuing discovery. (See Chapter 10 for more on discovery.) When it comes time to respond to the other lawyer's discovery requests, it is very important that you work closely with your lawyer. Be sure that the information he or she provides to the other lawyer is accurate.

Double Checking

It is very easy for an overworked or lazy lawyer to get it wrong. It is up to you to double-check the information provided to the other side. You may feel that your lawyer is being paid handsomely to do the job independently, and you may resent having to help. If so, feel free to trust that your lawyer will get it right. However, do not complain when mistakes are made. It is much better and easier to catch errors before they become problems.

Try to think of your case as a challenging game to succeed at, rather than a difficult job to avoid doing. You can think of yourself and your lawyer as partners, with you having special knowledge of the facts and your lawyer having special knowledge of the law. Your case is an opportunity to learn and grow, not just to make money.

Depositions and Trial Testimony

The most important phases of a personal injury case are depositions (Chapter 10) and the trial (Chapter 11)—preparation is key. Be sure your lawyer knows that you expect him or her to take all the time needed with you to ensure that no mistakes are made. If your case is an average personal injury matter, your deposition will probably last about an hour and a half. Your lawyer should spend at least an hour with you prior to the deposition getting you ready for it. Later, you will also need to prepare for your trial testimony. Again, you should spend at least an hour with your lawyer just before the trial in preparation.

If you are working through a firm, and the lawyer assigned to your case resists taking the time to prepare you, you may be in big trouble. Call the partner who attracted you to the firm in the first place and find out why you are not being given an adequate preparation session. Preparation for testimony is a very important part of your case. If you are being neglected, do not worry about ruffling the feathers of the associate handling the case. Call the partner and complain.

chapter four:
Various Kinds of Injury Cases

There are many different kinds of injury cases. These cases are sometimes referred to as tort cases. The word *tort* comes from the French word meaning *wrong*. The wrongdoer is known as the *tortfeasor*. Sometimes, injury cases are called negligence cases. *Negligence* is defined in injury law as the failure to exercise the care for the safety of another that a prudent person would ordinarily use. Negligence is an inadequate label, since some types of injury cases involve more than mere negligence. An example would be an injury caused intentionally, like an assault. For simplicity and completeness, all of these matters are here referred to as *injury cases*.

The concept of fault runs throughout any examination of injury cases. *Fault* must be proven before the injured party can obtain a legal remedy or judgment. The concept of *no-fault* refers to a system of payment of lost wages and medical bills resulting from an accident. The system was created to allow quick compensation without the need to fight over who was at fault. Fault does not need to be proven to collect these benefits, creating the term no-fault benefits. Auto accident victims are entitled to no-fault benefits even if they caused the accident.

This chapter reviews some of the different types of injury cases. Medical malpractice cases are discussed separately in Chapter 5.

INJURIES TO CHILDREN

A mother and father's worst nightmare is receiving a call from the hospital informing them that their child has been involved in an accident. While the physical and emotional suffering from such an event can never be set right by money, a lawsuit against the person at fault may be in the child's best interests. Handled properly, this type of case almost always results in fair compensation for the child.

While most people feel sympathy for injured children, do not expect obtaining financial compensation to be simple. In an automobile accident case for example, the insurance company typically takes the position that the child ran suddenly into the street and that the driver had no chance to react. The insurance companies refer to these cases as *pedestrian dart-out* cases. By labeling it this way, the insurance company hopes to create the impression that there was no way for the driver to avoid the accident. Personal injury lawyers, on the other hand, refer to these kinds of cases as *pedestrian knock-down* cases. You can clearly see the image your attorney hopes to create by using that label.

Regardless of what it is called, the best hope for litigation success when a child is hit by a car is a prompt and thorough investigation of the accident scene. The vital factors include the type of neighborhood where the accident happened, the length of time the child was visible to the motorist, and the age of the child. It is important to photograph the scene of the accident shortly after it occurs, if the photos will help to prove that the area was one in which children are likely to be present. Nearby playgrounds, schools, or shops that cater to children should be photographed since these put the motorist on notice that cautious driving is required. Traffic signs that warn motorists to watch for children must be photographed for the same reason.

If it can be proven that the child was visible to the motorist for more than a second or two, the chances for success in this litigation are greatly improved. The adult motorist is presumed to have the capacity to take steps to protect the safety of the child and must take them promptly in order to avoid responsibility on this claim. Children are often presumed incapable of negligence due to their tender years. The younger the child is, the stronger this presumption generally becomes.

A 12-year-old has a much weaker presumption of non-negligence than does a 6-year-old. Thus, if a 6-year-old is struck by a car, this child will almost certainly receive compensation for injuries suffered in the accident. Yet, even the 12-year-old is not held to the same standard of care as the adult driver. That is one reason why these cases are so easy to win when handled properly.

Similar rules apply to other accidents involving children, such as injuries on a dangerous piece of property or in a playground. The sooner you take pictures of the scene and get information from witnesses about the situation at the time of the accident, the better.

Juries, judges, and arbitration panels have special sympathy for children. They are much more likely to return large awards for children than they are for adults. Many feel that greed is the primary motivation when adults sue for personal injuries. This factor is far less prominent in the minds of jurors, judges, and arbitrators when it is a child who is injured.

In automobile cases, the medical bills resulting from the child's injuries are paid by the parents' automobile insurer. If there is no insurance in the household, the insurance for the driver has to pay these bills.

FALL-DOWN ACCIDENTS (SLIP-AND-FALLS)

Automobile accidents (see Chapter 1) and fall-down cases are the most common types of lawsuit for personal injuries. The legal principles involved with these types of cases differ greatly. Following are the hurdles that must be overcome in order to receive fair compensation for injuries suffered as the result of a fall.

Generally, the most difficult problem involves the question of notice. The injured victim must prove that the defendant either created the hazard that caused the injury or that the defendant knew or should have known of the hazard long enough before the accident to have removed or repaired it.

For example, when a pedestrian trips on a crack in a sidewalk, the personal injury attorney hopes to find someone who lives in the area who knows that the crack existed for a long time. Or, photos may show that the crack was not of recent origin. It is then easy to show that the property owner should have known of it and should have had the crack repaired.

The city where the accident happened may also have liability for failure to enforce the municipal requirements that sidewalks be kept in good repair. This is particularly important when the property owner carries no insurance on the property. In this situation, the government may be the only defendant against whom a money judgment can be collected. The city becomes the *deep pocket* or *target* defendant.

A thorough and prompt investigation can make all the difference in the outcome of fall-down cases. Witness statements must be obtained and photographs of the hazard must be taken. Even short delays can hurt the case, since memories fade rapidly and hazards get repaired quickly when injuries occur.

The discussion that follows sets forth the different classifications that some states use to describe fall-down accident plaintiffs. Although these exact classifications may not apply in your state, this discussion should at least enlighten you to some degree as to this subject matter. Be sure to consult the law in your own state.

Invitees

Property owners and their tenants owe the highest duty of care to individuals they invite onto their property. In some states, customers of businesses have the status of *business invitees*. The owner of the business is under the duty to protect the business visitor, not only against dangers the owner knows about, but also against those which with reasonable care he or she might discover. The business invitee enters the business' premises with the assurance that the business owner has taken steps for his or her protection and safety while on the business premises. The store customer is entitled to rely upon the business owner's performance of his or her duty to make the premises safe.

Licensees

A lesser standard of care is required with respect to *licensees*. In states in which that classification is used, a licensee may be defined as a person who may enter or remain on the property only by virtue of the consent of the possessor of that property. For example, social guests are licensees. Even though a social guest is normally invited, he or she is not on the property for business reasons. A person who cuts through a business parking lot to get to another location is also a licensee.

A possessor of land is subject to liability to his licensees for injuries caused by the possessor's *failure to exercise reasonable care* for their safety only under certain circumstances. The licensee must show 1) that the possessor should have expected that the licensee would not discover the danger and 2) that the licensee did not know or have reason to know of the danger. Thus, hidden dangers subject the possessor to liability, but open dangers do not.

Trespassers

A *trespasser* is one who enters the land of another without any right to do so or who goes beyond the rights or privileges which he or she has been granted by license or invitation. As a general rule, the owner or occupier's duty to a trespasser is to refrain from willfully or wantonly injuring the trespasser. However, foreseeable trespassers may, under certain circumstances, be entitled to greater protection. Thus, an *attractive nuisance*, such as an unfenced swimming pool, may subject the owner to liability if a child from the neighborhood wanders in and drowns. It is foreseeable that this might happen. Thus, the possessor must protect even trespassers from harm in this kind of case.

Comparative Negligence

The next issue that almost always comes up in these cases is the victim's own failure to be careful. This is called *comparative negligence*. (See Chapter 10 for a discussion of comparative negligence.) Defendants argue that the claimant should have seen the hazard and avoided it. While this argument often reduces the total amount of compensation received, it usually does not defeat the claim outright. There may be valid reasons that the hazard was not seen. For example, when a customer in a grocery store slips on grapes, the customer's attention may have been drawn by a catchy advertisement or display put up by the store. This is a reasonable explanation which, if believed, should enable you to receive full compensation.

DOG BITES

Another kind of personal injury case is for injuries arising out of a dog bite. Most states make it unlawful for the owner of a dog to fail to keep it either confined within the owner's premises or firmly secured by means of a collar and chain. A violation of such a law resulting in a dog bite is strong evidence of negligence. If you were bitten as a result of such a violation, it is likely that you can successfully pursue a personal injury lawsuit against the owner of the dog. In most cases, homeowners' insurance will cover such a claim.

One Free Bite Rule

Some states have what is known as a *one free bite* rule. This means that, under ordinary circumstances, the dog owner would not be responsible for the dog's first bite. You would have to prove that the dog had previously bitten another person or, at the very least, shown vicious propensities through fierce behavior in order to prevail in a dog bite case.

In other states, the *one free bite* rule has been abolished. The plaintiff is no longer required to prove that the dog showed vicious propensities prior to the attack. Essentially, you would simply have to prove that the dog owner was careless in confining or handling the dog and that this led to the attack.

Defenses

A typical defense in dog bite cases is that the plaintiff harassed the dog in some way, thereby leading to the attack. If, for example, a group of teenage boys were taunting and throwing rocks at a dog and the dog responded by biting one or more of the boys, the insurance defense attorney would argue that the attack was not the dog's fault. Under these circumstances, this would probably be an effective defense.

A small child, on the other hand, stands a better chance in this type of case, even if it is proven that his or her actions in some way incited the dog. Small children are considered less legally responsible for their behavior. It is possible in this kind of case that the attorney for the dog owner will enjoin the parents of the child into the litigation as additional defendants. In other words, this attorney will sue the parents as the responsible parties for their child's action and injuries. The two lawsuits are then consolidated so that they are tried before the judge or jury at the same time.

This attorney may claim that the parents failed to properly supervise the child thereby leading to the attack. If, in fact, the parents were negligent in their supervision of the child, it may well be that the child will end up collecting from the parents' own homeowners' insurance company. Or, if both the dog owner and the parents were negligent, the two insurance companies would have to share payment of the verdict or award.

Procedure

If you or someone you know has been injured by a dog bite, be sure to take photographs of the injury as soon as possible. If the scar worsens in appearance after you take the photographs, for example, through infection, take more photographs. It is important to try to get witnesses for this kind of case. If friends or neighbors know of the dog's history of biting, make sure you get witness statements, since this will help to get the case settled. Do not forget to contact the appropriate health authorities for dog bite injuries to ensure that the victim has not contracted rabies. The dog should be quarantined and tested by these health authorities.

During the litigation of a dog bite case, be sure to get complete veterinary records for the dog. The dog may have exhibited vicious behavior in the past, but the owners may not be willing to admit it unless you have documented proof. You may need to issue a subpoena in order to get these records. (see form 14, p.263.) The court in which you file will have its own form that you must use. It may also be possible to use a record production service to obtain documents you need to pursue your case. Court procedures for record production vary from state to state and county to county.

LEGAL MALPRACTICE

The issue of legal malpractice is relevant to every type of legal case. If a contract lawyer makes an important mistake in drafting a contract, the client can sue for legal malpractice. Similarly, if a personal injury lawyer errs when handling a personal injury case, the client should consider the possibility of suing the lawyer for legal malpractice. Personal injury litigation carries high potential for legal malpractice claims. The malpractice premium your lawyer pays to insurance carriers may reflect this fact. One reason is that people who sue for personal injuries are often particularly litigious. Such people may be looking for reasons to sue their own lawyers.

The most common mistake in personal injury litigation that leads to the malpractice claim is a blown statute of limitations. (See page 134 for a listing of the statutes of limitations for negligence cases.) If an attorney does not file the lawsuit by the statute of limitations deadline, there is a very good chance that he or she could be sued for malpractice.

Missing a statute of limitations date is objectively provable. Whether an error occurred is not a matter of opinion. However, other errors may be more subjective and therefore harder to prove.

Perhaps your lawyer failed to present evidence of lost earning capacity. If you suffered a severe injury and can no longer work in your chosen field, your lawyer may have needed to hire vocational or economic experts to fully prove your losses. Failure to do so may be malpractice.

Perhaps your lawyer failed to collect all the admissable medical records or failed to take the testimony of one of your key doctors. If this omission was the result of carelessness and it adversely affected the outcome of your case, your lawyer probably malpracticed.

Pay close attention to the rulings of the trial judge during your case. If the judge excludes an important piece of evidence or prevents an important witness from testifying, find out why. If the judge so ruled because your lawyer failed to take an important procedural step, that may be malpractice. You are entitled to an explanation. If the explanation does not satisfy you, you may need to consult a malpractice lawyer.

Most *mistakes* that a personal injury attorney makes are subjective. While you may feel that your lawyer should have handled your trial differently, in most cases it may come down to a matter of trial strategy. For example, your lawyer may have failed to ask a particular question of you or an adverse witness at trial, or he or she may have failed to call a particular witness to testify at all.

You may feel that this is a malpractice. Consider, however, that the lawyer may have had a very good strategic reason to avoid asking the question or bringing the witness to court. Perhaps asking the question carried risks the lawyer did not wish to take. Or perhaps the witness, once brought to court, may have hurt your case in other areas with his or her testimony. Your lawyer may well have been justified in how he or she presented your case.

It may be difficult to prove malpractice in this kind of situation. Unless you can prove that it was more likely that the result of your case would have substantially changed had the lawyer acted as you now claim he or she should have acted, it will be hard to prove that he or she committed malpractice. Clearly, legal malpractice claims can be complex and difficult.

Malpractice litigation is sometimes referred to as a *case within a case*. This is because to successfully prove a legal malpractice case, you have to show not only that the lawyer committed malpractice, but also that, had the lawyer not committed malpractice, you would have won the underlying case.

Example: Mr. Smith rearends Mr. Jones' automobile and Mr. Smith retains a lawyer to sue Mr. Jones. If this lawyer files suit against Mr. Jones after the running of the statute of limitations deadline, Mr. Smith will probably not be able to collect from either Mr. Jones' auto insurance company or from the lawyer's malpractice insurer.

Even if the lawyer had filed suit on time, the underlying lawsuit against Mr. Jones was probably not meritorious. Mr. Smith could not have collected from Mr. Jones' insurer. This will be the first line of defense presented by the lawyer whom the malpractice insurer assigns to defend Mr. Smith's original lawyer.

If, however, it was Mr. Jones who rearended Mr. Smith, Mr. Smith's lawyer will very much regret having failed to sue on time. It should be easy to prove both that this lawyer committed malpractice and that, had he sued on time, Mr. Smith would have won his case. The legal malpractice insurer might very well pay such a case without much of a battle.

Legal malpractice litigation is a specialty unto itself. There are lawyers who do nothing but sue other lawyers. (You can imagine how popular they must be at bar association conventions and parties.) It is essential that the malpractice lawyer you retain to sue your first lawyer understands fully both the law of legal malpractice itself and the law involved in the underlying lawsuit. Thus, Mr. Smith's malpractice lawyer should understand how to handle both malpractice litigation and personal injury litigation.

Most lawyers prefer not to sue other lawyers. Aside from the difficulty of having to prove both the legal malpractice and the merit of the underlying case, many lawyers simply do not wish to alienate a colleague by suing him or her. The lawyer may feel that *what goes around comes around.* Some day the lawyer being sued will be in a position to get back at the lawyer retained to sue him or her.

Similarly, you may realize in pursuing medical malpractice litigation, that it is very hard to find a doctor willing to testify that another doctor committed medical malpractice. Again, the doctor may worry the shoe some day will be on the other foot. Or, the doctor may simply feel a sense of loyalty to a colleague which deters him or her from testifying.

Most lawyers carry legal malpractice coverage. Assuming the insurance company is itself financially solvent, collecting on a settlement or judgment is not a problem. If, however, you find that you need to sue a lawyer who is not covered, you will be left with the unhappy task of having to collect from the lawyer's personal assets. Collecting from the personal assets of anyone you sue can be a serious problem. See page 176 for a discussion of collecting from an uninsured defendant.

Unless the *mistake* is fairly clear cut, like a blown statute of limitations and the underlying case is fairly significant in size, it may be difficult to find a lawyer who will handle a malpractice case with a contingent fee agreement. The complexity of these cases, the case-within-a-case aspect, the possibility that the malpractice insurer will disclaim coverage and the unpleasantness of a lawyer suing a colleague—all contribute to this difficulty.

If, however, you are able to pay a retainer based on an hourly fee, you will have no trouble at all finding a lawyer. In fact, in virtually every area of law, if you have the ability to pay a retainer, you will be able to find a lawyer to work with you. The question will always be whether it makes financial sense to do so.

Some people lose sight of what makes fiscal sense when they have been wronged. They may be willing to pay dearly to make their previous lawyer suffer, even if the amount they can conceivably recover will not cover their counsel fees. That is this person's right, and it will not be that hard to find a lawyer to assist such a crusade.

The lawyer should, however, make the financial risks clear at the outset. If the client wishes to proceed after this warning, he or she can do so. Most people will realize the ultimate futility of such a course of litigation, lick their wounds, and move on.

As you can imagine, even the threat of a malpractice suit is a distressing matter for any professional. Many lawyers hesitate before advising their malpractice carrier of a claim. They may fear that their insurance premium will dramatically increase. If the dispute is over a relatively small amount of money, the lawyer may be willing to compensate the client out of his or her own pocket, rather than putting the insurer on notice of the claim.

On the other hand, the lawyer may simply choose to represent him- or herself, thereby avoiding putting the insurer on notice. If he or she does this, you may be in for a very long, hard fight. As with suing a doctor for malpractice, lawyers take malpractice allegations very personally. Since the lawyer will have to pay any settlement or verdict out of his or her own pocket, he or she may call on his or her legal expertise to put up a long and difficult legal battle.

FOOD POISONING CASES

Food poisoning cases are difficult to pursue and usually settle for no more than *nuisance value*, a relatively small amount of money. Many personal injury lawyers refuse to take them. Because the lawyer is compensated only upon settlement, the relatively low value of most of these cases, along with the problems of proof, make them generally a poor investment of the lawyer's time and money.

If you have been severely harmed by a contaminated food product, you need to immediately find a good personal injury lawyer. For example, a negligently packed canned food product can cause serious bacterial diseases such as botulism. To prove a food poisoning case, you should go to a hospital for blood and stool samples. It is also helpful if the food is kept intact for examination by an expert. Keep it in a safe place where it will neither be thrown away or exposed to heat. Depending on the food product, it should probably be stored in the refrigerator or freezer. Your lawyer will instruct you as to the best way to handle this situation.

WORKERS' COMPENSATION

If you are injured on the job, you may be entitled to workers' compensation. Laws vary from state to state. The discussion that follows is the general view of most states, but you should consult an attorney in your area to be sure no important differences apply to your case.

Workers' compensation pays the medical bills and lost wages of individuals injured or killed in the course of their employment. It is not necessary to prove that your employer was at fault for the accident, because workers' compensation is administered under a no-fault system.

The tradeoff for receiving benefits without having to prove negligence is that you cannot sue your employer for compensation for your pain and suffering. Thus, workers' compensation cases differ from ordinary injury cases in two respects.

1. In a non-work-related injury, you must prove fault to collect, while in workers' compensation you need not prove fault.
2. You can collect for your pain and suffering in non-work-related accidents, but you cannot when you are injured at work.

There are some exceptions to these rules. If your employer does not carry workers' compensation insurance, you can sue your employer for your pain and suffering. If your injury at work was caused by some individual or company other than your employer or a co-worker, you can collect workers' compensation benefits from your employer's insurance. At the same time, you may still have a lawsuit for your pain and suffering against the individual or company that caused the accident.

Your attorney's involvement will also differ, depending upon whether your injury occurred during the course of your employment. In non-work-related accidents, the personal injury attorney hopes to get involved with the case at the very earliest opportunity so that a prompt investigation of the accident can be completed. In workers' compensation cases, the individual can generally pursue the claim without the services of an attorney. It is only when the claim is denied that it is necessary to obtain the services of an attorney.

The workers' compensation attorney generally receives 20% of the benefits paid. In non-work-related accidents, the personal injury attorney generally charges 33⅓ percent of the settlement or verdict.

SOCIAL SECURITY DISABILITY

Everyone knows that Social Security benefits are available to retired workers. But did you know that you might qualify for Social Security payments before you reach retirement age?

If you are disabled and unable to work, you may be eligible to receive Social Security benefits. There are two separate programs that pay disabled persons—*Social Security Disability* and and *Supplemental Security Income* (SSI).

To qualify for Social Security Disability benefits, you must work a minimum number of quarters (three months) and earn at least $500 in each quarter. If you do, the Social Security Administration (SSA) then applies a five-part analysis to determine if you receive benefits. The criteria for receiving SSI benefits are basically the same, except that a person with no work history may qualify to receive SSI benefits. The five-part analysis is as follows.

1. *Are you working?* If so, even part-time, no benefits are payable. As a general rule, you must be out of work to receive benefits.

2. *Do you have a severe medical impairment?* A severe medical impairment is one that significantly limits your physical or mental abilities to do basic work activities and is expected to last, or has lasted, at least twelve consecutive months, or will result in death.

   Physical limitations involve standing, walking, sitting, pushing, pulling, lifting, bending, carrying, reaching, handling, and the ability to see, hear, and speak. Mental limitations involve attention and concentration, the ability to understand and follow instructions, dealing with the public, handling work stresses, and the like.

   All physical and mental problems must be documented and supported by medically accepted tests and by available records and reports from treating doctors and hospitals.

3. *Does your medical problem meet or equal the listing of impairments maintained by the SSA?* The SSA publishes a seventy-page listing of

impairments by which it measures the severity of an impairment to determine if you will receive benefits. This determination is made without consideration of work history, skills, education, or age. This evaluation turns on the medical evidence available. If an impairment does not fit within the listing, the SSA goes on to Step 4.

4. *Does the medical impairment prevent you from returning to your past relevant work?* This means the job or jobs that you held within the fifteen years before the date of application. In reaching a decision, SSA will consider your physical and mental limitations and the job requirements of all jobs you held within the last fifteen years. If SSA concludes that you cannot perform past relevant work, it must proceed to Step 5.

5. *Does the medical impairment prevent you from performing other work that exists in the national economy?* In so deciding, the SSA must consider factors such as your age, education, and work experience along with your physical and mental limitations. The SSA also takes into account your *residual functioning capacity.* This involves evaluating your ability to sit, stand, walk, lift, carry, bend, push, pull, climb, and other physical activities. The SSA does not have to show that you could actually receive a job offer, nor does the SSA refer you to a specific job. All the SSA has to do is determine if you are capable of performing other work.

Based on this evaluation, the SSA will determine whether you can perform a job ranging from sedentary to heavy work. The SSA also takes into account whether skills you learned in prior jobs can be transferred to any other job.

Example: Alan is fifty-two years old, has a 12th grade education, and worked as a truck driver for twenty years in a job classified as medium work (one that routinely requires lifting of up to fifty pounds). Alan suffers from a chronic sprain of the lower back that keeps him from lifting more than ten pounds and from standing and walking for more than a few minutes at a time. His doctor clears him to perform sedentary work (mostly sitting). However, under SSA regulations, Alan would qualify to receive disability benefits.

Why? Even though Alan can still perform a sit-down job, his age (over fifty) is a factor that would make it difficult for him to find and hold a job. If he were forty-two years old, with all other factors the same, his benefits would be denied.

NOTE: *With private disability insurance, you are required only to show that you are unable to return to your former work.*

Applying for Benefits

The first step in applying for benefits is to visit your local SSA office and complete an application. You can find the address of your local office by checking the government section of your telephone directory or by calling the toll-free number for Social Security information at 800-772-1213 (be patient—you could be in for a long wait).

When you visit the office, you will be asked to fill out a lot of paperwork. You will describe in detail the physical requirements of each job you held (standing, walking, lifting, etc.) and your medical history. It is very important that the SSA have a complete list of your medical providers. Keep a record of the names and addresses of each of your doctors and of any hospital where you received treatment. Bring this with you when visiting your SSA office.

The SSA sends the completed paperwork to a designated state agency that assigns someone to obtain and review the medical evidence. Within three months, the SSA will send a written decision either granting or denying benefits. According to figures provided by the SSA, about 61% of all initial applicants for fiscal year 1993 were denied. Ten years later, about 60% of all initial applicants were still being turned down.

NOTE: *Social Security disability law and the criteria for receiving benefits is separate from and is not related to the Americans with Disabilities Act.*

Applying for Reconsideration

If your application is denied, the next step is to ask for reconsideration. Your local office has the forms. You must request reconsideration within sixty days after receiving the written notice of denial. If you do not, you have to start all over again. A majority of the requests for reconsideration are denied.

Requesting a Hearing

If you file for reconsideration and are denied, you can request a hearing before an *administrative law judge* (ALJ). You must file a request for a hearing within sixty days after receiving the written notice of reconsideration. Your local office has these forms (as do most attorneys who handle disability and SSI cases).

Your chance of receiving benefits improves greatly once you get to an ALJ hearing. According to SSA figures, ALJs granted benefits in 68% of the claims they heard in fiscal year 1993. Ten years later, almost two-thirds of appellants who were initially denied were ultimately granted benefits. This disparity between the high percentage of initial denials and high percentage of ultimately successful claimants suggests that something needs to be changed in the system. Persistence pays off when it comes to Social Security disability claims.

At a hearing, you get a chance to tell the ALJ your story and to present evidence in your favor. The ALJs are independent hearing officers with greater knowledge of applicable law and medical terms than the reviewers who decide initial applications and reconsideration.

Disability hearings are informal, fact-finding procedures. You and your attorney will appear before the ALJ to present your evidence. A hearing officer attends and records the hearing and handles your file. Sometimes medical and vocational experts attend and offer testimony about your case.

Your testimony will cover your age, education, vocational training, work record, and your physical and/or psychological disability. The ALJ considers your testimony along with the medical records, expert testimony, and your attorney's legal arguments before rendering a decision. You can expect to receive a written copy of that decision within ninety days after the hearing. If you win, figure on waiting an additional two to three months before you get your first check.

Appealing an Unfavorable ALJ Decision

If you have a hearing and the ALJ rejects your claim, you have the right to request review by the *Appeals Council* (within sixty days). The Appeals Council is composed of various ALJs who review the evidence and decide whether to uphold or reverse the decision, or to send the case to another ALJ for a new hearing.

If the Appeals Council rejects your appeal, you have the right to file a lawsuit in your local federal district court where you can ask that the court reverse the SSA and grant you benefits or a new hearing. This must be done within sixty days of the Appeals Council's decision. You may be able to request an extension if you have good cause, but it is best to file within the sixty day time frame.

You are entitled to legal representation at each stage of the process. Federal regulations limit attorney's fees to 25% of the benefits obtained for the client.

Be sure that any lawyer you retain specializes in Social Security disability litigation. This area of litigation is very different, procedurally, from car accidents, slip and falls, and other kinds of personal injury litigation.

Keep in mind that persistence and a good deal of patience usually pay off when dealing with the SSA.

PRODUCTS LIABILITY

Products liability law involves injuries resulting from defective products. These are often among the most serious injuries. Products liability cases arise when injuries occur because of a defectively designed, manufactured, repaired, or maintained product. For example, if a company designs automobile airbags that do not inflate properly upon impact, the laws of products liability apply to the injury lawsuits that are filed.

The Product

If you are injured by a defective product, hold on to the product for dear life. You must have access to the product to have the best chance for success in the lawsuit. If you do not have access to the product, contact a lawyer immediately. Your lawyer can assure that the product is not destroyed. If the product is lost or destroyed, neither your experts nor the company's experts are able to examine the product for defects. It is your burden to prove that the product was defective. So if the product cannot be examined, you may not be able to prove your case.

Strict Liability

The products liability law in your state may have the concept of strict liability. *Strict liability* involves the assessment of liability on the basis of the defect itself. The law permits liability to be assessed against the defendant on proof that the product was defective.

Cost

Products liability cases are very expensive to pursue. Expert engineers must testify concerning the defect in the product. The big corporations involved with the design, manufacture, etc., of the product have lots of lawyers and big budgets. They hope to *paper to death* the opposition with legal motions, petitions, etc. Your attorney must have the know-how and resources to do battle with the big boys. Many PI attorneys refer out the products cases that come to them if products liability is not their specialty. Be careful of others that take every case that walks in the door, intending to learn each new area of law as the need arises.

Because of the expense and time involved in the products liability war, the injuries must be serious for the case to be viable. As with medical malpractice cases (see Chapter 5), unless the case is worth $75,000 or more, it will be hard to find a reputable attorney who will take it.

INTENTIONAL INJURIES

Injuries that result from intentional action are resolved quite differently from injuries caused by negligent conduct. *Assaults*, threats or uses of force that cause fear of harm, and *batteries*, using force to cause harm, are the most common kinds of intentional injuries. Auto accidents also obviously sometimes result from purposeful conduct. The most important differences between negligence actions and lawsuits arising out of intentional injuries involve the assessment of punitive damages and the collectability of the judgment.

Damages

Intentional injuries can inflame a jury's passion such that it is moved to award punitive damages against the defendant. *Punitive damages* are assessed as a means of punishing the defendant for outrageous conduct. Punitive damages can be huge. Juries sometimes shock everyone involved with the litigation by awarding punitive damages that are way out of proportion to the actual damages suffered. You will read about such verdicts, since newspapers love to report large awards. But under the law, punitive damages must bear a reasonable relationship to the actual damages. What you will not read about is when the court reduces the award because the punitive damages were excessive.

Uncollectibility

Jury verdicts for intentional injuries are often uncollectible. Most insurance policies provide exclusions of coverage for intentional injuries. The courts uphold these exclusions since it is considered bad for society for individuals to be able to insure themselves against their intentional acts that injure others. The reasoning is that if you can insure yourself against assaulting others, the threat of a financially ruinous lawsuit will be reduced and you might be tempted to carry out your secret desire to assault the object of your disaffection. That is rightfully considered contrary to public policy and against the common good. Thus, the insurance company will not have to pay the judgment returned against its insured. That is why lawyers usually do not try to prove that the injury was caused intentionally, unless the individual defendant is wealthy.

If there is no insurance coverage, you must try to collect from the individual. This can be difficult, if not impossible, as well as time consuming and expensive. Even if you have the stomach to try to enforce a judgment by compelling the sale of the defendant's assets, you may be surprised to learn that the defendant has divested him- or herself of all such assets or never had any in the first place. Or you may find that the defendant has filed for personal bankruptcy to avoid your collection efforts. This is another example of winning the battle, but losing the war. You never declare victory in a personal injury case until the check clears the bank.

Libel, Slander, and Defamation

Libel, a false and damaging statement made in writing or broadcast, and *slander*, a false and damaging statement made orally, are also considered intentional injury cases. Both involve *defamation*, which is making a false statement to at least one other person, that damages the reputation of the person spoken about.

Although you often read about multi-million-dollar jury verdicts in these cases, large verdicts almost never stand up on appeal. The First Amendment makes it practically impossible for anyone but private individuals to collect for libel or slander. Thus, journalists, for example, are free to say practically anything they want about public figures (politicians, entertainers, athletes) without worrying about legal liability.

Slander suits between private individuals are not often profitable. Damages are difficult to prove since insults rarely result in actual financial losses. Further, collecting on a judgment against a private individual is difficult and unpleasant. Practically speaking, the only defamation case that is worth pursuing would be if a journalist prints a falsehood about a private individual and that defamation causes provable financial harm. For example, if a newspaper falsely printed that an accountant was arrested for drug trafficking, that would be a case worth investigating.

PSYCHOLOGICAL INJURIES

Psychological injuries can be an important part of a personal injury case. Post-traumatic stress disorder (also called post-traumatic stress syndrome) is a provable phenomenon that adds *value* to some cases. This disorder may involve headaches, nausea, dizziness, inability to concentrate, depression, irrational fears, etc. But this is also an area that is fraught with danger for you, the claimant.

The claim for a psychological injury opens your psychological history up for inspection. This can create issues that impede a favorable settlement. The insurance company's lawyer may be entitled to subpoena your psychologist's records. If these records disclose, for example, that the psychologist believes you are a liar, the insurance company has found a potent weapon for court. The company may become unwilling to offer a fair settlement now that it has this information.

Judges, juries, and insurance companies often view psychological injury claims with suspicion. Many people feel that these kinds of claims are usually either faked or exaggerated. Others feel that you should simply deal with *hurt feelings* and financial compensation should not be awarded. Finally, the jury might view you as greedy for pursuing a psychological injury claim.

It is not advisable for a client to pursue such a claim unless the psychological injury is serious and believable. When the claim is real and provable, and when damaging information that can come out during discovery is minimal, psychological injury claims can and should be pursued.

The law, in some states, seeks to weed out many of these claims by requiring that a *physical manifestation* accompany the psychological injury. For example, psychological injuries often occur in car accident cases. You may develop a fear of riding in cars after a serious accident. If there is a physical injury, the psychological injury can be pursued. But if there is no physical injury, in many states other physical manifestations must be present for you to be able to pursue a claim. Thus, at the very least, headaches, nausea, vomiting, etc., must exist to collect for this kind of claim.

chapter five:
Medical Malpractice

Often, people seek legal redress for a bad medical result for which there is no legal blame. Perhaps the patient simply felt that the doctor treated him or her with disrespect and wishes to get back at the doctor by filing a suit. The law does not provide a remedy for hurt feelings and it makes no economic sense to pursue a medical case unless the damages are severe and the liability fairly clear.

Medical malpractice litigation involves injuries suffered as the result of careless medical practice. There are two important points to understand about medical malpractice.

First, not every bad or suboptimal result from medical care or a medical procedure constitutes malpractice. Doctors are not guarantors of the medical care they provide. You cannot collect from the doctor's insurance company simply because an injury occurred. It must be proven in a legally sufficient way.

Second, even if you were the victim of medical malpractice, there are numerous factors that come into question of whether you have a winnable case. The fact that a doctor was negligent is only one of the many considerations. Because of the many complex issues that make up a medical malpractice case, medical malpractice is not the type of litigation a person should try to pursue without engaging a qualified lawyer.

DETERMINING WHETHER YOU HAVE A CASE

There are many factors that affect whether a lawyer will accept and pursue your case. First, despite what you may read in the newspapers, a medical malpractice case is not a guaranteed lottery ticket worth millions. A medical malpractice case is one of the hardest types of personal injury cases to win. The doctor is the winner in most cases that go to trial.

Since most cases take a number of years to resolve, the cost of preparing and presenting the case through trial is a major factor in whether a lawyer will accept your case. Medical malpractice cases are taken on a contingency fee. When the case is resolved, the lawyer is reimbursed for his or her expenses and paid a percentage of the award or settlement as the fee. (See Chapter 3 for a discussion of contingent fee arrangements.)

These cases are very expensive to pursue because they require the lawyer to gather the medical records and to hire medical professionals to review the records, write reports, and testify as expert witnesses. The lawyer must also pay the costs of pretrial preparation and trial. It simpy does not make sense to pursue a case that has a potential value of $50,000, if the estimated cost of pursuing and presenting the case is $50,000. Consequently, many smaller cases are not pursued, even if the negligence and causation is clear.

If the case is particularly difficult, the attorney may ask the client to put up at least some of the costs of the suit. This not only makes the case more economically viable for the lawyer, it causes the client to feel more invested in the process.

If the case is quite strong, the attorney may be willing to front the costs him- or herself. If he or she will not, continue interviewing lawyers.

Do not expect the case to settle quickly—it will not. Most of these cases must be tried before a jury before compensation can be obtained. This is primarily because, in many states, the doctor's insurance company cannot settle the case without the express consent of the physician. Since it is not the doctor who actually pays any judgment in the case, the doctor has little risk if the case actually goes to trial. The doctor may want to preserve his or her reputation for providing quality care, rather than accept a settlement that implies malpractice. The doctor's concern for his or her reputation is especially relevant in states that have open records on malpractice cases.

In assessing whether a case is winnable, the lawyer considers a number of other factors. The lawyer evaluates whether there actually was a breach in the standard of care that caused or increased the risk of harm to the patient. Equally important is the lawyer's ability to present proof of the negligent conduct at trial. If credible proof is not available, the case is likely not winnable.

The patient's medical records typically serve as the primary proof of the facts of the case. Medical records are often seen as more credible than the testimony of the patient. Consequently, even if you describe for your lawyer a clear case of negligence, if the facts are not documented in the medical records, the lack of documentation may persuade the jury that the negligent conduct did not occur.

Occasionally, a question will arise as to whether key medical records were altered or crucial entries deleted. It is not unheard of for medical professionals to alter or delete records in order to attempt to prevent documentation of malpractice. This is, of course, unethical and illegal.

This is another reason for hiring an expert to review the records in malpractice cases. It would be extremely difficult in most cases for a layperson to detect a missing or altered record. In some states, if it can be proven that medical records are missing or were altered, an inference is created that the missing or altered records contain information that is adverse to the physician.

Age may also be a factor in whether the case is economically viable. Although this may not seem fair, the law does not value the life of a 90-year-old the same as the life of a 20-year-old. When a jury is considering an award for a permanent injury, a younger plaintiff has to endure that permanent injury for more years than a senior citizen. Thus, the award should be higher, all other things being equal. The older a person is, the less likely the case has enough value to pursue.

In some states, damages for pain and suffering, loss of consortium, and other noneconomic damages are capped—that is, the defendant will not have to pay more than a legally set limit, regardless of the size of the jury verdict. There are states where the cap is so low that it is not economically feasible for an attorney to accept a case under a contingency fee arrangement, even if the malpractice is obvious and the injuries severe.

This is often problematic with a 90-year-old plaintiff, a homemaker of any age, or an unemployed plaintiff. For example, if an elderly plaintiff dies because of medical malpractice in a jurisdiction where noneconomic damages are capped by law at $100,000, the costs the attorney will have to pay to prepare the case properly for trial may also approach $100,000. The attorney here has no financial incentive to take the case.

Contrary to popular belief, extraordinarily large awards typically involve catastrophic injuries requiring a lifetime of medical care and expense. If the injury is only temporary or if the injury does not result in any impairment or disability that lasts a significant period of time, the value of the case to the lawyer may not be sufficient to make the claim worth pursuing.

HIRING AN ATTORNEY

It is important to select the right attorney for the case. Medical malpractice is a highly specialized field. Although one may be a very competent trial attorney, not every attorney has the experience or resources to handle a malpractice case.

It is important to actively question any lawyer you interview. You should ask about his or her years of experience handling this type of case, the percentage of his or her practice that is devoted to medical malpractice cases, the number of malpractice cases he or she actually tried, and whether the firm employs doctors or nurses to assist in preparing this type of case. These are common-sense questions to ask any lawyer holding him- or herself out as a medical malpractice lawyer.

Typically, there are certain firms in any locale that are recognized in the legal community as having a strong background and expertise in the area of medical malpractice. One way to locate a suitable attorney is to get recommendations from lawyers you may know who do not handle these types of cases. It is a good idea to interview two or three attorneys before hiring a malpractice lawyer.

THE NUTS AND BOLTS OF A MEDICAL MALPRACTICE CASE

A comprehensive discussion of medical malpractice litigation is beyond the scope of this book. Each case is unique and presents a multitude of issues. But, in the end, a medical malpractice case boils down to three elements that must be proven by the plaintiff. Proving less than three is insufficient and will result in a verdict in favor of the doctor, healthcare provider, or hospital you sued. *It is always the plaintiff's burden to prove all three propositions.*

Negligence

The first issue is *negligence*. Negligence in a medical malpractice case means that the defendant deviated from the standard of care that was required under the circumstances. The term *standard of care* is a term of art. It has no precise definition.

Standard of care generally refers to the type of medical care that a reasonable and prudent doctor would provide under the same or similar circumstances. Because medicine is an art and not an exact science, the standard of care is a guideline based on the facts surrounding your case and the prevailing medical practices in your local medical community.

The law applicable to medical malpractice case does not require doctors to be perfect or to practice with mathematical precision. As long as the art of medicine is practiced up to the standard of care, the doctor is verdict-proof, even if the medical outcome is poor.

In order to prove the standard of care, a medical malpractice case requires the plaintiff's attorney to engage the services of a physician, knowledgeable and experienced in the area of medicine at issue. In order for the case to have any chance of success, this physician must render the opinion that the care was *substandard*.

Thus, it is important to recognize that even if you and your lawyer think the doctor malpracticed, this does not mean your case is winnable. An opinion from a physician is almost always required. And even if an expert testifies that the care was negligent, this only means that you can present proof of negligence at trial. You still must convince the judge or jury that this is so.

There are rare cases in which an expert witness is not necessary to prove negligence. If the carelessness of the physician is obvious, expert testimony from a physician is not necessary. (The best example of this type of situation is where a sponge or some other medical device is left in the patient's body following surgery.)

Causation of Injury

Just as important as establishing the doctor's negligence, a plaintiff must also prove that this negligence caused injury. In short, it must be proven to a reasonable degree of medical certainty that the doctor's conduct was a substantial factor in bringing about the harm the patient suffered.

Proving *causation* in a malpractice case is difficult. There are complications that can arise from almost every type of medical care. Complications often happen, not because of negligence, but simply because there are inherent risks connected to most medical procedures or treatment.

In most medical malpractice cases, direct causation cannot be proven. For example, if a physician negligently fails to diagnose cancer at an early stage, and it is discovered later at an advanced stage, certainly one cannot say that the physician's negligence caused the cancer. Yet, the patient may have missed his or her window of opportunity to treat the disease. By failing to treat the disease early, the patient has lost a chance of a better outcome or cure.

In most, if not all states, the law allows the plaintiff to proceed in this type of case under a relaxed standard known generally as *increased risk of harm*. This means that even though one cannot prove that the doctor's conduct caused the harm, a plaintiff can satisfy his or her burden of proving causation by establishing that the doctor's negligent conduct increased the risk that the harm would occur or worsen.

Damages

The third proposition that must be proven is *damages*, that is, the actual harm caused by the malpractice. The objective of any case is to compensate the victim for the actual harm suffered. No matter how egregious the doctor's conduct, it is not a factor in valuing the patient's injuries.

The law generally categorizes the types of harm that may be compensated. They include economic harm, such as medical bills and lost wages, and non-economic harm, such as physical or mental pain and suffering, loss of the enjoyment of life's pleasures, embarrassment, and humiliation. (See Chapter 7 for a discussion of damages.)

If it turns out that any of the three elements (negligence, causation, or damages) cannot be proven to the degree legally required, the case will fail. A qualified malpractice attorney can usually determine within a short period of time if the case is winnable. If it is not, at least you should come to feel that your concerns have been taken seriously and that there simply is no feasible legal claim. This is a far more satisfactory situation than simply being left to wonder if a member of the medical community has wronged you or a family member. If your malpractice lawyer carefully explains to you why the claim cannot be successfully pursued and answers all your questions, you should be able to reach a measure of closure—not possible without having engaged the malpractice attorney.

THE FEE AGREEMENT

As noted, a medical malpractice lawyer works under a contingency fee agreement. Medical malpractice cases may warrant a higher contingency fee than garden-variety motor vehicle cases or slip-and-fall lawsuits. This is because the amount of work and the lawyer's own financial investment are usually significantly more.

Some states have laws that limit the lawyer's contingency fee. Some counties have laws that limit the lawyer's fee in cases involving children or in cases where the patient has died.

GETTING STARTED

No lawyer can properly evaluate or pursue a medical malpractice case without first obtaining the relevant medical records and interviewing available witnesses. If family members or friends accompanied you to doctor visits or were present during any of your interactions with the doctors, they should be interviewed. Your medical records are vital to your ability to prove a case. A lawyer who delays obtaining your records is, more often than not, not giving your case the attention it deserves. Check periodically to see that your lawyer has obtained records from your healthcare providers. However, know that it can take months to actually receive records.

It is important that your lawyer be aware of your most recent medical care. You must keep your lawyer informed of all the doctors you have seen. You only hurt your case by not keeping your lawyer updated on matters that are relevant to your case. If your medical care continues after the lawsuit is filed, it is the responsibility of both you and your lawyer to communicate regularly to make certain the attorney is up to date with your medical care.

Lawyers typically rely on their staff, namely their secretary or paralegal, to keep the file updated with current medical records. Typically, the secretary or paralegal is more available during the workday to receive telephone calls than the attorney is. It is a good idea to maintain an open line of communication with the legal staff as the case progresses.

EXPERT WITNESSES

One feature of a medical malpractice claim that distinguishes it from a garden-variety negligence claim is the use of expert witnesses. In the average motor vehicle case, most people have a sufficient understanding of the duties of a motorist on the highway. Most people already know that a driver must stop for a red light and that the failure to do so is considered negligence. It is not necessary for an expert to testify.

In medical malpractice cases, the issue of proper medical care is almost always complex. There is rarely a definitive statement in a medical textbook that will prove the case. Consequently, a lawyer must seek out an *expert witness* to provide an opinion as to what is proper or improper medical care.

An expert witness in a medical malpractice case is a physician who reviews the medical records, perhaps examines the plaintiff, speaks to the plaintiff's lawyer, and then renders an opinion on the medical issues in the case. When the issue is negligence, the expert will give an opinion regarding the standard of care owed by the physician to the patient and whether the physician's conduct has met the standard of care under the circumstances. If the issue is causation, the witness will render an opinion as to whether the doctor's conduct was a material factor in causing the harm that followed.

In addition to expert opinions on the issues of negligence and causation, expert testimony is often needed on other issues arising in a medical malpractice case. Typically, opinions from an economist or a vocational expert are required when the plaintiff contends that the injury has disabled him or her from employment. (See Chapter 7 for a discussion of loss of earnings and earning capacity.) If a person has a permanent injury, the plaintiff may be required to obtain an expert opinion regarding life expectancy so the jury can evaluate the length of time the plaintiff could have worked. If a person can continue to work despite a physical injury, but can no longer work at the same job or for as long as before the injury, a vocational expert (typically a psychologist with specialized training) is needed to give an opinion on the work the plaintiff could do before the injury and the limits that have resulted from the injury.

If a case involves a claim that the injury affects the plaintiff's future ability to earn a living, the expert who renders an opinion on loss of earning capacity will likely have to meet with the plaintiff. For example, if you had been a heavy laborer all you life, but your injuries require that you seek a new line of employment, a vocational expert will likely meet with you to review your educational and employment background in order to render an informed opinion.

Your attorney is responsible for scheduling the appointment for you. Ask your lawyer whether you will have to meet an economic or vocational expert, and whether he or she has taken steps to arrange the meeting.

One of the best indicators of whether your attorney is properly working on your case is his or her interaction with experts at various stages. For example, before suit is even filed, your attorney should review your medical care with an expert for a preliminary opinion of its merits. It is vital that he or she do so at an early stage of the litigation. In most cases, an attorney can make a negligence and causation assessment at the initial stages of the investigation by engaging an expert to perform a preliminary review of the case.

Too often, an attorney will accept a medical malpractice case and place it in suit without even knowing if a medical expert will support the view that the physician was negligent and the negligence caused the injury. After months, if not years of litigation, the client learns that the case has been dismissed because the lawyer could not find anyone to support the claim.

You must question your lawyer before suit is filed if he or she had your medical records reviewed by an expert. Once the case is in suit, periodically ask your lawyer if he or she has received a final opinion from the expert on the merits of the case. If he or she has not, find out why.

Once the attorney has completed pretrial discovery, (depositions, interrogatories, and request for production of documents), there are only a limited number of reasons why the attorney cannot have the file reviewed by an expert witness. Without a compelling reason, an attorney who has not obtained the necessary expert opinions will not be in a position to pursue your case through trial or even engage in a meaningful settlement dialogue.

No insurance company will settle a medical negligence case unless it is convinced that the plaintiff's attorney can prove the claim at trial. If the attorney has not produced a written report from an expert that the doctor was negligent, there is little chance that the insurance company will ever settle the case. More likely, the insurance company's lawyer will seek to have the case dismissed on the ground that the plaintiff is unable to prove the case.

Keeping track of your attorney's use of expert witnesses is one way to know that your attorney is giving your case the attention it deserves. In some jurisdictions, the court will establish deadlines by which each attorney must produce to their opponent reports from all expert witnesses they intend to present at trial. If your attorney misses the deadline, the court may dismiss your case.

In other jurisdictions, the court will not permit a case to be scheduled for trial unless all parties have produced their expert reports. In these venues, your case could go on for years and years if your attorney is not aggressively pursuing the matter and has not obtained or produced expert opinions. In either type of jurisdiction, find out if your attorney is meeting the deadlines and producing experts' reports in a timely manner.

NUISANCE VALUE

Attorneys who file medical malpractice lawsuits without thoroughly investigating them first do everyone a disservice. Malpractice lawsuits should only be filed after the records are obtained and reviewed by an expert. Some attorneys hope to harass doctors into settlements simply by filing suits. This is called going for *nuisance value*. While this might sometimes work with ordinary injury lawsuits, in medical malpractice cases, it usually leads to huge, lengthy, and bitter legal battles with the doctor, his or her insurance company, and his or her lawyer.

VALUING THE CLAIM

In medical malpractice cases, as in most personal injury cases, valuing a case is no simple task. There is no book, journal, or scientific study that tells lawyers that a broken arm is worth X or a torn rotator cuff is worth Y. The value of a case is based on many factors. Some of the factors that should be considered in valuing a medical malpractice claim are:

- the nature of the injury;
- the effect of the injury on customary and usual activities;
- the permanence of the injury;
- the treatment involved;
- the cost of the treatment;
- the effect on employment;
- the effect on life style;
- the credibility of the witness;
- the likely weight to be given to the witness' testimony;
- the weight of the medical science behind the claim; and,
- the jurors' potential feelings for the parties—sympathy for the plaintiff as well as sympathy for the defendant who has been blamed.

Many of the factors that go into valuing a claim cannot be properly evaluated at the beginning of a lawsuit. The lawyer cannot know how a jury may react to the doctor until he or she has had an opportunity to meet him or her at a deposition. Thus, it is unrealistic for any lawyer to advise the client of a specific dollar value of the claim before this stage.

Any lawyer who tells a client that the case is worth a specific amount at the very first meeting is more likely making a sales pitch than offering an educated opinion. Better attorneys know that at the outset of the case, one can really only provide a preliminary estimate of a range of values for the case. Even as the case progresses, better attorneys recognize that it is more accurate to discuss value in terms of a range than any one number.

SETTLING THE CLAIM

As a general rule, medical malpractice cases are difficult to settle for a number of reasons that have nothing to do with the merits of the case. First, many malpractice insurance agreements contain a provision that the insurance company cannot settle the case without the doctor's written consent. Since in most cases it is not the physician's personal assets at risk, there is little incentive for the doctor to consent to a settlement.

Second, unlike a car accident or a slip-and-fall case, malpractice cases deal with a person's professional reputation. Human nature being what it is, no one likes to admit making a mistake in performing professional responsibilities. Even when the doctor clearly has committed malpractice, he or she may be unwilling to admit this to the other side or even to him- or herself.

Doctors, quite naturally, are often extremely offended when they are contacted by medical malpractice attorneys concerning a possible claim. If the case is settled, it still shows up as a black mark on the physician's record. In sum, doctors tend to be extremely reluctant to settle these kinds of cases without a bitter battle.

Further, political action groups on behalf of physicians and insurance companies have propagandized that medical malpractice litigation is out of control and consistently results in unreasonably large awards to the plaintiff. This message has actually served as a grassroots form of tort reform, which instills in potential jurors a bias in favor of doctors. Jurors may fear that a plaintiff's verdict will somehow affect the medical community in general and, in turn, the jurors themselves. For example, the jurors may fear that a large malpractice award will drive doctors out of their community, making it more difficult for the jurors to be treated by the doctor of their choice.

Because of these factors, there may be very little desire for a defendant doctor or his or her insurance company to settle a case when they know that there is a good chance the jury, regardless of the strength of the patient's evidence, will find in favor of the doctor. If a doctor is willing to settle, remember that a settlement is a compromise. More often than not, a plaintiff who is considering a settlement offer must recognize that he or she will likely have to accept something less than he or she desired. Given the difficulty of winning a medical malpractice jury trial, you should strongly consider settling if the offer approaches the realistic value of the claim.

HOW TO HELP YOUR ATTORNEY

The attorney performs the vast majority of the work necessary to prepare a medical malpractice case without the client's involvement. There are, however, a number of ways you can assist your attorney throughout the course of the case.

Keep your attorney updated regarding your medical condition and treatment. Save all insurance statements and medical bills and periodically mail them to your attorney. This can be a big help in determining the amount of your medical expenses or the amount paid by your health insurer for your medical treatment. It can also ensure your lawyer is aware of all medical providers you have seen.

Another way you can help you lawyer concerns witnesses. Often, attorneys do not consider which witnesses to put on the stand until shortly before the trial begins. The attorney may not be aware of a neighbor or relative who can testify regarding the effect the injuries have had on your life. Provide your lawyer with the names, phone numbers, and addresses of individuals who are familiar with your situation and who are willing to testify on your behalf.

Also, keeping a diary of your medical care can be of great assistance to the lawyer. Many people keep a daily calendar in which they note the date and time of doctors' appointments. Consider copying your calendar and giving it to your attorney.

Generally speaking, the doctors who treat you for the injuries caused by malpractice will not want to get involved in your case. The medical community in most areas is small. It is quite understandable that one doctor may not want to testify against a colleague. However, there are occasions where a subsequent treating physician will wish to testify on your behalf. If your treating physician indicates a willingness to do so, pass this information along to your attorney. Most physicians will not call a lawyer and volunteer their services. Most lawyers will assume that a treating physician will not want to get involved. Consequently, you can greatly assist your lawyer by passing along information suggesting that your treating physician may be willing to testify on your behalf.

THE MEDICAL MALPRACTICE CRISIS

The insurance industry, in conjunction with business groups and medical associations, attempts to blame the civil justice system for the *medical malpractice crisis* in order to further its own agendas. The evidence, however, does not point to the civil justice system as a principal cause of the problem. The reality is that the legal, medical, and insurance fields play intertwining roles in this *crisis*.

The *American Trial Lawyers Association* reports that up to 98,000 Americans die each year because of medical malpractice. Only a small percentage of these cases results in lawsuits. In fact, the number of new medical malpractice claims filed annually declined nationally by about 4% since 1995.

You can find a wealth of information about the so-called medical malpractice crisis at ATLA's website, **www.atla.org**, in the "Consumer and Medical Resources" section of the website. ATLA reports that medical malpractice cases make up only 7.7% of all tort filings filed. Medical malpractice was the underlying cause of action in only 1% of punitive damage awards. Although multimillion dollar awards make the headlines, the median jury damage award from medical malpractice is only $254,000.

In the winter of 2003, President Bush proposed a $250,000 cap on noneconomic damages, like pain and suffering, in medical malpractice cases, declaring, *No one has ever been healed by a frivolous lawsuit.* While people who were working can recover lost wages, children, stay-at-home mothers, the unemployed, and the retired are much more limited. If they cannot recover for pain and suffering, there may be little compensation available to them.

The *medical malpractice crisis* is really an insurance crisis. The insurance industry itself admits that stock market losses and low interest rates have eaten up the reserves of many medical malpractice insurers. According to a press release dated January 7, 2003, from the North Central Pennsylvania Trial Lawyers Association, St. Paul Insurance Company lost $100 million on Enron bonds. St. Paul has left the medical malpractice market.

Mary Alexander, president of the Association of Trial Lawyers of America, says that tort reform is, "a misdiagnosis. We see this every ten to twelve years." Just as in the mid-1970s and mid-1980s, the insurance companies raise premiums to offset losses in the stock market.

The medical profession bears its share of the blame. Its reluctance to self-police is a major contributing factor to the *crisis*. According to the federal government's National Practitioner Data Bank, for Pennsylvania, 10.6% of its doctors have paid two or more malpractice awards to patients. These repeat offender doctors are responsible for 84% of all payments. Yet only 6.8% of doctors who made ten or more malpractice payments were disciplined.

chapter six:
Special Medical Concerns

This chapter explores the crucial questions involved in choosing the doctors and other medical providers who will treat your injuries. Also discussed is the importance of keeping track of your treatment so that you can assist your lawyer in gathering the medical information he or she needs to represent you properly.

CHOOSING YOUR HEALTH-CARE PROVIDER

If after an accident you will be seeking an attorney, it is helpful if you first choose your own doctor. Doing this helps to avoid the impression that your medical care was undertaken merely to build a legal case rather than to treat your injuries. When you make this choice, you generally will be choosing between a chiropractor, medical doctor, or an osteopathic physician.

Insurance companies and their lawyers are often very skeptical about the severity of the injuries claimed. Insurance companies tend to view the opinion of a medical physician as more credible than that of a chiropractor or an osteopath. Regardless of who actually provides the better treatment, initially selecting an MD may be in your best interest.

Nevertheless, the value of chiropractic and osteopathic care during the course of treatment for some personal injury plaintiffs is clear. There have been countless occasions over the years where the medical care offered by the MD proves insufficient. Often the only treatment that significantly relieves the trauma victim's pain is chiropractic manipulation. Thus, if a period of three to six months has elapsed without significant improvement in the client's condition, it is time to consider shifting the focus towards chiropractic or osteopathic care. Such a shift often results in an almost immediate improvement in symptoms. Each of the various disciplines has its strengths and weakness, and a flexible approach to this problem is best.

Managed Care

If your family's health insurance is through a health maintenance organization (HMO), you know of the problems of managed care. You know how difficult it can be to get a referral to a specialist. There may be financial disincentives for your primary care doctor to make such referrals.

If you are injured in a motor vehicle accident, you may be able to avoid this problem. Assuming that you have coverage for accident-related medical bills in your auto insurance policy, it is likely that your auto insurance coverage is primary to your health insurance coverage.

If your auto insurance is primary, you submit your bills first to the auto insurer and only any unpaid balance to the secondary health insurer. If your auto coverage is primary, you can select any doctor you wish and see any specialists that are necessary. Your auto insurance company will have to pay all reasonable and necessary bills for treatment related to your injuries. Only when your auto benefits are exhausted would you have to be concerned with your health insurance company's guidelines regarding the medical providers you can see. You should double check with your lawyer about this since, again, the law varies from state to state. The last thing you want is to be stuck with unpaid medical bills after you have settled your case.

If your auto insurance is not primary, you will need to carefully follow the guidelines of your health insurance company. If you fail to do so, it is very possible that all insurance companies involved in your accident will deny payments based on your failure to follow these guidelines.

If you were injured in a slip and fall accident, you will need to carefully follow the health insurance company's guidelines. In some states, if you fail to do so, the insurance company responsible for covering this accident will not have to pay your medical bills. Be sure to go to your primary care physician initially and then get any required pre-approval before you see any specialists. This is, again, an area where the law varies from state to state. You should think out this issue carefully before you choose your treating physicians.

PHYSICAL THERAPY

It is essential that you enter into a physical therapy program as soon as possible after either a motor vehicle or fall down accident. The muscles in the neck and back can go into spasm shortly after an accident in order to protect the area from further injury. Physical therapy helps to relieve the spasm and the accompanying pain.

During whiplash type injuries, ligaments in the neck can be damaged. Ligaments are very strong attachments that keep joints in alignment and limit joint movement to a normal range. Tight ligaments are essential to keep the cartilage firmly in place within a joint and to prevent excessive movement of body parts. Physical therapy teaches the muscles to support the skeletal system when the damaged ligaments have become stretched out. Physical therapists use any of a number of techniques to reduce spasm and pain and to rebuild the weakened musculature.

During the initial months of therapy, treatment generally involves moist heat, ice packs, massage, and ultrasound for deep muscle stimulation. As the body responds and the spasm is relieved, the therapy moves toward rebuilding the muscles that have atrophied during the initial therapy. The therapist supervises an exercise program to help the patient regain preaccident strength. Upon conclusion of the therapy program, the therapist instructs the patient in exercise techniques that can be undertaken at home or at a gym.

GOOD INJURIES

One of the more ironic, and telling phrases used by some personal injury lawyers is *good injuries*. This refers to chance of recovery of damages. An injury of sprains and strains usually is not as easy to collect on as one that is graphic (like broken bones) and elicits sympathy. So you may hear your lawyer say *good injuries* to a case in which, for example, a child is hit by a car and suffers a fractured femur that requires surgery to repair.

KEEPING TRACK OF YOUR TREATMENT

It is very important to make notes regarding your treatment and injuries. **Checklist 3** in Appendix B is a worksheet that should help you with this task. (see p.272.) Give your lawyer this worksheet when you conclude treatment. It will help him or her in many ways. It speeds his or her ability to gather all of your medical records. It provides information to put into the settlement demand letter he or she sends to the insurance company. If it becomes necessary to take depositions, it assists in preparing for that important part of the lawsuit.

chapter seven:
Damages

Some people object to the very concept of compensating injured accident victims with money. They might feel that individuals who have been injured should simply be strong and bear their losses. After all, their no-fault insurance should cover their medical bills and lost wages. It is a good bet that these people have never been seriously injured in an accident. Nor is it likely that anyone in their family has suffered such a fate. Nevertheless, it is fair to debate the issue of directly translating pain into dollars, which is called *damages*.

Some may feel that it demeans the value of human suffering to place a financial value on it. Yet that is the only method our legal system has to redress the injurious acts committed by negligent motorists, shop owners, corporations, etc. As long as this method of compensation is available, injured accident victims and their attorneys will seek to receive maximum financial redress for the injury.

Still others point to the added costs of doing business they feel that injury lawsuits cause. They believe that these added costs are passed on to the consumer in the form of higher prices. There is some merit to this argument, but many believe it is worth paying these higher prices in exchange for keeping the right to sue for compensation. Not only can financial compensation help to make the accident victim whole, but the threat of lawsuits keeps companies accountable for their errors. Consider also that even the Bible at Exodus 21:25 authorizes financial compensation for pain inflicted by another. There is nothing inherently wrong with seeking compensation for injuries caused by another person.

Pending further changes to our present set of negligence laws, individuals are free to look to the courts for financial compensation for injuries caused by the negligent acts of others. Given that this system, or some form of it, is likely to remain in effect for many years to come, the question becomes—*How much is an injury case worth?* Unfortunately, there is no way to know for sure what a case might settle for until the medical treatment is concluded and the doctor's prognosis rendered.

PLACING A MONETARY VALUE ON AN INJURY

Unless you have been in many accidents and sued many times, you probably have no idea of the amount for which a personal injury case should settle. Your fate, for all intents and purposes, is in the hands of your attorney. If the attorney, for whatever reason, wants to settle the case, even though fair value has not been offered, how will you know? There are no easy answers here, which is why it is vital to retain a lawyer you can trust. There are, however, some factors you should consider in understanding how your damages may be calculated.

Soft Tissue Injury Damage

Lawyers and insurance adjusters evaluate personal injury cases in many ways. For simple cases, such as neck and back sprains (soft tissue injuries) that heal over time, the key factors will be *length of treatment* and, perhaps, the *amount of the medical bills*. Some adjusters and lawyers just multiply the total of the medical bills by three or four to determine the settlement value. That is an overly simplistic approach that is used less these days than in the past. Yet medical bills still figure into the settlement evaluations in this kind of injury case. The bills are also considered to a lesser extent in more serious injury cases.

Perhaps the one rule of thumb for these *soft tissue injury* cases is $2,000 for each month of treatment. Thus, a soft tissue back and neck injury with three months of treatment will probably settle for between $5,000 and $7,000. There is a limit to this kind of computation. After perhaps six or seven months of treatment, the insurance company may begin to suspect that the claimant is prolonging the treatment just to drive up the settlement. It is totally inexcusable to stay in treatment one visit longer than is necessary to recover more from your injuries.

Inevitably, the insurance company hires a doctor to read the MRI showing the disc injury. Unless there is definitive proof that the injury is accident-related, the insurance's company doctor will undoubtedly say that the injury was degenerative and not accident-related.

Professional Medical Opinion

A credible medical opinion indicating that a hernia is degenerative reduces the value of the case by 50% or more. Your doctor will have to confront this adverse opinion head on for you to have any chance of connecting the disc injury to the accident. Unless you can credibly prove this causal connection, you cannot receive compensation for this injury. (Remember, the plaintiff has the burden of proof.)

You will need an MD to make this connection for you. A chiropractor's opinion will only get you so far. Perhaps a rebuttal by a chiropractor will add 10% back into the value of the case. A neurologist is best, although an ortho-pedic doctor or even a radiologist may suffice. A well-reasoned opinion by a respected neurologist, rebutting the insurance company doctor's opinion as to, say, arthritis, may bring the case back to 80% of its full value.

Aggravation

Remember also that just because the plaintiff has a medical condition that pre-dates the accident, if the accident *aggravated* that condition, this aggravation is potentially a collectible part of the case. There is a principal of law that states— *You take your victim as you find him.* Just because a defendant injured a per-son who was especially susceptible to that injury, the defendant is not entitled to special sympathy. Those who act negligently do so at their own risk.

Further, even if the plaintiff had a preaccident herniated disk, that injury might not have caused him or her any pain. The accident may trigger severe pain even if it did not objectively damage the disc. This pain is a collectible part of the plaintiff's case, but the plaintiff will have to testify very credibly since there is no objective evidence to support the claim.

Age

Age is a critical factor that affects the value of your injury. Older people take longer to recover from their injuries. Thus, the same injury to a 60-year-old gen-erally brings a higher settlement than to a 30-year-old. However, if the injury is permanent, a younger plaintiff does better since he or she has to live with the injury for a longer period of time.

Another factor age plays a part in is that juries tend to believe that an older plaintiff's complaints are more genuine than a younger plaintiff's. They are more likely to feel that the latter's complaints are simply not credible and motivated by hopes of financial gain.

Plaintiff Credibility

If the plaintiff is very credible, an adverse medical opinion as to, say, arthritis for an elderly plaintiff, may reduce the value of the case by only 10%. Conversely, if the plaintiff is not very credible in his or her testimony, that adverse opinion may influence the jury to award no damages at all. If a jury does not like a plaintiff, it will look for any reason at all to award only nominal damages (if that). Thus, if a jury awarded a plaintiff with a herniated disc $5,000, when the plaintiff sought $60,000, that would qualify as *nominal damages* and indicate clearly that the jury did not believe the hernia was caused by the accident.

Medical Records and Treatment

Perhaps the best way to convince a judge, jury, or arbitration panel that an accident caused the injury is through proof of the plaintiff's condition before the accident. Although the plaintiff's own testimony that he or she was feeling fine before the accident is helpful, prior medical records are even more persuasive. Thus, if the plaintiff's medical records indicate no previous complaints of pain, the accident, assuming it was a significant one, is very likely the cause of the disc problem.

If there was an MRI done prior to the accident, which can be compared to the post-accident MRI, this is very persuasive. If the two MRI's are identical, the accident obviously did not cause the problem. If there have been changes between the two MRI's, it is quite likely that the accident caused the injury. This is especially likely if the preaccident MRI was done no more than a few months before the accident and the post-MRI was done shortly after the accident.

The electromyography (EMG) test is also a very import diagnostic tool used in the treatment of traumatic injuries. The EMG searches for nerve-related injuries. Frequently an EMG will find that the plaintiff has suffered radiculopathy, which is defined as a disease of the nerve roots. A finding of either lumbar (back) or cervical (neck) radiculopathy adds considerable value to a personal

For auto accident cases, if your car was insured and you did not waive wage-loss benefits, you should be eligible to recover lost wages from your insurance company. If you have no wage-loss coverage, your lost wage claim is added to your settlement demand against the defendant.

The Defendant

The personality and actions of the defendant are yet another important factor. If the defendant's actions were particularly outrageous, the sky is the limit as far as the jury may be concerned.

> **Example:** Dave was struck in the back by a car as he was walking along the side of a country road. The *compensatory damages*, that is, the damages that were strictly to compensate him for his pain and suffering and out of pocket expenses for medical bills and lost wages, totalled about $75,000. However, the punitive damages part of the case made it interesting.
>
> The defendant had seen Dave when he was several hundred feet away. He nevertheless struck Dave in the back without altering the direction of his car. He testified at his deposition that he did so because he didn't want to go over the double yellow lines, even though there was no oncoming traffic. He reasoned that it would have been illegal to cross a double yellow line. He felt that it would be preferable to severely injure a human being than to break the law.
>
> He testified in a very calloused, unfeeling manner. He expressed no remorse for injuring Dave and seemed to deeply resent being forced to answer any questions at his deposition.
>
> This case eventually settled for $160,000. The insurance company knew that the jury was going to hate the defendant and would be inclined to award huge punitive damages.

A couple of other factors from the example went into Dave's decision to settle. First, punitive damages can be difficult to collect, as discussed in Chapter 4.

Second, the insurance company probably would have simply conceded liability for the accident and not presented this man as a witness at the trial. This would have prevented the plantiff's attorney from showing just how heinous this individual and his actions were.

Holding Out for a Better Settlement

The willingness you and your attorney have for holding out for top dollar is another important factor. Insurance companies always start with a relatively low offer and work their way up. Your attorney is ethically required to report each and every offer to you. If your attorney is experienced, he or she will tell you if the first offer is too low and ask you to be patient. This patience almost always pays off. The insurance company inevitably increases the offer if they are convinced that you cannot be bought off cheaply. Generally speaking, the longer you hold out, the higher the offer goes. Every case has its limit, though. If your lawyer has litigation savvy, he or she will settle when the offer reaches that limit.

> **Example:** Jack invited his neighbor, John, over for dinner. John slipped on a patch of ice while walking up Jack's front steps and he fell down the steps. Jack knew the ice was there, but since the front porch light was off, John was completely unaware of the danger.
>
> John is 42 years old, lives alone in a large urban city, has had no major prior medical problems, and works as a truck loader for a furniture company. Due to the fall, John herniated one disc, which impinges on the spinal cord, sprained his ankle, and required noninvasive back surgery. The ankle healed completely after three months of physical therapy.
>
> The doctor told him that he could not be on his feet, drive a truck, or lift anything until a month after the back surgery, and nothing over 50 pounds for three years. In addition, he will not be able to do major lifting for a full workday for the rest of his life, and occasionally, he will experience low back pain and spasms.
>
> John had established a solid earnings history as a truck driver during his twenty years in that job. He earned $45,000 in the year before the accident. His income was increasing at an average rate of 5% each year. He did not lose any health or retirement benefits because of the accident.
>
> Ultimately, John was out of work completely for two months, returned to light duty for the ensuing three years, and then modified full duty thereafter. His earnings for light duty started at $35,000 per year with 5% increases each year. His modified full duty pay was initially $5,000 less than he would have received but for the accident, with 5% increases each year. He planned to work to his retirement age of 65.
>
> A good settlement for John could be calculated as follows:

chapter eight:
The Settlement Process

The vast majority of personal injury cases ultimately are resolved through settlement, rather than through trial. There are various stages at which personal injury cases are most likely to settle. Knowing this will enable you and your attorney to concentrate your settlement efforts around these opportunities.

The first chance for settlement occurs shortly after the medical treatment is completed. After gathering your medical bills and reports, you or your lawyer evaluates your case and then informs the insurance company of the settlement demand. Sometimes that is all it takes to wrap up the litigation.

SETTLEMENT DEMAND LETTER
It is essential that you or your lawyer prepare a comprehensive and professionally written settlement demand letter. Three sample settlement demand letters can be found starting on p.117. The settlement demand letter summarizes the strengths of your case and alerts the insurance company to its potential financial exposure. As at all other stages of your case, you are trying to create a certain impression. If the settlement demand letter is not as close to perfect as possible, the settlement value of your claim, in the insurance company's eyes, will drop dramatically.

Professional Appearance
If your letter is well organized and professional in appearance, the insurance company will assume that you are likely to present an effective case at trial, thereby exposing the company to significant financial risk. That is the ultimate

goal of the settlement demand letter. If the letter has typos and is poorly worded and organized, the insurance company concludes that you will be similarly poorly organized for trial. The company will be less concerned about getting hit for a big jury verdict, since putting on an effective trial takes tremendous organizational and communication skills.

The letter must be prepared on a computer and printed on professional looking stationery. It must not have any typographical errors. Write the letter in the active voice to make all your points forcefully. A passively worded letter subconsciously affects the reader in a way that is to the writer's disadvantage. For example, you should write—*The impact injured my left shoulder* rather than, *My left shoulder was injured by the impact.*

You should not waste any words in this letter. Get right to your strengths, make your points, and then make your settlement demand. This is not a creative writing contest. You should use short sentences. If you are attempting to convey two separate ideas, use two separate sentences.

You should attempt as much as possible to write like a lawyer. That does not mean that you should throw in a lot of extra meaningless words like *heretofore* and *thereinafter*. That will only show your inexperience and insecurity. Rather, you should clearly, directly, and forcefully itemize all of your losses, damages, and reasons that you are entitled to a substantial settlement.

Attachments

Be sure to send organized copies of your medical bills and reports with your settlement demand letter. Arrange them in chronological order, beginning with the ambulance bill, the emergency room bill and report, the bills and reports of your primary physician, followed by the bills and reports of any specialist that you have seen. After this comes the physical therapy bills and reports, and then any bills and prescriptions for medical equipment you have received. You should send the property damage appraisal, your wage loss proof, original photographs of the property damage and/or of cuts, abrasions, scars, etc., on your face or body. You should also forward any other documentation that helps to prove the losses and damages you have suffered.

Getting a Response

It usually takes an insurance company a minimum of two weeks to review settlement demand letters and come up with a settlement offer. Frequently, your settlement letter and supporting documents are reviewed by various employees at different levels of authority of the insurance company. The larger the case, the more layers of review you can expect—and accordingly, the longer the delay before an offer is made.

Within a few days after you mail the settlement demand letter, contact the company to make sure they have received it. It is not unusual for important documents to get lost in the mail. This follow-up phone call can save you some aggravation down the road. Nothing is more frustrating than waiting two or three weeks for a settlement offer, only to discover that the insurance company claims that it never got your letter. If you send the letter by certified mail, you will have proof that it was received. Overnight mail ensures prompt delivery.

Within a couple of weeks after you have confirmed that the letter was received, it is wise to call the insurance company to see if they have a settlement offer for you. If you do not call, you may never hear from the insurance company. Many insurance companies simply put settlement letters on the back burner and wait for the follow-up call from the plaintiff or the plaintiff's lawyer.

Claims Representative

You can expect that, the first time you speak with the insurance company's claims representative about settlement, there will be some kind of excuse for why a settlement offer cannot be made at that time. That is standard operating procedure. It does no good to get frustrated or angry. If the explanation is reasonable, handle it professionally and courteously. You will know if you are being strung along if you are confronted with a series of lame excuses. If that happens, proceed directly to the next chapter of this book because it is time to file suit.

You want the claims representative to respect you. During your discussions with the claims representative, you must be professional and courteous, yet forceful and assertive (not hostile). You must be very clear in your resolve to take this case all the way to trial. You must also be ready to address any questions or concerns about your case that the claims representative may have.

If you are able to negotiate professionally, courteously, and assertively while effectively addressing all these questions and concerns, you are probably well on your way to settling your case for a relatively fair amount of money.

If you make an enemy of the claims representative holding the purse strings to your settlement, you will deeply regret it. Claims people do not settle with plaintiffs or plaintiffs' lawyers they dislike. They have the power to make your life miserable. Do not tempt them to do this.

Incomplete Information

At the time you send the settlement demand letter, the insurance company is operating with incomplete information. You have selectively presented them with only the strongest aspects of your case. For example, if you were in an accident just a year before the accident case you are trying to currently settle, you might choose not to admit that fact in your settlement demand letter. You are not legally required to do so at this stage. Your doctor, however, may have included that fact in his or her medical report, which would obviously alert the insurance company to this issue.

The insurance company knows that it is getting incomplete information. It is only after suit is filed and the discovery process is completed that the insurance company can know for sure that it has a complete picture of you and your case. These days, you cannot expect to settle your case for full value until after you have successfully made it through depositions and discovery. (See Chapter 9 for a thorough discussion of depositions and the discovery process.)

You might be asking yourself at this point why you should have even gone through the settlement demand letter process. You very well may have nothing to lose by simply skipping this step entirely and moving right to filing a lawsuit. However, if your injuries are relatively minor, you may be able to settle your case without filing suit. The settlement demand letter is indispensable if you hope to settle such a case without actually filing suit.

Skipping the Demand Letter

If your injuries are more serious, you may want to jump right to the lawsuit stage. That is the only way to get full value for a larger case. However, even in larger cases, going through the process of sending the settlement demand letter has benefits. Just writing the letter helps to organize the file and understanding of it. Organization is crucial, and a comprehensive settlement demand letter forces you to organize your thoughts and your file.

Also, if you bypass the presuit negotiation stage, you may offend the claims representative handling the case. It is improper protocol in some people's eyes to skip this stage. If the representative feels disrespected, it may be very hard to get a fair settlement offer from this person later.

Settlement Demand Letter—Represented by Attorney

October 19, 2005

GOOD HANDS INSURANCE COMPANY
1400 N. PROVIDENCE ROAD
SUITE 5055
PHILADELPHIA, PA 19151
ATTN: N. SURANCE,
CLAIM REPRESENTATIVE

RE: My Client: A. Ken Head
       Your Insured: Al Coholic
       Claim No: 1234567890000000

Dear Ms. Surance:

Enclosed are the following medical bills and reports for my client, A. Ken Head:

Suburban Primary Care	$59.00
Dr. David Smith	9,005.00
Main Line Open MRI	1,000.00
Philadelphia Neurology	1,350.00
Total	$11,414.00

This case involves a rear-end motor vehicle accident with clear liability. Your company has already paid $1,978.16, representing 100% of Mr. Head's property damage.

My client was severely injured on May 19, 2005, as a result of this accident. Joseph Anderson, M.D., of Suburban Primary Care, first examined him on June 5, 2005. Dr. Anderson diagnosed Mr. Head as having suffered a left paravertebral muscle strain and a probable leg strain.

On June 17, 2005, Mr. Head came under the care of Dr. David Smith. Mr. Head remained under Dr. Smith's care through April 6, 2005. He was treated consistently throughout this period of time.

At the time of Dr. Smith's initial examination, Mr. Head complained of headaches, neck pain, thoracic spine pain, left arm, leg, and hip pain. He had difficulty sitting, standing, and performing activities of daily living and work duties.

Because of the lingering nature of these injuries, Dr. Smith scheduled Mr. Head for an MRI and an EMG. The MRI was conducted on September 17, 2004, and was positive for bulging disc at L4-L5 and L5-S1 and spondylosis. The EMG was conducted on October 4, 2004. It was normal.

As of November 29, 2004, Mr. Head still had post-traumatic headaches and severe pain to his left cervical spine, low back, and left leg. He continued to make slight improvement with treatment through January 18, 2005, although his prognosis had not improved. In Dr. Smith's report of February 9, 2005, he notes that Mr. Head was progressing with treatment, but that he continued to complain of stiffness in the lower back and neck pain. In Dr. Smith's discharge report of April 6, 2005, he notes that Mr. Head still complained of lower back stiffness and right arm pain.

It was Dr. Smith's clinical opinion that, as of April 6, 2005, my client's condition had become permanent, and that further treatment would not necessarily elicit further improvement. He was discharged with a poor prognosis and was told that he would simply have to learn to live with his discomforts. It was Dr. Smith's clinical opinion within a reasonable degree of chiropractic/medical certainty that Mr. Head's injuries were a direct result of the accident of May 19, 1994, and that they are permanent.

In view of the clear liability and the severity of the damages sustained, settlement demand is hereby made in the amount of $65,000.00.
Please contact me after your review of this claim is complete.

Very truly yours,

EVAN K. AIDMAN

EKA/sb
Enclosure

Settlement Demand Letter—Represented by Attorney

April 24, 2005

SNAKE FARM INSURANCE COMPANY
1400 N. PROVIDENCE ROAD
SUITE 5055
PHILADELPHIA, PA 19151
ATTN: O.J. Kildum,
CLAIM REPRESENTATIVE

RE: My Client: G. Howett Hurt
        Your Insured: Scott Free
        Your Claim No.:   0123456789000000

Dear Mr. Kildum:

Enclosed are the complete medical bills and reports for my client, G. Howett Hurt. You are already in possession of original photographs taken of Mr. Hurt while he was standing at the accident intersection.

The medical specials are as follows:

Newtown Square Fire Co #1	$285.00
Newtown Community Hospital	181.66
M.E.P.S. Services	355.00
Dr. David Smith	12,455.00
Main Line Open MRI	1,000.00
Dr. Michael M. Johnson	1,525.00
Total	$15,801.66

Mr. Hurt was severely injured on February 9, 2004 as the direct result of the negligence of your insured, Scott Free. Mr. Free drove his motor vehicle directly into Mr. Hurt while he was lawfully crossing at the intersection shown in the photographs. Your insured struck my client without any warning of any kind.

Newtown Square Fire Company rushed Mr. Hurt to Mercy Community Hospital. He was diagnosed at the hospital with contusions of his left hand and left thigh.

The hospital notes document an abrasion on his fingers and a hematoma covering one third of his thigh. The x-rays at the emergency room were of his pelvis, lower back, fingers of the left hand, left hip, and left knee.

My client began treatment with Dr. David Smith on February 15, 2004. He had cervical spine x-rays on that date, since his neck had begun hurting after the day of the accident. Although these x-rays were negative for any acute fractures, Mr. Hurt did show a severely decreased cervical lordotic curve. Mr. Hurt complained at the time of Dr. Smith's initial exam of dizziness, pain to his head, neck, thoracic spine, lumbosacral spine, and left leg.

My client received consistent treatment from Dr. Smith through February 16, 2005. His treatment included soft tissue manipulation, electrical stimulation, ultrasound therapy, cryotherapy, hydroculator therapy, as well as osseous manipulation. He received ninety-four treatments during his year of therapy. The treatment helped Mr. Hurt slowly progress through his neck, left knee, and lumbosacral pain. The pain in the latter region radiated to his left lower extremity.

Dr. Smith reported that he experienced "slow, but steady improvement of his condition both objectively and subjectively. However, there were periods when the symptomotology was somewhat severe and as a result of the persistent symptomology he was referred out for neurological testing as well as an MRI study." Dr. Smith felt that his radicular symptoms and his radiculopathy were caused by this accident and that as of February 16, 2005, his condition had become permanent and stationary. He therefore elected to discharge my client at that time with a poor prognosis.

Dr. Smith referred Mr. Hurt to Michael Martin Johnson, M.D. Dr. Johnson examined Mr. Hurt on June 8, 2004, at which time Mr. Hurt complained of frequent headaches, neck pain, paresthesia, and numbness in his hands. Dr. Johnson noted his radiating lower back pain that moved into his right lower extremity down to the toes. His impression was bilateral lumbosacral radiculopathy, cervical strain, and post-traumatic headache syndrome. The EMG performed on June 8, 2004, was abnormal for both the right and left lower extremities for early subacute L5-S1 radiculopathy.

Mr. Hurt had only $5,000.00 in medical bill coverage. This was exhausted and claim is hereby made for the excess. In view of the clear liability and the severity of the damages sustained, settlement demand is hereby made in the amount of $75,000.00.

Please contact me after review of this claim is complete.

Very truly yours,

EVAN K. AIDMAN

EKA/sb
Enclosure

SETTLEMENT OFFER

Once the insurance company has finally made you a settlement offer, be prepared to say *no*. It is very rare for the first offer to be their best offer. When you go to purchase a car, you do not accept the first offer from the dealership. Similarly, the insurance company does not expect you to take their first offer, and that is why you can expect to initially receive a *low ball offer*. Unfortunately, you do not have the same bargaining power that you have when purchasing a car. When you begin to walk out of the auto dealership, things magically happen. The dealer knows you can buy the car elsewhere. Suddenly, the price drops and other extras are thrown in.

It is not so simple in negotiating the settlement of a personal injury case. You are stuck with the insurance company that is defending your case. You cannot shop around. Especially these days, it is very difficult to get full value out of insurance companies for personal injury cases. Whereas in the 70's and 80's, you could expect a substantial settlement within a few weeks after forwarding the settlement demand letter, in the latter part of the 90's and into the 21st century, casualty insurance companies around the country have gotten much tougher in settling cases.

Insurance companies invest a great deal more money in exhaustively investigating personal injury claims these days. Their investigations frequently turn up information they use against plaintiffs at trial. They may discover through the issuance of subpoenas that a claimant has been in several other accidents or that the claimant has criminal convictions for perjury or other crimes that negatively affect his or her credibility. (See form 14, p.263 for a sample subpoena.) Any of these factors can limit or even prevent a settlement offer.

If the firm refuses to make or raise their offer to a legitimate level, a lawsuit has to be filed. Once it is filed, the insurance company realizes that you are serious and that it will have to start paying its attorneys if it wants to continue to defend the case. This presents the second opportunity for settlement negotiations. It is common for the company to make a reasonable settlement offer immediately after your attorney files the lawsuit.

Depositions

Insurance companies know that jury verdicts, even for legitimate and substantial accident injury claims, are often much lower than they used to be. Thus, the insurance companies almost never offer full value until you have proven to them that they really have no other choice. That means having many aspects of your seemingly private life explored by means of subpoenaed documents.

It may also mean submitting yourself to a *deposition* under oath during which an insurance defense lawyer will ask you all about the accident, your injuries, and many other things that seem to be unrelated to your claim. If the case is not settled at this point, it will probably be several more months before further negotiations take place.

At the deposition, the insurance company's lawyer questions you under oath about the accident and your injuries. This is the first chance for the insurance company to evaluate you in person. How you present yourself at your deposition dramatically affects the settlement negotiations. If you have been properly prepared for the deposition by your attorney, it is very likely that the company will extend an increased settlement offer shortly afterwards.

Settlement Conference

The final opportunities for settlement occur after a settlement conference and *at the courthouse steps*. Judges almost always push hard for settlements at these conferences. The attorneys and their clients may find the judge's arm twisting irresistible and settlement may result. If it does not, the judge will order the case to trial. When faced head-on with this prospect, one side or the other may finally see the wisdom of settling out of court.

SETTLEMENT STRATEGY

Settlement attempts by your attorney are often perceived by the insurance attorney as a sign of weakness or desperation. This discourages serious settlement negotiations early in the litigation process. The insurance company may similarly feel that your attorney will see an early settlement offer as a sign of weakness. Relatively large personal injury cases almost never settle without the filing of a lawsuit. If you have been seriously injured in an accident and your lawyer is trying to push a settlement on you even before he or she has filed a lawsuit on your behalf, lights should flash and bells should ring in your head. There is a great chance that you will do much better with a lawyer who will file the lawsuit and hold out for a better offer.

Insurance Company's Strategy

The insurance companies often have a big bargaining advantage over you. The money rests in the company's bank account or investments drawing interest throughout the case. Your lawyer needs to push the firm to release its grip on some of that money. You, on the other hand, may badly need the money to pay your bills and live your life. Or worse, your lawyer may need to settle some cases for his or her own personal reasons. Insurance companies can smell desperation. If the insurance company senses that you or your lawyer are desperate to settle the case, it will make, at most, a small offer.

Delaying

Insurance companies use different tactics to increase their bargaining power over you. One such tactic is the *delay game*. The *subpoena game* is another annoying tactic. Insurance lawyers engage in extended *fishing expeditions* in which they subpoena documents from every imaginable area of your life, hoping to hassle, embarrass, or find something to use against you.

The insurance company hopes to find damaging information this way. They also use the subpoena game to intimidate plaintiffs into believing that no area of life is private. In reality, if the subpoena game goes too far, your lawyer can seek a protective order from the court prohibiting overly invasive subpoenas. For example, it is improper for the company to subpoena records from your psychologist where you are not making a claim for a psychological injury. Your lawyer should ask the court to *quash* such a subpoena.

Pushing Paper

The *paper game* is another favorite. The insurance company lawyer files essentially meaningless petitions and motions in an attempt to *paper to death* your lawyer. This tactic is especially useful against overworked plaintiff's lawyers. Such a lawyer might be willing to settle for less than full value just to reduce the workload.

Your Strategy

Experienced plaintiff's lawyers know that in cases involving serious injuries, full value will probably not be offered until after the discovery process has run its course. There is a caveat here though. If the insurance lawyer uncovers damaging evidence during discovery, the settlement value of the case may drop. The lawyer and client need to maintain clear lines of communication to keep unexpected surprises to a minimum.

Waiting

Your lawyer understands that the most favorable settlements are often reached by *waiting out* the litigation process. This helps to explain why so many settlements take place only after the parties reach the courthouse steps. Lawsuits become endurance tests in which each side attempts to wait out the other.

You and your lawyer want a prompt and fair settlement for obvious reasons. Insurance companies also prefer to settle cases without excessive litigation when it is clear that their insured was at fault and real injuries have been suffered. While insurance companies often use delaying tactics in order to hold onto the settlement money as long as possible, they prefer to settle when the only alternative is paying their lawyers large fees to defend meritorious cases. This is why it is absolutely vital that your lawyer demonstrate that it is in the best interest of the insurance company to settle the case quickly and for a fair sum of money.

Documenting

The best way to convince an insurance company to settle is by accurately and completely *documenting* both the severity of your injuries and the defendant's complete or substantial responsibility. This requires prompt investigation of the accident by your lawyer and his or her investigative team, and careful monitoring of your treatment and medical progress. It also requires clear communication between lawyer and doctor so that the opinions in the medical report are stated in a legally acceptable way.

An interesting and important dilemma arises when your doctor's report comes back with crucial errors or omissions. You or your lawyer may need to ask your doctor to correct any mistakes. How one deals with this problem can have a huge impact on convincing the insurance company to settle and on the future course of litigation.

For example, in some states the doctor's opinion must be stated to *a legal degree of certainty*. If those words are omitted from the report, the defense attorney may argue that the report does not pass legal muster and should be disregarded by the judge, jury, or arbitration panel. You or your lawyer must remedy this situation in advance of the day of trial. How you approach this problem is not as straightforward as it may appear.

The first question to ask yourself is how to communicate the need for a corrected report to the doctor. Realize that anything you put in writing to the doctor will probably end up in your file at the doctor's office. You can expect that the defense lawyer will subpoena your doctor's records. If there is a letter in your file that asks the doctor to change a report, the defense attorney may try to use it to attack you and your doctor's opinion at trial.

This lawyer may suggest to the jury that you were improperly trying to influence your doctor. Or, he or she may suggest that the doctor only wrote an amended report because of an inappropriate communication from you. Therefore, whenever you request a corrected report in writing, use the words *if justified*. For example, write to the doctor, *Please indicate, if justified by the medical evidence, that all opinions in your report are stated to a reasonable degree of medical certainty*. This way, it does not appear that you are trying to influence the doctor to say something that is not true.

Whenever you are writing to a medical provider, choose your words very carefully. Always assume that your written words will some day become known to the defense lawyer and the insurance company. Always assume that the defense lawyer will subpoena your doctor's records. Review the sample letters on pages 33 through 35 for acceptable letters to medical providers. Make you letter very generic. The less said, the better. What you do not say generally cannot be used against you.

Given the danger presented by letters to doctors, it is preferable that requests for corrected records be made over the telephone. In a telephone conference you can speak freely about the kinds of corrections that are needed in the medical report. One quick phone call will usually resolve the problem of an erroneous medical report.

Some doctors are not very receptive to changing their records. They may take offense that a lawyer or litigant is asking them to change a record. As long as you are not asking the doctor to say something that is not true, there is nothing wrong with asking a doctor to amend a report. But the doctor may not see it that way. If the doctor will not amend the report, you are going to have to approach the problem from a different angle.

> **Example:** I recently had a case in which a doctor and client were not on good terms. For some reason, there was simply a personality conflict between them. I needed the doctor to make a reasonable correction in his report and he refused to do so. I had no choice but to find another doctor to make the correction, and to have my client examined by this second doctor strictly for purposes of the litigation. After this doctor examined my client and reviewed all of the medical records, he wrote a report that helped the case.

Bringing a doctor in to the case for litigation purposes is a last resort. This doctor's testimony will be subject to attack on the grounds that he or she is a *gun for hire*, that is, that his or her opinion is for sale to the highest bidder. The defense lawyer will argue that the opinion was offered only because of the litigation and that it is tainted in this respect. That can be a devastating attack, especially if the opinions stated in the report are controversial.

Nevertheless, if there are no other options, you should not hesitate to seek a second opinion. You can be sure that if your opponent hires a doctor to examine you or review your records, the doctor will be inclined to say what your opponent wants him or her to say. That is the reality of personal injury litigation. (See Chapter 9 with regard to the defense medical examination.)

Errors in doctors' reports are extremely common. Most of the errors are not problematic. The date of accident may be recorded as *11/7/58* when it actually occurred on November 7, 1998. You really do not need to correct this error since the defense lawyer in unlikely to attack your case on this basis. This error can easily be explained away at trial if necessary. Clearly, this was simply a clerical error. There is nothing wrong, however, with asking the doctor to correct this kind of error.

FINALIZING SETTLEMENT

Once the case is finally settled, there are some procedures that must be taken care of before the insurance company will send you the settlement check.

Offer

It is absolutely unethical for a lawyer to fail to immediately notify the client of any settlement offers. Even if the offer is extremely low, the client must be notified and given the option of accepting the offer. Some lawyers may withhold this information out of fear that the client will force the acceptance of a low offer. Perhaps the client is desperate for cash. The lawyer may feel that the case is worth a lot more money and he or she may not be eager to settle cheaply. Nevertheless, it is 100% your call on when to settle and for how much. Of course, it is the lawyer's job to counsel you about the advisability of accepting a certain offer.

Release

Once the insurance company makes an offer of settlement, the ball moves into your court. If the insurance company's offer is acceptable, you must sign a legal document that sets forth the terms of the settlement. This document is called a *release*. By signing a release you give up the right to ever bring additional claims against the insurance company, even if your injuries turn out to be more severe than you thought at the time of settlement.

It is to your advantage to know the nature of the insurance company with which you are dealing. Many insurance companies will treat you fairly. Unfortunately, some insurance companies *low ball* every claimant, no matter how legitimate the case is, and get you to sign a release with a very poor settlement. These same insurance companies may do the same thing to your lawyer, even if an experienced PI attorney represents you.

General Release

KNOW ALL MEN BY THESE PRESENTS that I, D. Rick Testimonee, for and in consideration of the payment to us of $10,500.00 and other good and valuable consideration, have remised, released, quitclaimed, and forever discharged and by these presents do, for myself, my heirs, executors, and administrators remise, release, quitclaim, and forever discharge Manny and Les Bucks and Acme Insurance Company, their heirs, executors, administrators, successors and assigns, and all of them, of and from all actions, causes of action, demands, damages, costs, loss of services, expenses, compensation, and all consequential damage arising out of or in any way growing out of any and all personal injuries resulting or to result from an incident that occurred on or about November 1, 2004, at or near Ridge Avenue and Glennwood Avenue, Birmingham, AL. IN WITNESS WHEREOF, I have hereunto set my hand and seal this 12th day of January, 2005.

_____(SEAL)

D. RICK TESTIMONEE

Court Notification

If you filed a lawsuit before settlement, you must file a legal document with the court advising that the case has been settled so that the court can remove the case from the dockets. Otherwise, the case stays on the dockets and a trial is scheduled. In Pennsylvania, for example, you would file an **Order to Settle, Discontinue and End** with the court. If you are unrepresented, you will have to contact the court for the appropriate form for your jurisdiction.

If a lawsuit was not actually filed, you do not have to file anything with the court, since the court has had no involvement with your case. The possible exceptions to this rule are if the plaintiff is either a minor or is mentally incompetent to handle his or her legal affairs. To settle these kinds of cases, you may need special permission from the court even if the case settled prior to suit. If the case involved a death, you may also have to obtain the court's permission to settle the case. The procedure varies from state to state. Your lawyer will know what the procedure is. If you are unrepresented, you should call the court and, hopefully, some sympathetic civil servant will guide you.

Time Frame

It usually takes the insurance company about two weeks from the time it receives the signed release before it sends the settlement check to you or your lawyer. If two weeks have passed without having received the check, call the insurance claims representative to inquire. That is usually all it takes to get things moving.

Keeping Communication

It is not a bad idea to call the insurance company a couple days after you send the release, just to make sure that it was received. It is not unusual for important documents to get lost in the mail. This follow up phone call can save you some aggravation down the road. Also, you might want to send these documents by certified or overnight mail. It costs a little extra, but may prove to be worth the expense.

ALTERNATE DISPUTE RESOLUTION

Jury trials are expensive and painful affairs. *Alternate dispute resolution* (ADR) techniques try to ease this pain and expense, while also reducing court backlogs.

There are numerous forms that ADR can take. The principal forms are *mediation*, *binding arbitration*, *nonbinding arbitration*, and *high-low arbitration*. Only the imagination limits the possibilities here. As long as both sides agree, ADR can take place in virtually any setting, utilizing virtually any procedure.

Mediation

Mediation involves bringing the sides together before a neutral third party. This third party can be a judge, an ex-judge, a practicing attorney, a professional mediator, or any other individual upon whom both sides agree.

The mediator helps the parties find common ground. He or she does not make a decision like a judge. Instead, he or she helps to get each side to see the merit in the other side's positions. He or she also points out weaknesses that the parties may not realize exist in their own case. By bringing the parties together in this setting, the mediator hopes to expedite settlement of the case or, at least, bring the sides closer together.

The mediator's neutrality is his or her power. This neutral perspective may give both sides the first truly independent evaluation of the case. It can greatly influence the way the parties view the case for settlement purposes.

Mediation is most appropriate where both sides see the possibility for settlement. When one or both sides are firmly entrenched in their position, it is unlikely that mediation will be useful.

Arbitration

Arbitration is a better settlement device when the sides are entrenched. Arbitration usually involves a mini or summary trial. The rules of evidence are relaxed to permit admission of evidence without the formalities required in jury trials. For example, medical reports, rather than actual medical testimony, may be used to prove damages. This greatly reduces the time and expense of litigation.

If the arbitration is *binding*, the ruling of the arbitrator ends the dispute. If it is *nonbinding*, the ruling is advisory only. Both sides will learn a great deal about the case and its merit during the course of the arbitration. Often, settlement takes place shortly after a nonbinding arbitration.

High-low arbitrations are a special kind of arbitration in which each side submits a monetary figure. The arbitrator selects either the high figure, which, of course, is the one submitted by you, or the low figure submitted by the insurance company. He or she will not split the difference.

The reason for this is that it makes both sides submit their absolute best offer, because if they are too far off, the arbitrator will choose the other side's figure. If the arbitrator could split the difference, then each side would exaggerate their position. It is kind of like when a parent lets one child break the candy bar in half and lets the other have first pick. Both take great care and precision to achieve the best result.

There are various kinds of high-low arbitrations. This is just one kind. Again, imagination is the key to finding a process on which both sides can agree.

chapter nine:
The Lawsuit Process

This chapter explores the initial stages of the lawsuit process. It examines statutes of limitations deadlines, choice of trials, choice of venue, and the initial legal filings you can expect from the insurance company or individual or entity you have sued.

STATUTES OF LIMITATIONS

A sad moment for lawyer and client occurs when it becomes clear that a *statute of limitations* deadline has passed. Statute of limitations deadlines are legal time limits that control when lawsuits must be filed. If the lawsuit is not filed before the statute of limitations deadline, it will be subject to dismissal by the court. It is, therefore, extremely important that you find out the deadline for your case and keep it in mind when negotiating.

Statutes of limitations vary from state to state and occasionally are changed by legislatures. On the following pages is a list of the deadlines for negligence cases as of the time this book was written, along with the statute citations. To be sure of your deadline you should check the law for your state or ask a personal injury attorney.

This list applies *only* to negligence cases. Thus, if you have been injured in a motor vehicle accident or slip-and-fall accident involving negligence, you can check this list for your statute of limitations deadline. If your injury involves medical malpractice, a defective product, assault and battery, slander or liable, or any other kind of injury, a different statute of limitations deadline may apply to your case. You will need either to check the law yourself or contact a personal injury attorney. A quick trip to your local library should be all it takes to research this important issue.

Even if you are pursuing a negligence lawsuit, this list may not suffice. For example, in Kentucky where a one-year statute of limitations applies to negligent cases, an exception exists that may extend the deadline significantly. In California, in certain cases, the limitations period is one year and in others it is two years. In Colorado, it is two years for slip and fall cases but three years for motor vehicle accidents.

> **NOTE:** *This list is only a starting point in your research. If you are concerned about a statute of limitation, you should either contact a personal injury lawyer in your state or go to a law library and look up the statutory section cited in this list.*

Alabama	Code of Alabama §6-2-38	2 years
Alaska	Alaska Statutes §09.10.070	2 years
Arizona	Arizona Revised Statutes §12-542	2 years
Arkansas	Arkansas Stat. Annotated §16-56-115	5 years
California	Civil Civ. Procedure Code §340, §335.1	1 or 2 years
Colorado	Colorado Revised Statutes §13-80-102	2 years
Connecticut	Connecticut General Statutes §52-584	2 years
Delaware	Delaware Code Annotated §§8107, 8119	2 years
District of Columbia	District of Columbia Code §12-301	3 years
Florida	Florida Statutes §95.11	4 years
Georgia	Georgia Code Ann. §3-1004	2 years
Hawaii	Hawaii Revised Statutes §657-7	2 years
Idaho	Idaho Code §5-219	2 years
Illinois	Illinois Statutes Ann. §13-202	2 years
Indiana	Indiana Code Ann. §34-11-2-4	2 years
Iowa	Iowa Code Annotated §614.1	2 years
Kansas	Kansas Statutes Annotated §60.513	2 years
Kentucky	Kentucky Revised Statutes Ann. §413.140	1 year
Louisiana	Louisiana Civil Code Ann. Art. 3492	1 year
Maine	Maine Revised Statutes Ann. §752	6 years
Maryland	Maryland Ann. Code §5-101	3 years
Massachusetts	Massachusetts General Laws Ann. Ch. 260, §2A4	3 years
Michigan	Michigan Compiled Laws §600.5805S	3 years

Minnesota	Minnesota Statutes Annotated §541.07	2 years
Mississippi	Mississippi Code Annotated §15-1-49	3 years
Missouri	Missouri Statute Annotated 35 §516.120	5 years
Montana	Montana Code Annotated §27-2-204, §27-2-207	2 or 3 years
Nebraska	Revised Statutes of Nebraska §25-208	4 years
Nevada	Nevada Revised Statutes Annotated §11.190	2 years
New Hampshire	New Hampshire Revised Statutes Ann. §508:4	3 years
New Jersey	New Jersey Statutes Annotated §2A:14-2	2 years
New Mexico	New Mexico Statutes Ann. §37-1-8	3 years
New York	N.Y. CIV. PRAC. R. §214	3 years
North Carolina	General Statutes of North Carolina §1-52	3 years
North Dakota	North Dakota Century Code §28-01-16	6 years
Ohio	Ohio Rev. Code Ann. §2305.10	2 years
Oklahoma	Oklahoma Statutes Annotated Title 12 §95	2 years
Oregon	Oregon Revised Statutes §12.110	2 years
Pennsylvania	42 PA Con. Stat. Annotated §5524	2 years
Rhode Island	General Laws of Rhode Island §9-1-14	3 years
South Carolina	South Carolina Code Ann. §15-3-530	3 years
South Dakota	South Dakota Comp. Laws Ann. §15-2-14	3 years
Tennessee	Tennessee Code Annotated §28-3-104	1 year
Texas	Texas Civ. Prac. & Rem. Code Ann. 2 §16.003	2 years
Utah	Utah Code Annotated §78-12-25	4 years
Vermont	Vermont Statutes Ann. Title 12 §512	3 years
Virginia	Virginia Code §8.01-243	2 years
Washington	Revised Code of Washington Ann. §4.16.020	3 years
West Virginia	West Virginia Code §55-2-12	2 years
Wisconsin	Wisconsin Statutes Annotated §893.54	3 years
Wyoming	Wyoming Statutes Annotated §1-3-105	4 years

Consult an attorney in your state if you fear that the statute of limitations has passed in your case. There are some exceptions you may need to be aware of. For example, minors generally have two years from the date they reach their 18th birthday to file, although, again, this varies from state to state.

In cases involving repressed memory, the court may suspend the statute of limitations during the time that the memory was repressed. Similarly, many states suspend the statute of limitations during periods that the plaintiff suffered from insanity or mental incapacity. Thus, this period of time would not count toward the deadline.

Even if memory was not repressed, in cases involving victims of childhood sexual abuse, a civil lawsuit for damages might have a very long statute of limitations deadline. In Pennsylvania, the legislature passed a law in June 2002 changing the statute of limitations in these types of cases to twelve years after the plaintiff reaches age 18, the age of majority.

This forward-thinking legislation recognizes that even if the victim of childhood sexual abuse has not repressed any memories, he or she may not have the ability to act to protect his or her legal rights for a very long time after becoming an adult. It may take many years before this person has worked through the trauma enough to move forward with legal action. (See **www.smith-lawfirm.com/remedies.html** for an extended discussion of these issues.)

If you are relying on a recent change by the legislature in the statute of limitations, be sure to research whether the change applies only to cases that occur after the effective date of the new law or whether it applies retroactively. If the change in the law does not apply retroactively, you may not be able to revive a case that was time barred by the previously existing statute of limitations deadline.

For obvious injuries, like those resulting from car accidents, the time period begins when the injury occurs. However, different deadlines apply to certain kinds of cases. In medical malpractice cases, most states set the start time on the date you first discovered or should have discovered the malpractice. It is a good idea to start the suit within two years from the alleged malpractice since this may be the date on which you should have discovered it.

One of the most difficult types of calls a personal injury attorney can get is when a potential client says he or she was badly injured and the statute of limitations runs out next week. A busy attorney will often decline to take such a case because he does not want to take the risk that the suit cannot be filed on time or that he or she will have to file a suit before knowing if there are actual grounds for filing.

Learn your deadline as soon as you can and mark it on all of your calendars. If you delay hiring an attorney, be sure to contact one at least a month before the deadline.

Attorney Errors

Occasionally an attorney will simply miss a deadline. This is an embarrassment and a financial disaster for the attorney. Some try to cover up their error by telling the client that their case had to be dropped because it was not as good as they had thought. Others put up some of their own money and tell the client that it was the only settlement they could get. Still others stall for time by telling their client that suit was filed and that the litigation is progressing.

If you believe your attorney has missed your statute of limitation deadline through his or her own fault, then you should contact a legal malpractice lawyer or your state's bar association disciplinary committee.

(See Chapter 4 for an extended discussion of legal malpractice.)

CHOICE OF TRIALS

The first major choice that must be made regarding the filing of a personal injury lawsuit involves the type of trial you wish to have. You and your lawyer must determine whether to demand a jury trial, a trial before a judge without a jury, or a hearing of a more informal nature. The choice you make may determine how quickly your case is decided and the maximum amount of money you can receive to compensate you for your injuries.

If you and your lawyer select an informal hearing, many states provide an arbitration procedure as the forum for the resolution of your dispute. To illustrate, in Philadelphia Common Pleas Court arbitrations, your case is judged by a panel of three attorneys. These lawyers are chosen at random from a list of all qualified lawyers who practice in Philadelphia County. The Arbitration Center tries to assure that the arbitration panel has one plaintiff's lawyer, one insurance defense lawyer, and one lawyer who does neither plaintiff's nor defense work.

The average Philadelphia personal injury arbitration takes no more than two hours to complete. The lawyers submit medical reports to prove the extent of the injuries. The rules of evidence are greatly relaxed so that the case can be tried quickly and efficiently. The arbitrators reach their decision immediately upon the conclusion of the hearing. This decision is communicated to the lawyers within four days in most cases. Jury trials, on the other hand, can take weeks or longer. Doctors and other expert witnesses must actually testify, and strict adherence to the rules for admission of evidence is required. Trials before judges, also known as *bench trials*, take much less time than jury trials but considerably more than arbitrations.

The amount of money damages you can obtain in an arbitration hearing may be limited to a certain dollar amount. This will vary from state to state and county to county. Trials before juries or judges without juries have no such limitations. If you have suffered a serious injury due to someone else's negligence and there is adequate insurance coverage, you will want either a jury trial or a trial before a judge.

These types of trials are considerably more expensive than arbitration hearings. You will probably also have a longer wait before your case comes to trial if you choose a jury trial over an arbitration. Again, in arbitrations you may be able to prove your pain and suffering through your testimony and your medical reports alone. The added expense in jury and judge trials comes from the expert witness fees charged by doctors and other expert witnesses. This, as you might imagine, can cost several thousand dollars. Thus, if your case is on the borderline, that is, if the arbitration limit is $50,000, and you think the case is worth somewhere between $40,000 and $50,000, you will undoubtedly elect to have your case filed as an arbitration.

If the case is clearly worth more than $50,000, it is probably worth the wait and the additional expense involved with a jury trial. Your lawyer may be able to work out an arrangement with your doctor so that you do not have to pay the doctor's fee for his or her testimony until your case settles.

CHOICE OF VENUE

Often there is a choice of counties in which the lawsuit may be brought. This is known as *choice of venue*. For example, if the accident happened in one county, but the defendant resides in another county, your case probably can be filed in either county. In some areas, one county has an advantage over other counties because the awards are generally higher. For example, awards are generally higher in inner-city counties than in suburban counties. Thus, even though you may wait longer for trial in a large city, the higher money awards make it worth the wait.

When the accident involves federal law, there may be an additional choice, namely, federal court. For instance, if you are in an accident with a U.S. Mail truck or if you fall and are injured on federal property, the suit must be brought in federal court. Cases based upon civil rights violations, such as policy brutality, may also be pursued in federal court. On average, cases decided in federal court result in lower money awards than those brought in state court in large metropolitan areas.

Money awards are highest in big cities because of the characteristics of its residents. In general, the more urban the setting, the higher the average verdict returned by jurors. It seems that big city dwellers are more liberal and more comfortable with socking it to insurance companies than people who live in rural areas. Also, salaries and costs of living are higher in big cities. This apparently makes it easier for big city residents to fully grasp and come to terms with the compensation owed to the injured plaintiff.

POST-FILING BATTLES

Now that the lawsuit has been filed, what happens next? Sometimes the insurance company immediately makes a settlement offer. The lawsuit papers may be just the thing to get the insurance company's attention. Often the case has not settled simply because the insurance company just has not gotten around to evaluating the case. Once it is served with the suit papers, it will be squarely faced with a choice. If it chooses to contest the case, it will have to pay its attorneys to defend it. Rather than pay its lawyers and then the claimant at the end of the case, the company may begin to seriously consider making a fair offer of settlement.

If the insurance company does not yet want to settle the case, it will send the suit papers to its attorneys so that a response to the lawsuit can be filed with the court. Lawyers sometimes refer to the suit papers as the **Complaint**. The insurance company's lawyers may file an *Answer* to the **Complaint**, or it may file some form of objections to the **Complaint**. Objections are filed when the complaint is in some way technically defective.

Once the preliminary objections are out of the way, the lawyers will file an *Answer* to the **Complaint**. An *Answer* is a legal document that admits or denies the allegations contained in the **Complaint**. The *Answer* rarely sheds any light on the conflict because it generally contains nothing but blanket denials. The *Answer* typically denies everything except that which cannot possibly be disputed (such as the names and addresses of the parties). Once these preliminaries are out of the way, the attorneys begin the discovery process. That is where the essence of the conflict begins to emerge.

chapter ten:
The Discovery Process

In the old days, trials were even more like war than they are now. Modern discovery rules have put an end to the sneak attacks that until recently characterized litigation. These days, each side is required to respond to the other side's requests for information concerning the case. If it fails to do so voluntarily, the court, upon the motion of the requesting party, will order the recalcitrant party to provide discovery. If the attorneys do their jobs properly, 90% of what happens at the trial can be anticipated and planned for.

The discovery process involves three stages:

1. interrogatories and exchange of documents;
2. depositions; and,
3. the independent medical examination.

INTERROGATORIES AND THE REQUEST FOR PRODUCTION OF DOCUMENTS

The first stage of discovery consists of answering written questions (called *interrogatories*), and the exchange of relevant documents. Each side submits a written request for all relevant documents, as well as for answers to these interrogatories.

Forms 3 and 4 are sample sets of **Interrogatories**. (see form 3, p.203. and form 4, p.219.) Unfortunately, these written questions generally do not yield much useful information. Lawyers typically answer them in a vague manner to avoid having these answers used against their clients later in the litigation.

Example: An interrogatory may ask how fast the defendant was traveling when he first saw your car. The defendant may tell his attorney that he was going 35 m.p.h. at that time. The defense attorney may, however, choose to be less specific when answering this interrogatory. He may indicate in the answer that the defendant was traveling *within the speed limit at the time he first saw the plaintiff's car.* If, at the defendant's deposition, the defendant testifies that he was going 25 m.p.h. at that time, an inconsistency has been avoided.

There is a sample **Request for Production of Documents** in Appendix A. (see form 5, p.236.) The exchange of documents is very useful, since each affects the settlement value of the case.

Depending on the nature of your case, other documents may be relevant and exchanged at this time. The documents that are exchanged during this stage of the proceedings include:

◆ the police report;
◆ ambulance report;
◆ all medical records;
◆ witness statements;
◆ property damage appraisals;
◆ photographs of the cars;
◆ photographs of the scene;
◆ diagrams of the accident scene; and,
◆ insurance policies.

The rules of civil procedure require a response to these requests for information within a short period of time, typically thirty days, although this varies from state to state. If the responses are late or inadequate, the attorney who submitted the requests can file a motion with the court requesting that the court order the other side to provide the documents. There is a sample **Motion to Compel Discovery** in Appendix A. (see form 6, p.238.) There is also a sample of the order the judge would sign. (see form 7, p.239.)

Once this stage of discovery is completed, it is time to begin preparing for stage two of the discovery process—depositions. It is here that the lawyers get the clearest idea yet of the strengths and weaknesses of their case and of their opponent's case.

DEPOSITIONS

The *discovery deposition* is one of the most important stages in the litigation of a personal injury lawsuit. It is during the discovery deposition that the insurance company's lawyer gets the opportunity to question the accident victim in person about the accident and the injuries suffered. Similarly, at the defendant's deposition, your lawyer is able to discover much about the insurance company's version of the accident. A sample list of deposition questions was presented on p.24. Success on deposition day vastly improves the chance of a prompt and fair settlement.

The discovery deposition gives the attorney the chance to pick the mind of the individual who is being deposed. Depositions are usually held in the office of one of the lawyers. The testimony is taken under oath and is recorded by a stenographer. Thus, extreme care must be taken to accurately describe the accident and resulting injuries. By confronting an individual at trial with clearly erroneous deposition testimony, an attorney can devastate that individual's credibility in the eyes of the judge, jury, or arbitration panel. That is why thorough preparation prior to deposition day is a necessity.

Telling the Truth

Perhaps the most important advice your lawyer can give you during preparation for the deposition is to tell the truth. Even the craftiest lawyer has trouble tripping up an individual who speaks the truth and sticks to it. Clients sometimes think they can outsmart the other lawyer by bending the truth in their favor. More often than not, the other lawyer can figure out when this is happening and can expose the lie. An otherwise meritorious case can be lost by a small lie. Juries, judges, and arbitration panels have no sympathy for liars, even injured ones.

Guessing

It is also vital not to guess during a deposition. Frequently the other lawyer asks questions to which the witness simply does not have the answer. It is important to remember that a deposition is not a multiple choice test. You do not score points by occasionally guessing correctly. Stick to the facts and testify only to that which you personally know.

Every trial lawyer has seen his or her client's case reduced in value by an incorrect guess. *I do not know* is a fair answer if it is true. The time spent preparing for the deposition will ensure that the witness does not have to rely on this answer too often. *I do not remember* is also fair if you truly do not remember. Sometimes depositions are taken years after the accident. It is nearly impossible to recall the minute details attorneys routinely seek during a deposition. Again, preparation will minimize the need to rely on this answer. It is far better to admit that you do not know the answer to a question or that you do not recall the answer, than to venture a guess.

Stopping Answers

Another key to a successful deposition is to know when to stop answering. Often the defense lawyer uses the deposition as a *fishing expedition* to hook anything of use to the defense case. That is why many questions that seem completely irrelevant to the accident are asked. Believe it or not, this is generally permitted by the courts.

Since the other lawyer is attempting to pick your mind, you must not make his or her job easier by responding to each question with a long, drawn out answer. If a question can fairly be answered with a *yes* or a *no*, by all means do that and say no more until the next question is asked. Your lawyer may even tap you on the shoulder or use a prearranged signal if your answers are getting too detailed. This signal lets you know to keep your answers brief. If you give the other lawyer enough ammunition, you increase the likelihood that eventually he or she will find something to use against you. That is why brief answers are usually best.

Understanding

It is vital that you completely understand each question before attempting to give an answer. It is not possible to give a truthful and accurate answer to a misunderstood question. The defense attorney will repeat or rephrase the question if requested to do so.

Speaking Clearly

It is important to speak loud enough so that all in the deposition room can hear the testimony. You should keep your hands away from your mouth. To some attorneys a hand in front of the mouth implies that you have something to hide. Questions cannot be answered with a nod of the head or an *uh-uh*. You must say *yes* or *no* so that the stenographer can record the response.

chapter eleven:
The Trial

If the personal injury case does not settle shortly after conclusion of the depositions, it is time to begin preparing for trial. It is necessary for you and your lawyer to meet in advance of trial to prepare. There is nothing wrong with a lawyer and client meeting to run through possible questions and answers.

Every lawyer prepares his or her witnesses. Good lawyers prepare exhaustively in hopes of accurately forecasting opposing counsel's questions. If your lawyer is unwilling to spend the necessary time preparing you to testify, you may want to think about looking for a new lawyer. Witnesses testify much more compellingly when they are confident that the other lawyer will be unable to surprise them with unexpected questions. Preparation helps to assure this confidence.

The preparation session also helps to refresh your memory and suggests additional areas of inquiry the lawyer may not have thought of already. It lets the lawyer see the areas to avoid.

Some people think it is unnecessary to prepare for trial. Many resist taking the time to prepare and insist that everything will work out if they simply tell the truth. While having the truth on your side is critical, it is not enough to ensure fair compensation at trial. Careful preparation helps you (or any other witness) to relax so that you can offer testimony in an organized, thoughtful, and convincing way. This helps the jury to understand your testimony, to relate to it and to you in a positive way, to recall it accurately during deliberations, and most importantly, to be motivated to return a large award that fully compensates you.

The substance of your preparation session with the lawyer is privileged information. The defense lawyer is not permitted to inquire about it during cross examination. In fact, all communications between lawyer and client are privileged and private, unless the client waives that privilege.

SELECTING THE JURY

An important stage in the course of a jury trial takes place at the very outset of the proceedings, namely, the *voir dire* (generally pronounced *vwa dear*) of the jury. *Voir dire* consists of questions the attorneys ask the potential jurors in order to determine which of them will actually sit on the jury panel. There is a sample set of *voir dire* questions in Appendix A. (see form 11 p.248.) *Voir dire* procedure varies from judge to judge. Sometimes the judge asks all the questions with input from the attorneys, other times the attorneys do the questioning.

Your Role

You have a very important role to play during *voir dire*. You can provide your lawyer with your reaction to the various potential jurors. If your gut tells you that a certain individual would be unsympathetic to you and your case, you need to let your lawyer know that. Even a sideways glance by a potential juror can tip you off to some unstated hostility he or she may have for you. Your lawyer will greatly appreciate this information.

You should conduct yourself during *voir dire*, and throughout the trial, in a respectful and appropriate manner. The jury will begin appraising you and your credibility from the moment it first files into the courtroom at the beginning of *voir dire*. If your jury feels that you are judging them, they may feel offended. You should therefore strain to avoid this appearance. You should express your feelings about the jury to your attorney in as private a way as possible. Be sure to have a pen and note pad handy to make notes during *voir dire*. You can use these notes to help you later recall your reactions to the various jurors. You can also scribble off messages to your lawyer during *voir dire* to advise him or her of your opinion concerning individual jurors. Written messages are a better way to communicate with your lawyer than a tap on the shoulder or a whisper.

Your Attorney's Role

The first set of questions your lawyer will ask may involve whether any of the potential jurors know you or the defendant, any of the witnesses in the case, the attorneys, or the judge, or if any of the jurors have heard anything about the case. This kind of knowledge probably excludes an individual from sitting on the jury, since they may have preconceived notions about the case. It is considered undesirable in our jury system for jurors to have such notions.

The attorneys inquire during *voir dire* into the background and attitudes of each potential juror. These questions are not intended to invade the individual's privacy, although sometimes it may seem that way. The questions are asked so that the attorneys can attempt to assess how the individual will view the case. Your attorney wants people on the jury who are sympathetic to accident victims. The insurance company's lawyer wants just the opposite.

For example, your lawyer may ask if there is anyone who has been sued for personal injuries, and, if so, if that experience created feelings of resentment against people who file personal injury lawsuits. Your lawyer will remove anyone who feels that way from the panel.

He or she may also ask if anyone on the panel works for an insurance company. This question serves a double purpose. First, people employed by insurance companies tend not to be especially sympathetic to accident victims. Second, your lawyer may simply be trying to communicate to the potential members of the jury that the defendant is insured. Juries tend to award more money if they feel that an insurance company will have to pay the award rather than an individual.

It is actually highly questionable whether this technique is proper, since the jury is not supposed to know of the existence of insurance. Nevertheless, many plaintiff's lawyers employ this technique as a way of influencing the jury. Similarly, the insurance company's lawyer phrases questions to the jury panel in such a way as to suggest that accident victims should not receive much in the way of compensation. Thus, *voir dire* is important not just because it determines who sits on the jury, but also because it presents the attorneys with their first opportunity to influence the jurors. This is a key opportunity.

Many other questions are asked during *voir dire*. This process may seem quite dull to the average juror. The lawyers, however, are extremely interested in the responses, since the make up of the jury has a momentous effect on the handling of the case. Experienced trial lawyers give this process extremely close attention. In large cases, professionals who specialize in jury analysis may be brought in to prepare a profile of the ideal juror for that case. This helps the lawyer to select favorable jurors and to eliminate those who do not fit that profile.

Yet many lawyers will tell you that after studying all of the jury research into the type of juror who will favor his or her client's cause, the lawyer picks the jurors his or her gut tells him or her should be on the jury. If the jury gives the lawyer a friendly, accepting look or a favorable nod of the head during *voir dire*, that lawyer will probably want this juror, even if jury research indicates that he or she will be an unfavorable juror.

The attorneys seek a promise from the jurors during *voir dire* that they will be fair. The lawyers repeatedly speak of wanting nothing more than a fair jury. This is happy-sounding nonsense meant only to convince the jury that the lawyer is a reasonable fellow. The reality is that each lawyer wants jurors who are sympathetic to their client's cause and unsympathetic to the other side. A jury that is unfairly prejudiced against the other side is ideal.

The lawyer's business is serving the client's best interests, while always acting within the bounds and strictures of the ethical rules for lawyers. The American system of jurisprudence is adversarial in nature and lawyers are expected to practice in an adversarial manner. Theoretically, truth and justice emerge after a legal battle in which each attorney zealously presents the evidence in the light that is most favorable to that attorney's client. It is a nice theory but hardly scientific in its accuracy.

Peremptory Challenges

Each attorney in a one plaintiff/one defendant case is permitted during *voir dire* to eliminate or *strike* a set number of jurors from the jury without stating the reason. These are called *peremptory challenges*. In cases with multiple plaintiffs or defendants, the judge decides the number of strikes available to each attorney. There are many different theories that attorneys study in deciding on which jurors to strike peremptorily.

For example, Jewish people, African Americans, and individuals with ancestry from the Mediterranean countries are generally considered sympathetic to plaintiffs. Germans, Englishmen, and people from any of the Scandinavian countries are often preferred by defense attorneys. People who have been sued in the past or who have families employed in the insurance industry or in other exacting professions are thought typically to be unsympathetic to personal injury plaintiffs. Married men and women are preferred by attorneys representing minor plaintiffs. Female jurors are considered by many to be unsympathetic to female litigants, especially young, attractive litigants. The preferred age for a juror from a plaintiff's perspective is someone who is between thirty and fifty-five years of age.

The attorneys are basically free to strike potential jurors who fit into certain profiles, subject of course, to the limit in the number of peremptory strikes available. The one exception involves race. If a pattern of striking emerges that appears to be based solely on race, this can be challenged legally by the other side. However, this form of challenge is most frequently made in criminal cases.

Remove for Cause

Jurors who appear through their answers to be prejudiced in some way concerning a matter of importance in the trial can be removed *for cause*. There is no limit to the number of jurors who can be struck for cause. If, for example, a juror admits that he or she believes that people who have been injured due to the negligence of another person should not be able to sue for their pain and suffering, that juror will be struck from the jury for cause. Or if a juror admits that he or she believes insurance companies should always have to pay, regardless of who caused the accident, that juror will be struck *for cause*.

After all of the strikes have been utilized, the jury is set and the trial can begin. The jury in personal injury cases consists of active and alternate members. The alternates hear the case, but take part in the deliberations only if an active juror is removed from the jury during the trial for sickness or for some other reason.

OPENING STATEMENTS

Jury trials begin with the attorneys' *opening statements*. Your lawyer addresses the jury first. The defense lawyer can choose to address the jury immediately after your lawyer finishes or wait until you have finished presenting all of your evidence. Most defense lawyers open immediately after your lawyer's opening.

Opening statements are an extremely important stage of the proceedings. The attorneys are permitted here to tell the jury what the case is about and what the evidence will show. It is also the second opportunity the attorneys have to influence the jurors. The attorneys seek to build upon the trusting relationship they began cultivating during voir dire. The idea here is to get the jury to identify with the lawyer's client and his or her case.

Jury research indicates that 80% of jurors make up their minds as to liability for the accident after the opening statements and never change those initial beliefs. Accordingly, smart trial lawyers treat this area of the trial with careful preparation and deep respect.

It is absolutely crucial that the opening statement be interesting to the jury. The trial lawyer's worst nightmare is a boring opening address. It is extremely difficult to persuade an inattentive jury. Experience has shown that one of the best ways to get and keep the jury's attention is to turn the opening address into the telling of a story. The skillful trial lawyer attempts to weave a tale concerning the events of the accident and the plaintiff's injuries that gives the jury an interesting context for the case. A boring car accident case can be enlivened by this storytelling technique.

Perhaps the opening address might begin as follows.

April 11, 1997, began as an ordinary day in the life of John Jones. He awoke, made his coffee, talked to his wife and kids, and got ready for work. Little did he know that the events of that day would change his life. Come with me as we journey back to that momentous day in John Jones' life. Come with me as we watch the events unfold that would leave John Jones with the shattered life and dreams he must cope with today.

What juror could sleep through that?

Lawyers often choose a theme for the case that they first refer to during the opening statement. This gives the jury an interesting point of reference that hopefully will make the evidence easier to understand and apply during deliberations. The lawyer then returns to this theme during the closing argument in order to create a sense of completeness and closure in the jury's mind.

For example, for a grocery store slip-and-fall case, your lawyer may use the theme of consumer expectations. He or she will speak of the store's failure to meet those expectations and how the accident resulted from that failure. Adding this theme element makes the story more interesting to the jury than a dry recitation of what the evidence will be.

The attorney may also weave interesting and familiar analogies into the opening address. He or she may analogize a scarred face to a damaged work of art. He or she may point out the economic value society places on art in the hope that the jury will value an intact human body even more. The trial lawyer will do whatever it takes to get and keep the jury's attention and empathy during the opening statement. You should feel free to suggest to your lawyer appropriate themes, analogies, or stories for your case.

Lawyers make certain promises to the jury in the opening about what the evidence will show. It is a foolish lawyer that makes a promise that he or she cannot keep, since the opposing lawyer will pounce on unkept promises. If the trial has gone as planned, the lawyer reminds the jury during his or her closing argument of the promises made during opening statements and how those promises were kept. This helps to tie the whole process together in the jury's mind and helps it reach clear conclusions about who should prevail and for how much.

Burden of Proof

Insurance company lawyers love to talk to juries about how the plaintiff has the *burden of proof* in personal injury cases. This is true, but generally rather meaningless. The burden of proof in civil cases requires you, the injured plaintiff, to prove your case by a *preponderance of the evidence*. To win in a personal injury case, your evidence needs merely to outweigh, by any amount, the defendant's evidence. In criminal cases, the prosecution's burden of proof is *beyond a reasonable doubt*, which is a much more onerous burden.

Your lawyer should remind the jury, during both the opening and closing statements, of the easy burden that you must sustain. He or she will also probably ask the jurors during *voir dire* if anyone has a problem with the concept that you need to prove your case by a mere preponderance to prevail. It is a very important point that needs to be hammered home so that the jury decides the case in accordance with the law.

YOUR TESTIMONY

Your case usually begins with your testimony, both on direct and cross examination. Your testimony is perhaps the most important part of the trial. No matter how skillful and prepared the lawyer is, if the jury does not like or does not believe you, the result will not be favorable.

Direct Examination

Direct examination involves your testimony in response to your lawyer's questions. The initial questions typically are simple and concern background information, such as education, family, and employment. These simple questions give you a chance to relax on the witness stand in the role of plaintiff. They also provide the jury with information that may help them relate to you. Your lawyer wants the jury to like you so that it will want to compensate you generously for the losses and damages you suffered in the accident.

After the initial background questions, the testimony might turn to the facts of the accident. Your lawyer attempts to elicit a favorable and believable recitation of these facts. Hopefully, this will fix a version of the accident in the jury's mind that will stay cemented in place all the way through to the conclusion of the jury's deliberations.

After testifying about the accident, your lawyer may ask you to discuss how you felt physically and emotionally at the accident scene and whether emergency room treatment was required. If the defendant made statements at the scene, this would be an appropriate place for them to come into evidence. Even a simple apology from the defendant at the scene can influence the jury's view of liability for the accident.

The testimony then moves to the days and weeks following the accident. Eventually, the jury will hear about the full course of medical treatment and, of course, how you are currently feeling. You may testify about the effect the accident has had on your life and on your family. Employment losses are also examined. Any other relevant aspect of your losses and damages are discussed before the conclusion of direct testimony.

Your lawyer may attempt during direct testimony to take the sting out of unfavorable evidence. If, for example, you have a preexisting medical condition that calls into question the causal relationship between the accident and the injury claim, your lawyer may gently ask you about this medical condition during direct. This gives you the opportunity to discuss the prior condition and perhaps explain the effect the accident had on you. This can defuse an otherwise troublesome aspect of the case. By confronting the problem directly, you avoid the situation in which the jury first hears about the damaging information during the defense lawyer's accusatory questioning. This preemptive strike takes some of the wind out of the other lawyer's sails.

Cross-Examination

After direct testimony concludes, the defense attorney *cross-examines* you. This attorney attempts to discredit you, if possible. He or she may try to show that your version of the accident is unreliable. He or she will also undoubtedly try to prove that your losses and damages are not as bad as you would like the jury to believe. This is where the deposition testimony is so important. If you testified differently at your deposition than at trial, the defense lawyer makes this clear to the jury. If possible, this lawyer also brings out additional deposition testimony that hurts your case. (Your lawyer makes similar use of the defendant's deposition when he or she cross-examines the defendant.)

The importance of how you respond to the cross-examination of the other lawyer cannot be emphasized enough. Cases are sometimes won or lost in the blink of an eye.

> **Example:** A panel of arbitrators found against a party because of the seemingly arrogant way that party responded to a single line of questioning. It seemed like he was trying to outsmart the cross-examining lawyer, as if he was trying to avoid something. He should have just answered the lawyer's question directly.

You must, at all costs, avoid appearing arrogant or evasive during the entire course of the trial. It is also helpful to avoid becoming defensive, argumentative, or extremely informal. Just answer the questions to the best of your ability in a conversational tone of voice.

One of the main purposes of cross-examination is to set up the closing argument. Sometimes the lawyer asks questions on cross that seem unimportant to the outcome of the case. The importance may be made clear only during the closing speech. For example, the defense lawyer in a grocery store slip-and-fall case may bring out during cross-examination that your shopping cart was empty at the time of the accident. During closing, the defense lawyer might argue from this that you should have seen the liquid you slipped on, since it was not blocked by any groceries in the cart. Rather than pressing the issue during cross-examination to make its relevance clear then and there, saving the issue for closing allows this lawyer to avoid the risk that you will explain away the problem.

This technique is employed frequently during the cross-examination of a medical expert. The lawyer does not expect to destroy the doctor's credibility. In real life, the lawyer hopes to make a few points during cross-examination and then to attack the doctor's credibility or opinion during closing argument. The technique of a fleet-footed boxer is much safer here than directly confronting the doctor with a series of impeaching questions, especially if the doctor is experienced as a trial witness. The doctor's superior medical knowledge may allow him or her to talk his or her way through difficult cross-examination.

The traits of the witness affect the way a lawyer conducts cross-examination. The jury may deeply resent the scathing cross of a sympathetic witness. For example, the jury may have great sympathy for an elderly plaintiff who was seriously injured in an accident. Similarly, juries view children with sympathy. A jury will punish the lawyer who attempts to torch such a witness during cross-examination. It would be better for the lawyer to make his or her points in a relatively gentle, respectful way and then sit down.

The same rules and strategies of direct and cross-examination apply to eye-witnesses, experts, family, friends, police officers, and all other witnesses. The investigating police officer may testify if he or she witnessed key events at the scene of the accident. An accident reconstruction expert may testify if it will help to clarify who caused the accident. This expert relies upon evidence at the scene and witness statements to reconstruct the events leading to the accident.

Your lawyer may offer the testimony of members of your family or others familiar with the effect the accident has had on you. On cross-examination, your friends and family members are subject to questions about their relationship to you. These questions seek to show bias of the witness in your favor. Similarly, defense witnesses who are related in some way to your adversary can expect cross-examination concerning that relationship.

Redirect and Recross-Examination

After the conclusion of cross-examination, your lawyer has the chance to ask additional questions on what is called *redirect*. Redirect testimony is supposed to be limited to matters that were discussed during cross-examination. The object of redirect is to rehabilitate you in the eyes of the jury or to answer questions raised by the cross-examination. For example, if the defense attorney forces you to admit during cross-examination that some part of your deposition testimony was different than your trial testimony, on redirect you may be able to offer a reasonable explanation for the difference or you may explain why the difference is irrelevant to the accident. The defense lawyer is permitted to conduct *recross* as to any issue raised on redirect, and so on until all the questions have been asked.

consortium not stated in a convincing way, the jury might decide that you and your spouse are greedy for pursuing a loss of consortium claim.

Also, many people prefer not to have this very personal aspect of their life subjected to the searching cross-examination of an insurance company attorney. Many people prefer that the most personal aspects of their marital life not be discussed in open court. A loss of consortium claim potentially opens up this kind of inquiry. The defense attorney may be entitled to inquire into the spousal sexual relations that existed before the accident so that this can be compared to the post-accident relations. This is obviously the type of claim which you, your spouse, and your attorney need to discuss in depth before pursuing.

Loss of consortium claims are limited to husbands and wives. Thus, if the injury occurs before the plaintiff's wedding, even if it is just hours before, the spouse is unable to make a loss of consortium claim.

CAUSATION

It is not enough to show that a defendant engaged in negligent or careless conduct. To recover in a personal injury case, you must prove not just negligence, but also that this negligence was the *legal cause* of your injuries. Legal cause is shown if the negligence was a substantial factor in producing the harm. An act is not considered a substantial factor in producing the harm if other factors actually caused the harm and the defendant's act was harmless until acted upon by those other factors. The law in your state may vary in some degree, but essentially that is the way causation works.

To help illustrate legal causation, look at the following example in which one of the defendants claimed that his acts were not the legal cause for the accident.

Example: Sara was driving along the freeway. A tow truck ahead of her dropped a tow dolly on the road. The dolly was negligently fastened to the tow truck. Sara was able to bring her vehicle to a halt without striking the dolly. Unfortunately, her vehicle was then struck in the rear by another vehicle.

The lawyer for the tow truck company claimed that his client's negligence was not a substantial factor in producing the harm. He claimed that, but for the unsafe conduct of the striking motorist, the negligent fastening of the tow dolly was quite harmless.

The judge agreed, as Sara was able to stop without hitting the dolly. Even though the tow truck driver's actions were negligent, and even though that negligence led directly to Sara's severe injuries, he had no legal responsibility whatsoever. The full brunt of the liability fell upon the striking motorist.

THE DEFENSE CASE

When all your evidence has been presented, your attorney rests your case. The defense attorney may then ask the judge to dismiss the case for insufficient proof. This virtually never works, yet for technical reasons the insurance company's lawyer often makes this request. Then the presentation of the defense case begins.

The first witness presented by the defense is usually its strongest. Since your evidence has dominated the first half of the trial, the defense seeks to take away your momentum by offering up testimony that is as compelling as possible in favor of the defense. The first defense witness might attack either your version of the accident or the injury claim itself. Perhaps the defendant will testify about how the accident happened from his or her viewpoint. An eyewitness may testify.

If the defense is not contesting fault for the accident, or if it does not have a strong witness on liability, it may put a doctor on the stand to testify about the severity of your injuries.

The defense will have carefully prepared its witnesses for testimony. The defense lawyer hopes to persuade the jury to return either a defense verdict or a low monetary award. Carefully prepared testimony will help.

Your lawyer gets the opportunity for cross-examination after the insurance attorney finishes questioning each defense witness on direct. The roles the lawyers played during the presentation of your part of the case are now reversed. The defense lawyer presents the evidence and your lawyer then attempts to punch holes in the believability or significance of that evidence.

The defense attorney presents the testimony of all witnesses it has to oppose the plaintiff's case. In addition, the defense offers any other evidence it possesses to support its defense to your claim, such as photographs of the vehicles showing very little property damage. This will work to rebut your claim that the collision caused a serious injury.

In cases involving serious personal injuries, the insurance company frequently engages in surveillance. It may retain an investigator to spy on you. If you are involved in personal injury litigation you need to be on your guard against this kind of tactic. The insurance company may attempt to videotape you engaging in physical activities in order to show the jury that you are not as injured as you claim. Insurance companies have been known to flatten the tires of the plaintiff's car and then videotape him or her changing the tire.

Comparative Negligence

One of the primary defenses to a personal injury case involves the concept of *comparative negligence.* To understand this concept, you must first consider that the total amount of negligence involved in the accident equals 100%. This total is divided between the negligence of the defendant (or defendants) and the plaintiff's comparative negligence. Your recovery is reduced by the comparative negligence.

For example, if the defendant rear-ended your stopped car, the defendant's negligence represents 100% of the total negligence. The verdict is not reduced under this scenario. If, however, the accident involves a defendant who ran a red light, comparative negligence may figure in. If it was determined that you were speeding at the time of the accident and this contributed to the accident, the jury might find that the defendant was 80% negligent and you were 20% comparatively negligent. If the jury determined that the damages justified a verdict of $10,000, the judge would reduce the award by 20% and you would receive $8,000.

Assumption of Risk

A standard defense is the claim that you *assumed the risk* of injury and therefore, should not be able to recover damages from the defendant. This is a valid defense to many injury claims. For example, most skiing accidents are not compensable because skiing is an obviously dangerous activity involving frequent injuries. The law in your state may not permit personal injury lawsuits for skiing accidents unless truly reckless conduct can be shown. For example, if the ski resort knew that the design of its slopes was extremely dangerous and failed to warn skiers, it is possible that you would not be found to have assumed the risk of an injury on these slopes.

If you get struck by a batted ball at the ballpark, you should probably forget about suing the team, the stadium, or anyone else. When you entered the stadium you assumed the risk that a ball would fly into the stands, possibly injuring you. If you are aware of an obvious danger, purposely elect to abandon a position of relative safety, and place yourself in the zone of danger under circumstances showing a willingness to accept the risk of injury, you cannot collect for your injuries. That is what assumption of risk is all about.

This defense doctrine is often asserted in fall down accident cases. For example, if you are aware of an isolated patch of ice in a parking lot, park your car next to it, and then slip on it—you are probably not going to get any awards. You assumed the risk of falling when you knowingly parked next to the patch of ice. However, if the entire lot was icy and you had no reasonable alternative route, you can still sue for your injuries.

The assumption of risk defense is generally successful only in the most extreme cases. Do not assume it will bar your lawsuit unless you fit clearly into one of these scenarios. It is a defense that is often asserted, but rarely prevails.

OBJECTIONS

Objections are the trial lawyer's tool for preventing the admission of unfair evidence for the jury's consideration. Some of the most frequently made objections are that the question is leading, irrelevant, beyond the scope, argumentative, assumes a fact not in evidence, or has been asked and answered.

Leading Questions

A *leading question* is one that improperly leads the witness to the answer sought by the lawyer. For example, "You were driving under the speed limit, weren't you?" is clearly leading. The appropriate wording for such a question is, "How fast were you driving?"

Leading questions are permissible when asked of the witness on the other side. Thus, a plaintiff's lawyer can ask the defendant on cross-examination in a car accident case, "You were driving faster than the speed limit, were you not?" Similarly, the insurance company's lawyer is permitted to ask that question of the plaintiff.

If a witness your lawyer presents testifies contrary to your interests, your lawyer can ask the judge to declare him or her a *hostile witness*. If the judge grants this request, your lawyer can use leading questions. This allows tougher questioning and permits greater control over the witness.

Judges have great discretion in ruling on the leading question objection. Many leading questions are asked simply to save time concerning matters that are either relatively unimportant or not in serious dispute. Thus, "Was it sunny on the day of the accident?" is a question that might be permitted by the judge, even though it is leading. In fact, the opposing attorney probably would not object to this question. Attorneys do not assert objections unless they feel there is a good reason to do so. Objections that serve no real purpose, even if they are technically proper, can aggravate the judge and jury, perhaps even creating the impression that the lawyer is trying to hide the truth.

Irrelevant

Irrelevant is a commonly made objection. A question is relevant if the answer really matters to the case. Conversely, a question is irrelevant if the answer does not make the facts more or less true than they would be without that answer.

Sometimes the answer may have some relevance to the case but would be so unfairly prejudicial that the judge will not permit it. For example, if the defendant in a personal injury case had an accident while driving home after an extramarital tryst, the judge will probably exclude evidence of the affair. While the defendant's preaccident activities may have some bearing on his her state of mind and therefore, on his or her operation of the vehicle, this evidence might so prejudice the jury against him or her that it might blind them to the rest of his or her testimony. Trials are supposed to be about the events leading directly to the conflict between you and the defendant, not morality plays about private lives.

Beyond the Scope

The objection that a question is *beyond the scope* generally occurs in redirect and recross-examination. These are the stages of the testimony that take place immediately after the conclusion of direct and cross-examination. Redirect is supposed to be limited to subjects that were explored on cross-examination. It is not another opportunity to have the witness restate the testimony elicited on direct. Nor is it a chance to ask questions that slipped the lawyer's mind during direct. If the lawyer attempts to achieve either of these ends, the opposing lawyer should object that the question goes beyond the scope of cross-examination.

Recross is supposed to be limited to the issues raised on redirect. Re-redirect should be limited to subjects raised on recross—and so on. In this way, the inquiry is progressively narrowed until all appropriate questions have been asked. Yet the judge has great discretion here to overrule this objection. Even where the question is clearly beyond the scope, the judge may permit the question for any number of reasons. Every judge has his or her own practice when it comes to this and every other objection. That is one reason it pays to have a lawyer who tries a lot of cases. Familiarity with the tendencies of judges is a big advantage.

Technically, the objection of beyond the scope is available during cross-examination. Thus, your lawyer may object to an opposing counsel's question on the basis that it is beyond the scope of direct testimony. Realistically, the judge is very unlikely to sustain this kind of objection, since cross-examination represents the defense lawyer's first round of questioning. Practically any inquiry that is relevant to the case and is otherwise not objectionable is fair game during cross-examination, even if not raised on direct examination. For example, even if your lawyer does not question you about a prior car accident during direct examination, the defense lawyer can certainly ask about this on cross-examination. Even though technically this area of inquiry might be beyond the scope, no judge would sustain this objection. It would be foolish for a lawyer to even offer this objection. Again, beyond the scope is an objection typically heard during redirect and recross-examination.

Argumentative

The objection that a question is *argumentative* is a powerful weapon in the trial lawyer's arsenal. Attorneys tend to get quite carried away during cross-examination. This objection reigns in some of the more hotly worded questions. For example, the question, "Do you want this jury to believe that you were only going 25 m.p.h. at the time of the accident?" is argumentative and should be objected to. Questions are supposed to be worded simply, directly, and with the purpose of eliciting useful information concerning the accident. Questions that argue with the witness' statements are objectionable as argumentative.

Asked and Answered

The objection that a question has been *asked and answered* seeks to avoid repetition. Attorneys frequently ask a witness during direct examination the same question over and over in order to hammer a favorable point home to the jury. Many judges will sustain the asked and answered objection here. This objection is also used during cross-examination. If a lawyer does not like the answer a defendant gave the first time asked, he or she may ask it again later in the cross. The astute lawyer on the other side will object that the question has already been asked and answered.

Assumes Facts not in Evidence

Assumes a fact not in evidence is an objection the attorney must keep at the ready. The question, "How fast were you going when you struck the plaintiff's car in the rear?" is inappropriate if it has not first been established that the defendant actually rear-ended you. This is sometimes also referred to as a *foundational* objection. The foundational evidence (a rear-end hit) must first be proved before the question may be asked. The objection here would be either, *The question lacks the proper foundation* or *The question assumes a fact not in evidence.*

Objections in General

Objections have other uses as well. Sometimes trial lawyers object to questions that are probably proper simply to send a message to the witness that the question is one of particular importance. The objection communicates to the witness that he or she needs to take extra care in formulating the answer. The objection gives the witness a couple of extra moments to do just that.

The proper time to make an objection is just as the other lawyer finishes asking the question. If the attorney waits until the question has been answered, the damage may have already been done. The attorney then can only object and *move to strike* the answer. This request asks the judge to instruct the jury to disregard the answer. Lawyers typically compare this to trying to *unring the bell*. It is an inadequate remedy that the lawyer hopes to avoid relying upon.

If the answer was so egregiously improper that it may unfairly influence the jury's deliberations, the lawyer may ask the judge to declare a mistrial. If this request is granted (which rarely happens), the trial ends then and there. The parties then must decide if they want to resume settlement discussions or begin preparing for another trial with a new jury.

CLOSING ARGUMENT

The *closing argument* represents the lawyers' last chance to directly influence the jury. As opposed to an *opening statement*, the closing address is more than a statement of the evidence—it is an *argument*. Whereas the opening statement sets the stage for the trial by informing the jury what the evidence will show, the closing statement goes much further. The lawyers during closing not only sum up the evidence that has been presented, they also argue to the jury about what the evidence means to the case. It is objectionable to make argumentative statements to the jury during the opening address. During closing, they are indispensable.

Each lawyer during closing highlights the most favorable evidence presented during the trial and argues from that evidence certain inferences that are favorable to the lawyer's client. For example, if photographs of the accident vehicles have been presented to the jury and the damage is severe, your lawyer asks the jury to infer from the photos that the collision caused the severe injuries you claim. Further, each lawyer argues that the evidence and inferences mandate that the jury decide the case in favor of their client.

While the comments made during either an opening statement or closing argument can be objected to, most lawyers hesitate before interrupting their adversary's opening statement or closing argument. The fear is that the judge, jury, or both will be offended by the interruption. Many judges feel that it is extremely discourteous for a lawyer to object during opening or closing, and the judge may scold the objecting lawyer in the presence of the jury. This is the lawyer's worst nightmare since jurors generally look to the judge as a respected authority figure. Jurors look to the judge for guidance. If they feel that the judge favors one side or the other, the jurors will, consciously or not, be swayed toward that side.

During closing arguments the lawyers usually remind the jury of the promises made during opening statements about what the evidence would show. The lawyers then suggest to the jury that the evidence indeed showed all that was promised and that the jury, therefore, should return a favorable verdict. The lawyers may also refer to the promises the jurors made during jury selection to be fair and to return a just verdict.

The closing argument generally ends with a brief expression of thanks by the lawyer for the jury's attention and a request for a verdict favorable to that lawyer's client.

JURY INSTRUCTIONS AND DELIBERATIONS

The judge's instructions to the jury represent the very last stage of the trial before the jury retires to decide the case. In his or her instructions, the judge advises the jury about the law that applies to the case. The judge uses certain standard instructions but may also permit the lawyers to influence which instructions are given and how they are worded. A sample set of *Jury Instructions* is in Appendix A. (see form 10, p.242.) Jury instructions are also sometimes called *points for charge*.

If, for example, the accident involves a slip-and-fall occurence, the judge advises the jury of the degree of care that the defendant was required to exercise for your safety. The judge defines such legal terms as *negligence* and *circumstantial evidence*. The judge advises the jury of your burden to prove the case by a *preponderance of the evidence* in order to receive a favorable verdict. The judge may explain that a *preponderance of the evidence* is a far easier burden of proof than *beyond a reasonable doubt*, the standard of proof required in criminal cases. *Preponderance of the evidence* requires that your evidence outweigh the defendant's evidence by even the slightest amount. If it does, an award in your favor is appropriate.

The judge advises the jury of the various items of damages it can award. For example, the jury is instructed that, if it believes the defendant is liable to you for the accident, it must award a certain amount of money damages. That amount must fairly and adequately compensate you for the physical, emotional, and financial injuries caused by the accident. The judge advises the jury that past, present, and future pain and suffering should be considered. The judge may also advise the jury to include your medical bills in the award.

If one of the lawyers objects to any part of the jury instructions, the objection must be made before the jury retires to deliberate. That gives the judge the opportunity to correct the instructions, if necessary. If the objection is not made by then, the lawyer waives this objection and may not assert it on appeal. If the objection is made in a timely manner and the judge overrules the objection, the issue is preserved for the appellate court to rule on, if an appeal is filed. If the judge erred in failing to correct the instructions, the appellate court can order a new trial.

THE VERDICT

Now it is the jury's turn to get active. After possibly years of waiting, countless phone calls, letters, doctors' visits, consultations with your lawyer, pretrial preparation, and the grueling drama of the trial, the jury finally has the case, and your legal fate, in its hands. The answer to the question, *How much?* may be just minutes away.

Sometimes the verdict comes back quickly, and sometimes there are hours or even days to agonize while waiting for the jury to return with the verdict. When it does, the jury foreman announces the decision and the trial is at an end.

POSTTRIAL MOTIONS

Either the plaintiff or defendant may file a motion for a new trial after the jury has returned its verdict. This action is appropriate when the verdict was against the weight of the evidence or a party has suffered injustice or has been denied substantial rights. Typically, a party must move for a new trial to correct errors or irregularities during the course of the trial. If he or she fails to do so, the court may rule that the issue is waived.

A *motion for judgment notwithstanding the verdict* may be filed on the theory that the verdict should, as a matter of law, have been in favor of the moving party. This might be based upon the party's belief that there was not sufficient evidence to submit the case to a jury. For example, if the evidence shows that the plaintiff rear-ended the defendant, but the jury, nevertheless, returns a verdict in favor of the plaintiff, the court may grant a motion in favor of the defendant notwithstanding the verdict. This motion differs from the *motion for a new trial* in that the former seeks an actual verdict in favor of the moving party while the latter seeks a whole new trial.

Defendant's counsel may file a *motion for remittutur* when he or she believes that the verdict is so excessive and unconscionable as to shock the conscience of the court. Plaintiff may move for *additur* to increase an inadequate jury award.

Either party may move for an award of attorney's fees due to dilatory, obdurate, or vexatious conduct. For example, if one of the attorneys prolonged the trial through frivolous objections, multiple witnesses who testified about matters already sufficiently established, or otherwise was particularly discourteous to the other party or his or her attorney, the court may award attorney's fees to the moving party.

The plaintiff may also file a motion for delay damages to assess interest on top of the jury's verdict. This would be particularly appropriate when the defendant unnecessarily delayed the onset of the trial through various litigation tactics. In some jursidictions, delay damages may be awarded even if the trial began promptly. You should check your local rules since delay damages can be very significant.

THE APPEAL

Just when you thought you were finally free of this legal process, you get the news from your lawyer that there is going to be an appeal. Appeals from jury verdicts are taken for various reasons. Perhaps the judge excluded an important piece of evidence for a reason one of the lawyers felt was improper. If one of the lawyers made inappropriate remarks during his or her closing argument that were not adequately corrected by the judge, an appeal may be sought. Or possibly, the judge refused to allow one of the lawyers to ask certain questions of the jury during *voir dire* and the lawyer feels this deprived his or her client of a fair jury. All of these are appealable issues.

Another appealable issue is the amount of the jury's verdict. Just because a judge or jury makes a decision about an award, that is not necessarily the final word.

Example: There was outrage over the jury that awarded nearly $3 million to the woman who spilled hot coffee in her lap after leaving McDonald's drive through.

McDonald's appealed the verdict. In the end, this woman, who received severe burns from coffee that McDonald's knew was much hotter than it was supposed to be, received far less compensation than was publicized.

A vascular surgeon had determined that this woman suffered third degree burns over 6% of her body, including her inner thighs, perineum, buttocks, and genital and groin areas. She was hospitalized for eight days and underwent skin grafting. She originally tried to settle her claim for $20,000, but McDonald's refused.

Instead, the jury awarded $2.7 million in punitive damages and $200,000 in compensatory damages. When McDonald's appealed the award, the compensatory damages were reduced to $160,000 because the jury found the plaintiff to be 20% at fault in the spill. The trial court reduced the punitive award to $480,000, even though the judge called McDonald's conduct reckless, callous, and willful.

A new trial will not be awarded on appeal unless the appealing attorney can prove to the appellate court that something seriously wrong happened at the trial. For example, if you clearly suffered serious injuries, the defendant was obviously at fault for the accident, and yet the jury awarded no damages, the appellate court will order a new trial. If your attorney made a reference in his or her closing argument that was seriously improper, such as mentioning that the defendant had insurance to cover the claim, a new trial will be awarded.

(The judge will probably *sanction* (levy a fine against) the attorney who made this clearly improper remark.)

Appeals are often taken for tactical reasons. Even though the party that filed the appeal does not truly believe a new trial will be awarded, he may file an appeal to try to force the other side to accept a settlement that is less favorable than the jury's verdict. Insurance companies often use this strategy. They figure that if you are desperate for money, you will take whatever you can get. Meanwhile, the money is sitting in the insurance company's bank account (or more likely tied up in investments) drawing interest. It is a cynical approach, but, after all, litigation is war. The appeal can be a very powerful weapon in the war of attrition that PI lawsuits often become.

COLLECTING FROM AN UNINSURED DEFENDANT

The operation was successful, but the patient died. This is how a litigant feels after obtaining a judgment against an uninsured defendant from whom it is impossible to collect. When settling a personal injury claim with an uninsured defendant or a self-insured entity, such as a government entity or a wealthy company, it is almost always a matter of weeks between settlement and receipt of the settlement monies. Such is not the case when settling with the vast majority of uninsured defendants.

Many, if not most, uninsured defendants are judgment proof. This means that it is next to impossible to collect in full, or perhaps even in part, on a judgment against such a defendant. If the person you have sued and taken a judgment against does not own real estate, valuable personal property, such as a car or expensive jewelry, does not have a large bank account or a salaried job, your collection efforts may prove not only fruitless and deeply frustrated, but also expensive.

You and your lawyer can spend a great deal of time and money trying to collect on such a judgment. The expression, *throwing good money after bad,* often describes this process. Most lawyers will not even take a personal injury case unless the defendant is insured or has substantial collectible assets.

Even if the injuries are very serious and the liability clear, you win the battle but lose the war if you cannot scoop up the pot of gold at the end of the rainbow. You should seriously consider right at the outset the wisdom of pursuing such a case. Ending up with an uncollectible judgment only adds insult to injury.

If you have a judgment against an uninsured individual, what should you do to try to collect? While collection law varies from state to state, the best hope for collecting money in such a case is when the defendant is the sole owner of real estate. You may be able to take two different steps against this property. First, you could try to execute on this judgment and force a *sheriff sale* of the property to satisfy the judgment. Realize that you may be putting a person out on the street if you do so. Not everyone has the stomach for forcing a sheriff sale on a defendant's home. If you do, you may be able to collect the money from the sale, up to the amount of your judgment.

Second, if you record your judgment, it will appear on any title report for the property. When the defendant goes to sell or refinance the property, your judgment will act as a *cloud on the title*. The defendant may need to satisfy the judgment, that is, pay you for your damages, before the cloud is lifted. He or she may not be able to sell or refinance the property without paying off the judgment.

If the defendant is only a co-owner of the property, it may be impossible to take these steps. Since someone other than the defendant is also an owner, and since you do not have a judgment against that co-owner, you may not be able to force a sheriff sale or cloud the title on this property. Check the laws in your state to be sure of this.

If the defendant is the sole owner of a car, expensive jewelry, or other valuable property, you can try to force the sale of those assets in order to satisfy your judgment. It is easy to do an investigation through the Department of Motor Vehicles in order to determine if the defendant owns a car. If that car has 12 to 14 for documents that may be useful in obtaining the sheriff's assistance in executing upon the defendant's real estate or personal property.

Determining whether the defendant has other valuable property is going to take some sleuthing. It really depends on how hard you want to work at this, how good a private investigator you hire, and how much money you want to spend chasing down this property.

One step you can take is to send **Interrogatories** to both the defendant and to any bank at which you suspect he or she may have an account. See Form 12 for a sample set of of **Interrogatories** that you can send to the defendant. These **Interrogatories** can help you locate collectible assets.

If the defendant refuses to reply, you will need to file a **Discovery Motion** asking the court to order the defendant to reply. See Form 6 for a **Discovery Motion** that you can adapt to this situation.

See Form 13 for a sample set of **Interrogatories** that you can send to every bank in the defendant's town. These **Interrogatories** will help you determine whether the defendant has money at these banks.

If the defendant has a salaried position, you may be able to *attach* his or her wages. This forces his or her employer to send you a portion of the defendant's paycheck every week until the judgment is paid off. Each state has its own rules and procedures for this type of action.

Another useful collection tool that some states offer involves car accident cases. If you obtain a judgment in such a case and the defendant refuses to pay, you may be able to get his or her driver's license suspended. The defendant will be required to show proof that the judgment has been paid before the suspension is lifted.

ONLINE PERSONAL INJURY SETTLEMENTS*

Online settlement companies are now involved in settling personal injury claims. These companies preach quick and easy settlements, whether you are represented by legal counsel or not. But before you log on to such companies as **Cybersettle.com** or **Namadr.com**, remember the maxim—*caveat emptor*—let the buyer beware. These dot-com entrepreneurs raise questions about the role of the civil justice system on the Internet, consumers' rights, the involvement of the insurance industry in the process, and the neutrality of cyber-mediators.

Particularly subject to close scrutiny are companies that attempt to persuade accident victims to proceed without help of a personal injury attorney. Many of these sites imply that consumers can successfully work through this process without a lawyer. While this may be tempting, especially for those looking for quick cash, unrepresented individuals have no basis upon which to negotiate a personal injury claim. Claims involving particularly serious injuries are especially inappropriate for computer-generated resolution over the Internet.

These companies typically offer some type of *blind-bidding process*. This system begins when one of the parties submits a case for negotiation. Each side has a confidential password and can make bids day or night over secure software. The computer automatically settles the case if the offers are within a certain percentage of each other. **Namadr.com** also offers traditional in-person mediation.

One must question how any computer-generated settlement is truly in the best interest of the plaintiff. Insurance companies settle cases only if it is in their financial interest to do so. For example, if you rely on the settlement statistics that the online companies provide in mediation, your risk is that those statistics are biased toward the insurance companies. You cannot trust your case to a mediator provided by one of these companies unless you are sure that the mediator is truly neutral. It is a question of credibility.

Compared to traditional dispute resolution companies, whose impartiality can be checked, based on performance over the years, the services provided by these companies may be unknown.

Online Injury Settlements Raise Questions About Consumers' Rights, Craig Giangiulio, PaTLA News, Volume XV, No. 1, April 2001.

chapter twelve:
Insurance Fraud and Other Problems

People often wonder about the extraordinarily high cost of auto insurance, particularly in big cities. You will not be surprised to hear that there is blame to go all around. The people who bring fraudulent claims and their lawyers contribute mightily to the problem. Doctors who knowingly over-treat plaintiffs in order to build personal injury cases are also at fault.

The insurance industry and its lawyers deserve a large share of the blame, too. They frequently refuse to offer fair compensation until the parties reach the courthouse steps. Insurance companies and their lawyers force extended delays before offering fair compensation while they exhaustively investigate every possible suspicion of fraud. This greatly, and often unnecessarily, increases everyone's litigation costs. While no one can blame the defense for having a certain amount of skepticism, everyone loses when the meritorious case is treated like a potential fraud. Everyone also loses when reasonable settlement efforts are not made until all of the time and money has been spent preparing for trial.

The widespread public perception of fraud in personal injury cases badly hurts average, honest citizens, and the reputable lawyers and doctors who work to assist them in achieving medical and financial relief from their injuries. Jurors who read in the newspaper about the allegations of fraud can be expected to return lower money verdicts when they decide personal injury cases.

There is no easy answer to the problem of insurance fraud. Stepped-up investigation by the Justice Department and state prosecutors is an important start. It is useless to hope that those responsible for the problem will voluntarily change their methods. Yet only through each individual taking care to conduct him- or herself in an honorable way can the situation begin to be rectified.

It is absolutely inexcusable for citizens, lawyers, and doctors to present anything but totally legitimate personal injury claims. If you have been injured due to the negligence of another, you need to be sure you select a lawyer and a doctor who are respected for their integrity. Otherwise prepare for a very long wait before you receive compensation for your injuries. Never forget that justice delayed may very well be justice denied.

IMPROPER INSURANCE PRACTICES

Insurance companies are in the business of making money. Make no mistake about that. They fight hard to hold onto their money as long as possible and pay out as little as possible. That is just the way it is and there is nothing inherently wrong with that from a strictly legal point of view.

Occasionally, however, insurance company employees, in their enthusiasm for maximizing company profits, step over the line into improper insurance practices. If you feel that the insurance company you are dealing with has stepped over this line, you should consider contacting the Insurance Board in your state. In some states, the Insurance Board is nothing more than a mouth piece for the insurance industry. This type of Insurance Board is quite toothless and unwilling to help the individual who has an insurance complaint.

However, in some states the Insurance Board has a real mission that can help the individual who is confronted with an insurance company engaged in unfair insurance practices. It certainly does not hurt to contact the Insurance Board in your state, but do not be surprised if you end up getting a run around.

Hopefully, the Insurance Board in your state is consumer-oriented, staffed by aggressive, energetic employees who will help you stand up to the insurance company. Check your phone book for your local Insurance Board if you wish to take this step. It may be called the Department of Insurance, the Insurance Commission, or some other similar name.

Unfair Insurance Practice Statute

If you have truly been treated unfairly by an insurance company, you may be able to pursue a legal remedy under an unfair insurance practices statute. Many states have an *Unfair Insurance Practices Act* or at least a *Consumer Protection*

Law that provides some degree of protection against wrongful conduct by an insurance company.

If an insurance company tries to deceive you about coverages or some other important matter, you may be able to pursue a bad faith lawsuit under such a statute. It would be very difficult to pursue such a claim without a lawyer since the law is fairly technical. Even the average personal injury attorney hesitates before taking on a bad faith lawsuit. The unfair treatment would have to be quite egregious and the damages substantial before the average attorney would take on this kind of battle.

AMBULANCE CHASERS

An accident can be a very traumatic event. An accident can leave you feeling vulnerable and at loose ends. Ambulance-chasing lawyers prey on this feeling. These lawyers, or their underlings, mysteriously pop up at the scene of accidents hoping to lure the accident victim.

Some lawyers peruse police reports of auto accidents. These reports are often available for little or no charge at law enforcement agencies. They then contact the individual who appears not to have caused the accident and suggest that he or she pursue an injury claim.

Some lawyers have people on the streets looking for accidents. It is a simple thing to buy a radio that picks up police calls. Many people report being approached after an accident by one or more people who offer to take them to a lawyer's office. These people often arrive even before the police. They may have a whole system set up that at first seems attractive. They might offer to drive you to a body shop they know of, then to a hospital emergency room, and then to the lawyer's office. They might even suggest that the lawyer will lend you money.

You might be tempted to choose a lawyer who will lend you money. Resist this temptation. It is unequivocally unethical for a lawyer to lend a client money. You should select a lawyer because he or she is a good lawyer, not because he or she will lend you money. The dollars you receive up front as a loan may pale next to the small settlement you receive at the end of the case because your lawyer does not know what he or she is doing or does not have your best interests at heart.

Glossary

A

agency. A legal principal supporting liability against one party for actions taken by another.

answer. The legal document filed by the defendant that responds to the Complaint.

arbitration. A relatively informal means for resolving a dispute. Arbitration is generally much less expensive and time consuming than a jury trial.

assault. A violent physical or verbal attack.

assumption of risk. The defense that a plaintiff should not be allowed to collect from a defendant after engaging in an activity that he or she knew to be dangerous, but voluntarily engaged in that activity anyway.

B

battery. The causing of harm to someone through impermissible contact.

burden of proof. The standard of proof that the plaintiff must sustain in order to make a case and defeat a motion for judgment.

C

causation. The connection that shows that the other party's act was a substantial factor in producing the harm.

challenge for cause. Disqualifying a juror because of perceived prejudice concerning matters relevant at trial.

closing argument. Final address made by each side summing up the evidence and events of the trial in the light most favorable to that side.

comparative negligence. The percentage of negligence attributable to the injured party. (It reduces the amount recoverable from the defendant by the same percentage.)

compensatory damages. Compensation for all proven injury or loss, such as medical bills, lost earnings, or automobile property damage.

complaint. A legal pleading that starts a lawsuit, which states the nature of the plaintiff's claim, the request for damages, and the basis for the court to hear the case.

contingent fee. The amount an attorney charges for handling a personal injury case. It is calculated as a percentage of whatever the client is awarded.

costs. Money expended in the pursuit of a lawsuit. It includes the cost of obtaining medical records, filing the lawsuit and any motions, investigating the accident, obtaining expert testimony, taking depositions, procuring the attendance of witnesses, etc.

cross-examination. The questioning of a client by the adverse attorney. All witnesses are subject to both direct and cross-examination.

D

damages. The sum of money that an injured party claims the other party owes for all losses, expenses, and harm to property or persons.

defamation. The harming of a person's reputation by making a false statement to another person, either in writing or orally.

defendant. The party against whom the plaintiff takes legal action.

deliberations. The time during a jury trial when the jury leaves the courtroom to weigh and analyze the facts in the case, in order to ultimately reach a verdict.

demand letter. A correspondence in which an injured party explains its side of a legal dispute and requests a sum of money to settle the case.

deposition. The out-of-court procedure at which the attorney has the opportunity to question the opposing party or any other potential witness under oath.

direct examination. The questioning of a client by one's own attorney. All witnesses are subject to both direct and cross-examination.

discovery. The stage of the lawsuit in which each side obtains answers to interrogatories, responses to request for production of documents, and depositions. It is the process by which each side learns of the strengths and weaknesses of the other side's case.

discovery motion. A motion through which one party attempts to obtain the court's assistance in forcing the other party to produce information about the case.

E

emotional distress. The mental reaction (anguish, grief, fright) to another person's actions. It may only be recoverable as damages when it is accompanied by physical manifestations (such as nausea, vomiting, dizziness).

excessive damages. An unreasonable or outrageous award of money by a jury that is subject to reduction by the court.

expert witnesses. Those witnesses whose special expertise is required regarding a matter of relevance to the trial. Doctors, engineers, accident reconstructionists, statisticians, economists, vocational specialists, nurses, etc., are all examples of expert witnesses.

F

fact witnesses. Those witnesses who will testify concerning the facts of the accident.

fee agreement. A contract between an attorney and client that spells out the terms of the legal representation.

future damages. The money awarded for additional medical treatment, future pain and suffering, or loss of earning capacity.

G

general release. A legal writing setting forth the terms of the settlement. It prevents the plaintiff from seeking further legal redress.

H

hearsay. Generally inadmissible as evidence in court, it is the statement a witness makes about what he or she heard another person say.

I

inadequate damages. A jury award that does not fairly compensate the plaintiff for the injuries and losses proved. The court's remedy may be to award a new trial.

independent medical examination (IME). A term used by the insurance industry for medical examinations conducted by doctors paid by the insurance company to examine the plaintiff. (IME's are performed strictly for litigation purposes.)

insurance adjuster. The insurance employee who handles some or all aspects of the investigation, negotiations, and settlement of the claim.

insurance board. The supervisors of the insurance business conducted in a state.

intentional injury. The harm inflicted as the result of intentional conduct, as opposed to negligent conduct. (An example are the injuries suffered in an assault and battery incident.)

interrogatories. The written questions that one party submits to the other party during litigation in order to gather factual information relevant to the case.

invitee. A person who has an expressed or implied right to be on the premises, such as a business associate or a restaurant patron. The owner of the premises has a duty to inspect the premises and to warn the invitee if there are any dangerous conditions.

J

joinder. A legal process by which two separate lawsuits are joined together into one litigation.

jurisdiction. The legal authority of a court to preside over a case.

L

liability. A legal responsibility to another.

libel. A defamatory statement expressed in a fixed medium, such as a writing, art, or the Internet.

licensee. One who has an express right to be on the premises, but is not there for the owner's benefit, such as a social guest. An owner has a duty to warn the licensee about dangerous conditions, if they are known to the owner.

litigation. All of the strategies and communications involving the prosecution or defense of a legal claim.

loss of consortium. The loss of the affection, sexual relations, aid, services, and companionship that one spouse is entitled to from the other spouse.

loss of future earning capacity. The loss of the ability to earn future wages as the result of an accident.

lost wages. The money that an injured party is awarded for the time he or she lost from employment due to the injury.

M

mediation. An alternative to court involving a neutral third party who assists the parties in settling the case.

motion. A legal document that requests that the court issue an order pertaining to the case.

motion for judgment. A motion filed by one party during the trial asking the court to rule in its favor regarding some or all of the issues in the case.

motion in limine. A motion filed by one party to prevent the other party from using certain evidence at the trial of the case.

N

negligence. The failure to act with the degree of care ordinarily expected of the average person.

no-fault benefits. Those benefits obtainable from one's own insurance company, usually for medical bills and lost wages. (This is sometimes also known as PIP benefits or first party benefits.)

O

objective evidence of injury. An injury that is directly provable generally through radiological methods, such as MRI, X-Ray, or EMG testing.

opening statement. The opening address given by each side before the testimony begins. It serves to summarize the evidence and orient the jury to the case it is about to hear.

P

preemptive strike. Disqualifying a juror for no stated reason.

plaintiff. The party that was injured and who seeks compensation from the defendant.

product liability. The legal liability caused by a defective product.

proximate cause. Conduct so closely related in time and space to the injury that it is legally determined to be the cause of that injury.

proximate damages. The amount of money awarded for those injuries and losses that flow immediately and directly from the defendant's conduct.

punitive damages. The amount of money awarded to the plaintiff if the defendant acted recklessly, intentionally, outrageously, or fraudulently. The award is over and above the actual damages and is intended as a deterrent.

R

request for production. A written request from one party to another asking for specific documents and other things for reviewing and copying.

S

service of process.   The formal delivery of a legal notice.

settlement. The resolution of a legal dispute in which the parties agree on the amount the defendant must pay the plaintiff.

slander. A defamatory statement made orally.

soft tissue injury. Injuries such as neck or back strains and sprains involving damage to the connective tissues. This type of injury does not show up on radiological testing and is therefore often considered by the insurance company to be faked or at least exaggerated.

special damages. The damages for past, present, and future medical bills, property damage, and lost earnings.

statute of limitations. An established time limit within which an injured party can sue the defendant.

statutory damages. The money awarded because statutory law requires it.

subjective evidence of injury. The proof of an injury in which objective evidence is not available. This most commonly takes the form of the plaintiff's own testimony concerning pain and suffering and limitations in function and range of motion.

subpoena. The legal document used to compel the attendance of a witness or the production of documents.

subrogation. The right of recovery for amounts already paid. For example, your insurance company may pay you for your property damage under your collision coverage and then assert its right of subrogation to recover that money from the insurance company for the driver who caused the accident.

T

third party benefits.   Those benefits obtainable from the other party's insurance company.

tort.   A wrongful act, damage, or injury for which a civil lawsuit can be brought.

tort reform.   The phrase coined by the insurance industry characterizing its efforts to change the laws regarding personal injury litigation.

tortfeasor.   The individual who caused the accident.

trespasser.   One who has no consent or right to be on another's property.

V

venue.   The place where a trial can properly take place. Proper venue is usually found where the accident happened or where one or more of the defendants lives or does substantial business.

voir dire.   The point early in the trial when the lawyers and judge question potential jurors to see if they are desirable as jurors.

W

workers' compensation.   A state system that allows employees to recover payment for lost wages and medical bills for injuries sustained at work.

appendix a:
Sample Forms

Form 1:   Complaint—Car Accident 196

Form 2:   Complaint—Fall-Down Accident 199

Form 3:   Interrogatories—Car Accident 203

Form 4:   Interrogatories—Fall-Down Accident 219

Form 5:   Request for Production of Documents 236

Form 6:   Motion to Compel Discovery. 238

Form 7:   Order for Discovery 239

Form 8:   Authorization to Release Records. 240

Form 9:   Contingent Fee Agreement 241

Form 10:   Jury Instructions. 242

Form 11:   *Voir Dire* Questions 248

Form 12:   Interrogatories—Execution 252

Form 13:   Interrogatories—Attachment 260

Form 14:   Subpoena 263

Complaint—Car Accident

YOUR ATTORNEY
Identification Number 1234567   ATTORNEY FOR PLAINTIFF
24 North Lawyer Row
My City, My State 98765-4321
(123) 555-5555

_____

MANNY BUCKS   COURT OF COMMON PLEAS

    v.   CIVIL DIVISION

N. SURANCE

    and   DOCKET NUMBER: 1234567

D. POCKETS, INC.
              CIVIL ACTION—PERSONAL INJURY
               MOTOR VEHICLE ACCIDENT

1. Plaintiff, Manny Bucks, is an adult individual who resides at 3000 N. 7th Street, Philadelphia, PA 11111.

2. Defendant, N. Surance, is an adult individual who resides at 2000 Levick Street, Philadelphia, PA 11112.

3. Defendant, D. Pockets, Inc., is a Pennsylvania Corporation with an address for service of process at 123 Wister Street, Philadelphia, PA 11113.

4. On or about January 6, 2000, at approximately 5:00 p.m., plaintiff, Manny Bucks, was operating a motor vehicle in a northerly direction on Whitaker Avenue at or near its intersection with Roosevelt Boulevard in the City and County of Philadelphia, Commonwealth of Pennsylvania.

5. At the aforesaid time, date and place, defendant, N. Surance, was operating a motor vehicle on Roosevelt Boulevard at or near the said intersection when, suddenly and without warning, defendant side swiped plaintiff's motor vehicle.

6. The plaintiff did not own a motor vehicle at the time of the accident, nor did he reside in a household in which a motor vehicle was insured.

7. The Full Tort option applies to plaintiff, and he is therefore eligible to receive compensation from defendant without regard to the severity of his injury.

8. The said accident was caused solely through the defendant's negligence and was due in no manner whatsoever to any actions taken by the plaintiff.

9. At all relevant times, defendant, N. Surance, acted as the agent, servant, workman, and/or employee of defendant, D. Pockets, Inc., and/or in the alternative acted on his own behalf, and was acting within the course and scope of his authority.

10. The negligence of the defendants consisted of the following:
   (a) operating the motor vehicle at a high and excessive rate of speed;
   (b) failing to have the said motor vehicle under proper and adequate control at the time;
   (c) failing to give proper and sufficient warning of the approach of the said vehicle;
   (d) operating the said vehicle without due regard for the rights, safety, and position of the plaintiff at the point aforesaid;
   (e) violating the various ordinances of the City of Philadelphia and the statutes of the Commonwealth of Pennsylvania pertaining to the operation of motor vehicles; and,
   (f) with plaintiff's motor vehicle in plain view, failing to exercise care and vigilance so as to avoid the collision.

11. Solely as the result of the defendants' negligence, the plaintiff sustained severe personal injuries to his head, body, and limbs; more particularly, he suffered: post-traumatic cervical sprain and strain, post-traumatic headaches, lumbosacral strain, shock and injury to his nerves and nervous system, and he was otherwise injured.

12. All the above injuries are serious and permanent except those of a superficial nature. All of the foregoing injuries have rendered the plaintiff, sick, sore, lame, prostrate, disabled, and disordered and have made him undergo great mental anguish

and physical pain, as a result of which he has suffered, yet suffers, and will continue to suffer for an indefinite time in the future.

13. As a further result of this accident, plaintiff may in the future continue to suffer great pain and agony and he may be prevented from attending to his usual daily work and occupation to his great financial damage and loss.

WHEREFORE, plaintiff, Manny Bucks, demands judgment against defendants, N. Surance and D. Pockets, Inc. in an amount not in excess of FIFTY THOUSAND ($50,000.00) DOLLARS, plus costs of this suit.

_____

YOUR ATTORNEY
Attorney for Plaintiff

Complaint—Fall-Down Accident

YOUR ATTORNEY
Identification Number 2345678   ATTORNEY FOR PLAINTIFF
24 North Lawyer Row
My City, My State 98765-4321
(123) 555-5555

C. Ewan Court   COURT OF COMMON PLEAS
and
D. Vorce Court   CIVIL DIVISION

    v.

U.R. Richman, Inc.

                    DOCKET NUMBER: 9876543

CIVIL ACTION—PERSONAL INJURY
PREMISES LIABILITY, SLIP AND FALL

1. Plaintiff, C. Ewan Court is an adult individual who resides at 123 Apple St., Annandale, VA 22333.

2. Plaintiff, D. Vorce Court is the wife of Plaintiff, C. Ewan Court, and she resides at 123 Apple St., Annandale, VA 22333.

3. Defendant, U.R. Richman, Inc., is a business entity licensed to do business in the Commonwealth of Virginia with an address for service of process at 200 Curtis Avenue, Alexandria, VA 22335.

4. On or about January 25, 2005, at approximately 11:15 A.M. and for a long time prior thereto, there existed a patch of ice in the parking lot of the defendant's grocery store located at 6000 North Broad Street, in Alexandria, which presented a substantial impediment to travel.

5.   The defendant knew or should have known of the said patch of ice in the parking lot, and the fact that it presented a substantial impediment to travel sufficiently prior to the said time and date to take such action as would cure the said condition.

6.   On the date and time aforesaid, defendant had under its care and direction the supervision, control, and maintenance of the said property and had the duty to keep it free from snow and ice and safe for travel for those lawfully traversing the said area.

7.   On the date and time aforesaid, plaintiff, C. Ewan Court was lawfully traversing the said area, at which time he slipped and fell to the ground after he stepped onto the said patch of ice, thereby sustaining certain injuries which are hereafter more particularly set forth.

8.   The said accident was the result of the defendant's negligence, and was due in no manner whatsoever to any act or failure to act on the part of the plaintiffs.

9.   The negligence of the defendant consisted of the following:
   (a)   allowing a patch of ice to remain in the said area;
   (b)   failing to make the said area safe for travel for those lawfully upon the said premises;
   (c)   failing to maintain the said area in a condition that would protect and safeguard persons lawfully entering the area;
   (d)   filing to have the said area inspected at reasonable intervals in order to determine its condition;
   (e)   failing to warn persons lawfully traversing the said area of the dangerous condition of such;
   (f)   disregarding the rights and safety of plaintiff, C. Ewan Court at the time he was traversing the said area;
   (g)   violating the codes and ordinances of the City of Alexandria and the statutes of the Commonwealth of Virginia pertaining to property maintenance and condition of public walkways;
   (h)   otherwise failing to use due care under the circumstances, as well may be pointed out during the discovery and trial phases of this matter;
   (i)   directing plaintiff, C. Ewan Court to park his car directly next to the said patch of ice; and,
   (j)   failing to spread rock salt, dirt or any other substance on the said parking lot in order to make it safe for guests of the defendant's grocery store.

COUNT I

10. The allegations contained in paragraphs 1 through 9 above are incorporated by reference as though set forth in full.

11. Solely as the result of the defendant's negligence, plaintiff, C. Ewan Court sustained severe personal injuries to his head, body, and limbs; more particularly, he suffered: right distal fibula fracture, right knee abrasions, shock and injury to his nerves and nervous system, and he was otherwise injured.

12. All the above injuries are serious and permanent except those of a superficial nature. All of the foregoing injuries have rendered plaintiff, C. Ewan Court sick, sore, lame, prostrate, disabled, and disordered and have made him undergo great mental anguish and physical pain, as a result of which he has suffered, yet suffers, and will continue to suffer for an indefinite time in the future.

13. As a further result of this accident, plaintiff, C. Ewan Court may in the future continue to suffer great pain and agony and he may be prevented from attending to his usual daily work and occupation to his great financial damage and loss.

14. As a further result of this accident, plaintiff, C. Ewan Court has suffered an injury which is in full or part a cosmetic disfigurement which may be permanent, irreparable, and severe.

15. As a further result of this accident, plaintiff, C. Ewan Court has suffered other financial losses which are hereby claimed from the defendant.

WHEREFORE, plaintiff, C. Ewan Court demands judgment against the defendant, in an amount in excess of FIFTY THOUSAND ($50,000) DOLLARS, plus costs of this suit.

COUNT II

16. The allegations contained in paragraphs 1 through 15 above are incorporated by reference as though set forth in full.

17. Solely as a result of the foregoing negligence of the defendant, plaintiff, D. Vorce Court, has been deprived of the aid, comfort, assistance, society, companionship and services of her husband, and she may be deprived of the same in the future, all of which is to her great damage and financial loss.

18. As a further result of this accident, plaintiff, D. Vorce Court has been or will be obliged to expend various sums of money or to incur various expenses resulting from the aforementioned injuries suffered by plaintiff, C. Ewan Court and she may be obliged to continue to expend such sums or incur such expenditures for an indefinite time in the future.

WHEREFORE, plaintiff, D. Vorce Court demands judgment in her favor and against defendant, in an amount in excess of FIFTY THOUSAND ($50,000.00) DOLLARS, plus costs.

_____
YOUR ATTORNEY
Attorney for Plaintiffs

Interrogatories—Car Accident

YOUR ATTORNEY
Identification Number 1234567   ATTORNEY FOR PLAINTIFFS
24 North Lawyer Row
My City, My State 98765-4321
(123) 555-5555

WARREN PEACE   COURT OF COMMON PLEAS
    and
SUE U. DALEY   CIVIL DIVISION
    v.
NOAH FAULT   DOCKET NUMBER: 200000

INTERROGATORIES
ADDRESSED TO DEFENDANT

Demand is hereby made that you answer the following interrogatories under oath or verification pursuant to state law within thirty (30) days from service hereof. The answering party is under a duty to supplement their responses under the following conditions:

The party must supplement his response with respect to any question, directly addressed to the identity and location of persons having knowledge of discoverable matters and the identity of each person expected to be called as an expert witness at trial.

A party or expert witness must amend a prior response if he obtains information upon the basis of which:

(a) he knows that the response was incorrect when made or

(b) he knows that the response, though correct when made, is no longer true.

I.   DEFINITIONS

The following definitions are usage that apply to all of the Interrogatories contained herein:

A.   The singular and masculine form of any noun or pronoun shall embrace, and be read and applied as, the plural or feminine or neuter as circumstances may make appropriate.

B.   "Document" refers to all types of written, recorded, or graphic matter, however produced or reproduced.

C.   "Person" refers to any person, firm, corporation, partnership, proprietorship, association, or agency.

D.   "Plaintiff" refers to either or both parties bringing this action as circumstance may make appropriate.

E.   "Identify" when used:

1.   In reference to a person, means to state the full name, full title, last known resident address, last known business address, and last known occupation and business affiliation.

2.   In reference to documents, means to state with respect to each and every document, the type of document, author's name, recipient's name, date of preparation, present or last known custodian and location, and title and identification code or number of the file in which the document is kept.

II.   INTERROGATORIES

1.   State:

(a)   your name, age, date, and place of birth;

(b)   any other name by which you have ever been known;

(c)   your present address and your address at the time of the accident;

(d)   your marital status at the time of the accident;

(e)   your present marital status;

(f)   your Social Security number;

(g)   whether you are a licensed driver, and if so, where and when you were first licensed;

(h)   any and all restrictions on your driver's license at the time of the accident and at present;

(i)   your operator's license number;

(j)   whether you have any physical defects, and if so, their nature and duration;

(k)   whether you had taken any medication within the 24 hours preceding the accident. If yes, identify the medication and the condition for which it was taken;

(l)   whether you had taken any other drugs within the 24 hours preceding the accident. If yes, identify the drugs so taken;

(m) whether you had consumed any alcoholic beverages within the 8 hours preceding the accident. If yes, state when, what type of alcoholic beverage, where you consumed it, and how much you consumed;

(n) whether you were under the care of a physician, psychiatrist, or psychologist at the time of the accident and, if so, the name and address of the physician, psychiatrist, or psychologist;

(o) whether or not you have ever been convicted of a crime of moral turpitude or crimen falsi, and if so, please state the county, court, term, number, and charges; and,

(p) whether you ever served in the Armed Forces. If so, state the date, branch, rank at discharge, any infirmities at discharge, any claims made and any benefits received for infirmities, and your Veteran's Administration Claim Number.

CIRCUMSTANCES SURROUNDING THE ACCIDENT

2. State the date, time, and exact location of the accident.

3. With reference to the trip you were taking at the time of the accident herein, state:

(a) where it started;

(b) when it started;

(c) where it was scheduled to end;

(d) the route followed to the accident scene and any stops made along the way; and,

(e) the purpose of the trip.

4.   Did you have passengers in your vehicle at the time of the accident? If so, state:

   (a)   their names and addresses;

   (b)   their relationship to you; and,

   (c)   where they were located in your vehicle at the time of the accident.

5.   State as to the motor vehicle involved in the accident:

   (a)   the make, model, and year;

   (b)   the serial number;

   (c)   the mileage at the time of the accident;

   (d)   whether it had previously been in any accidents, indicating the date thereof and the parts damaged;

   (e)   the type of brakes, their condition, and the date they were last repaired or adjusted;

   (f)   whether the horn was in operating condition and when it was last used before the accident; and,

   (g)   whether the windows were open or closed and whether you were able to see through them clearly.

6.   As to the road on which your vehicle was being operated at the time of the accident, state:

   (a)   the type of road surface (*i.e.*, concrete, blacktop, etc);

   (b)   the surface condition (*i.e.*, dry, wet, muddy, etc);

   (c)   whether there were any defects in the road. If so, describe the same;

   (d)   whether the road was a one-way or a two-way street;

(e)   the number of lanes;

(f)   whether the road was a divided highway;

(g)   whether any buildings were located on either side of the road;

(h)   whether there was any road construction, and if so, describe the same;

(i)   the grade of the road;

(j)   the straightness or curve of the road; and,

(k)   the lighting conditions at the time of the accident.

7.   State:

(a)   the weather conditions prevailing at the time of the accident;

(b)   the exact intersection or highway where the accident occurred;

(c)   the position of all vehicles at the time of the accident;

(d)   the distance from you when you first observed the other vehicle and/or vehicles;

(e)   when and where you applied your brakes;

(f)   the distance traveled between the point when the brakes were applied and the point of impact;

(g)   an estimate of the respective speeds of the vehicles at the time of impact; and,

(h)   the initial point of impact for each vehicle.

8.   Describe how the accident occurred, including the actions of the respective parties and particularly detail any action you took to avoid the accident.

9. At what point in time did you first realize that the accident was going to occur?

10. State the name and address of the owner or owners of the motor vehicle you operated or occupied at the time of the accident.

11. State whether or not you were acting on behalf of your employer or in the course of your employment at the time of the accident referred to in the Complaint.

12. Did your vehicle carry any cargo and/or loads? If so, describe:

    (a) what the cargo or the load was and

    (b) its location in the vehicle.

13. Do you wear glasses or contact lenses? If so, state:

    (a) whether you were wearing them at the time of the accident;

    (b) as accurately as you can, the condition for which they were prescribed;

    (c) your visual acuity without glasses; and,

    (d) your visual acuity with glasses.

14. State:

    (a) whether there were any obstructions in your view when approaching the scene of the accident, and, if so, please describe each such obstruction in detail, giving its location with relation to the site of the accident;

    (b) whether at the time of the accident your vision was impaired or obscured in any manner, either from inside of the vehicle or from external factors and, if so, in what manner your vision was impaired or obscured.

15. State whether or not prior to the time of the accident you had traveled the road upon which the accident occurred. If so, please state the frequency and the last time that you traveled the road prior to the accident.

16. Where were you looking just prior to the time of the accident?

17. State where the point of impact was, giving the distance in feet with reference to the nearest intersection and/or other established points.

18. Describe the movement of your motor vehicle within the last 30 seconds immediately prior to the occurrence.

19. State whether you gave any warning of your approach. If so, state in detail the nature of the said warning.

20. Describe all physical evidence, including its location, which you observed at the scene of the accident after the collision, including but not limited to dirt, debris, etc.

21. State whether any skid marks were made by any vehicle involved in the accident. If so, state as to each vehicle:

    (a) the length and direction of the said skid marks and

    (b) the point of beginning and ending of the said skid marks.

22. State the type and color of any traffic signal controlling the street on which your vehicle was traveling when you first noticed it and:

    (a) the distance in feet the traffic light was from the vehicle at the time;

    (b) whether or not the signal had changed between the time you first observed it and the accident;

(c)   if the light did change, from what color to what color did it change; and,

(d)   the exact location of all traffic signals.

23.   At or immediately following the time of the accident, was there any conversation relevant to the accident or injuries sustained which you engaged in or heard? If yes, state:

(a)   the identity of the speaker;

(b)   the substance of what was said; and,

(c)   the identity of all persons within hearing distance.

24.   State how all the parties involved in the accident were removed from the accident, including the name, address, present whereabouts, and job classification of all persons assisting in their removal.

25.   State whether the accident was caused by any broken, defective, or unworkable device, or by the breaking, absence, misplacement, or malfunction of any equipment, or of any similar condition. If so, state:

(a)   the particular things involved and the precise nature of the defect;

(b)   when the defect first arose;

(c)   what caused the defect;

(d)   when you learned of the defect for the first time;

(e)   if the said defect existed prior to the accident, state how long it existed prior thereto; and,

(f)   what, if anything, was done to remedy this defect after the accident?

PROPERTY DAMAGE

26. State the condition of your vehicle at the time of the accident, describing specifically any damage that existed prior to the accident.

27. When and where was that vehicle last inspected prior to the accident in question and what, if any, repairs were made or parts replaced at the time of inspection?

28. Describe specifically what parts of your vehicle were damaged in the accident, listing the damage to each of those parts.

29. Did you obtain estimates for the repairs of these damages? If so, give the names and addresses of the repair shops and the amounts of the estimates.

30. If the damages were repaired, state:

    (a) the date or dates on which repairs were made;

    (b) the name and address of the person who made the repairs; and,

    (c) the total cost of repairs.

31. Please attach a copy of all repair bills or estimates.

32. State whether any damage to property other than the motor vehicles involved resulted from the accident, and if so, describe such damage.

INJURIES RELATING TO THE ACCIDENT

33. State in detail all injuries you sustained in the accident or as a result thereof.

34. Have you contacted anyone regarding injuries sustained by any other party in this action? If so, state the name of such persons and the substance of any information received from said person.

35. State whether you saw either plaintiff subsequent to this accident in question and, if your answer is in the affirmative, set forth:

    (a) the date you saw either plaintiff;

    (b) the places at which you saw either plaintiff; and,

    (c) the identity and condition of the plaintiff at this time.

WITNESSES AND THOSE WITH KNOWLEDGE OF THE ACCIDENT

36. State the names and addresses of all persons who you or anyone acting on your behalf, including but not limited to, attorneys and insurance adjusters, know or believe:

    (a) actually witnessed the accident;

    (b) were present at the scene of the accident immediately after its occurrence; and,

    (c) were within sight or hearing of the accident.

STATEMENTS

37. Please state the nature of any oral statements made by either plaintiff concerning the occurrence. Please state when, where, and to whom the statements were made.

38. Have you or anyone acting on your behalf obtained from any person any statement (as defined by the Rules of Civil Procedure) concerning this action or its subject matter?

If so, please:
    (a) state the names and addresses of each such person;

(b) state when, where, by whom, and to whom each statement was made, and whether it was reduced to writing or otherwise recorded;

(c) state the names and addresses of each person who has custody of any such statements that were reduced to writing or otherwise recorded; and,

(d) attach a copy of each such statements to these Interrogatories.

39. Do you have knowledge of any transcript or of testimony in any proceeding arising out of the occurrence? If so, please identify it.

STATEMENTS MADE BY PARTY TO WHOM INTERROGATORY IS ADDRESSED

40. Have you given any statement as defined by the Rules of Civil Procedure concerning this action or its subject matter?

If so, please:

(a) state the names and addresses of each person to whom a statement was given;

(b) state when and where each statement was given;

(c) state the names and addresses of each person who has custody of any such statements that were reduced to writing or otherwise recorded; and,

(d) attach a copy of each such statement to these Interrogatories.

DEMONSTRATIVE EVIDENCE

41. Are you or anyone in your behalf in possession of maps, models, plans, diagrams, or drawings relating to the accident complained of, showing the locale or surrounding area of the site of the accident or any other matters involved in the accident? If so, attach a copy of said map, plan, or diagrams to these Interrogatories and state:

(a) the date(s) when such maps, models, plans, diagrams, or drawings were taken or made and what they are;

(b) the names and addresses of the person or persons taking or making the same;

(c) the subject that each represents or portrays; and,

(d) the name, address, and job classification of the person having possession or custody of the same.

42. Are you or anyone acting in your behalf, including but not limited to attorneys and insurance adjusters, in possession of any photographs, motion pictures, or video recordings relating to the accident complained of, showing the local or surrounding area of the site of the accident or any other matters or things involved in the accident? If so, attach a copy and state:

(a) the dates when such photographs, motion pictures, or video recordings were taken or made;

(b) the names, addresses, and job classifications of the person or persons taking the same;

(c) the subject that each represents or portrays;

(d) what location each was taken from; and,

(e) the name, address, and job classification of the person having possession or custody of the same.

TRIAL PREPARATION MATERIAL

43. Have you or anyone on your behalf, including but not limited to attorneys and insurance adjusters, conducted any investigation of the accident that is the subject matter of the complaint? If the answer is in the affirmative, please:

(a) state the names and addresses of each such person, and the employer of each person, who conducted any investigations;

(b) state the subject matter of the investigation;

(c) state the dates of the investigation;

(d) describe all notes, reports, or other documents prepared during or as a result of the investigations and the identity of the persons who have possession thereof; and,

(e) attach copies of any and all documents, memoranda, notes, photographs, and statements obtained as a result of the investigation.

EXPERTS

44. Identify by name and address any experts with whom you have consulted who will not be called upon to testify.

45. Identify by name and address any experts with whom you have consulted who will be called upon to testify at trial.

46. As to the experts in question No. 45 state:

(a) the background and qualifications of each said expert, listing the schools attended, years of attendance, degrees received, and experience in any particular field of specialization or expertise;

(b) the subject matter upon which each expert will testify;

(c) the substance of all the facts and all the opinions to which each expert will testify; and,

(d) the grounds for each expert's opinion.

INSURANCE

47. State whether you are covered by any type of insurance, including any excess or umbrella insurance, in connection with this accident;

    If the answer is affirmative, state the following with respect to each policy:

    (a) the name of the insurance carrier(s) that issued each policy of insurance;

    (b) the named insured under each policy and the policy number;

    (c) the type of each policy and the effective dates;

    (d) the amount of coverage provided for injury to each person, for each occurrence, and in the aggregate for each policy;

    (e) each exclusion, if any, in the policy which is applicable to any claim thereunder and the reasons why you or the company claims the exclusion is applicable; and,

    (f) whether you have made a claim under the policy and if so, set forth the nature of the claim, the amount recovered, and the date of recovery.

48. Did you make an oral or written report or give any other notice of the accident to any insurance company, or agent, or broker? If so:

    (a) state if the report was written or oral and

    (b) please attach copies and/or transcriptions of said reports.

49. State whether or not any insurer has a file on the accident herein, and if so, where the file is located.

50. Did you receive any compensation from, or make a claim under, any Workers' Compensation Insurance Plans as a result of the accident in question? If your answer is in the affirmative, please state:

    (a) the name of the insurance company or companies providing such coverage;

(b) the date of the claim and the policy or claim number involved;

(c) the name of the insurance adjuster or supervisor handling the claim and his office address; and,

(d) if any claim was disallowed, please state the specific nature of the claim made and the reason(s) given by the insurance company for the denial.

51. Identify and give the home and business addresses of all witnesses who you anticipate will testify at the trial of this matter.

52. If you are not the registered owner of the motor vehicle you were driving at the time of the accident, state by what authority you were driving the said motor vehicle.

53. Were you performing any duties or acts on behalf of any person or entity other than yourself at the time of the accident?

54. If the answer to the preceding interrogatory is yes, state the name, home address, and business address of each such person and/or entity.

55. Identify and give the home and business addresses of all persons having knowledge of any discoverable matters.

BY: _____

_____
Attorney for Defendant

YOUR ATTORNEY
Attorney for Plaintiff

Interrogatories—Fall-Down Accident

YOUR ATTORNEY
Identification Number 1234567   ATTORNEY FOR PLAINTIFF
24 North Lawyer Row
My City, My State 98765-4321
(123) 555-5555

AXEL DENT   COURT OF COMMON PLEAS
v.   CIVIL DIVISION
D. FENDANT   DOCKET NUMBER: 123456789

PLAINTIFF'S INTERROGATORIES ADDRESSED TO DEFENDANT

Demand is hereby made that you answer the following interrogatories under oath or verification pursuant to state law within thirty (30) days from service hereof. The answering party is under a duty to supplement his responses under the following conditions:

The party must supplement his response with respect to any question, directly addressed to the identity and location of persons having knowledge of discoverable matters, and the identity of each person expected to be called as an expert witness at trial.

A party or expert witness must amend a prior response if he obtains information upon the basis of which:

(a) he knows that the response was incorrect when made or

(b) he knows that the response, though correct when made, is no longer true.

I. DEFINITIONS

The following definitions are usage that apply to all of the Interrogatories contained herein:

A. The singular and masculine form of any noun or pronoun shall embrace, and be read and applied as, the plural or feminine or neuter as circumstances may make appropriate.

B. "Document" refers to all types of written, recorded, or graphic matter, however produced or reproduced.

C   "Person" refers to any person, firm, corporation, partnership, proprietorship, association, or agency.

D. "Plaintiff" refers to the plaintiff in this matter.

E. "Identify" when used:

1. in reference to a person, means to state the full name, full title, last known resident address, last known business address, and last known occupation and business affiliation and

2. in reference to documents means to state, with respect to each and every document, the type of document, author's name, recipient's name, date of preparation, present or last known custodian and location, and title and identification code or number of the file in which the document is kept.

II. INTERROGATORIES

1. Were you aware, prior to the filing of the Complaint in this action, that plaintiff was injured while on the premises made reference to in the Complaint?

2. Did you receive notice of this accident from the plaintiff?

If so, state:

(a) the date, time, and place you received the notice and

(b) whether this was written or oral, and if written, the name and address of the person who now has custody of it.

3.   Did you receive notice of the accident from any other person?

     If so, state:

     (a) the date, time, and place you received the notice;

     (b) the name, address, and telephone number of the person from whom you received the notice; and,

     (c) whether the notice was written or oral, and if written, the name and address of the person who now has custody of it.

4.   If you will do so without a Motion to Produce, attach a copy of each written notice to your answers to these Interrogatories.

5.   What is the name and address of each person who, on the date of the accident, was the owner of the real property located at the premises made reference to in the Complaint?

6.   What was the nature and extent of each person's ownership interest?

7.   What financial interest did each owner of the real property have in the said premises?

8.   Were the premises made reference to in the Complaint subject to any lease on the date of the accident? If so, state the name and address of the lessors, lessees, and sublessees.

9.   What is the name and address of each person who managed and controlled these premises on the date of the accident?

For each such person, state:

     (a) his or her job title;

     (b) a description of his or her duties;

     (c) what his or her financial interest in these premises is;

(d) the inclusive dates of his or her management up until the present time;

(e) a description of his or her qualifications and experience in managing such a business; and,

(f) the name and address of each other business at which he or she has been employed, and the inclusive dates of such employment.

10. State the name, address, and job title of the person who was in charge of these premises at the time plaintiff was injured:

11. Where was such person located at the time of the accident?

12. Was any person responsible for supervising the area in which plaintiff was injured at the time of the accident?

If so, for each person state:

(a) his or her name and address;

(b) his or her job title;

(c) a description of his or her duties; and,

(d) his or her location at the time of the accident.

13. Were there any employees on these premises, or other person, on duty at the time of the accident?

If so, for each such person state:

(a) his name and address:

(b) his job title;

(c) a description of his duties; and,

(d) his location at the time of the accident.

14. Does the area of the premises where the accident occurred have a particular designation? If so, what is the designation?

15. Describe the accident site.

16. Was there a defect or collection of debris in the area where the accident is alleged to have occurred? If so, for each collection of debris or defect, give a description of it.

17. If you will do so without a Motion to Produce, attach a copy of each written complaint, warning, or other notice with regard to the area of the premises where the accident occurred.

18. Were inspections made prior to the accident to determine whether the area where the plaintiff was injured was in a safe condition for use by workers or other occupants of the area?

    If so, state:

    (a) the frequency of such inspections;

    (b) the date and time of the last inspection prior to the accident;

    (c) the name, address, and job title of the person who made the last inspection;

    (d) the substance of the findings that were made on the last inspection; and,

    (e) whether any instructions were given as a result of the last inspection to remove, clean, or alter anything in the area of the accident, and if so, a description of the instructions, and the name of each person to whom such instructions were given.

19. Was any inspection made of the scene of the accident subsequent to the accident?

If so, state:

(a) the date and time it was made;

(b) the name, address, and job title of each person who made the inspection; and,

(c) what findings were made.

20. Did you or any employee receive any complaint, warning, or other notice concerning a dangerous or defective condition on the premises prior to the accident?

If so, for each complaint, warning, or other notice, state:

(a) the date and time it was received;

(b) whether it was written or oral, and if oral, the substance of it;

(c) the name or other means of identification and address of the person by whom it was given;

(d) the name, address, and job title of the person who received it;

(e) the nature and location of the danger or defect to which it related; and,

(f) Whether any action was taken as a result of it, and if so, a description of the action, and the time at which it was taken.

21. Was any warning given to plaintiff or any other person concerning any danger in the area where the accident occurred?

If so, for each warning state:

(a) the warning that was given;

(b) the name or other means of identification and address of the person who gave the warning;

(c)   the name or other means of identification and address of each person to whom it was given;

(d)   the form in which it was given; and,

(e)   the reason it was given.

22.   Was there any guardrail, sign, or other marking in the area where the accident occurred?

If so, for each such marking, state:

(a)   a description of it;

(b)   its location;

(c)   its purpose; and,

(d)   whether it was in use at the time of the accident, and if not, the reason it was not in use.

23.   Has any other accident occurred on your premises in the same area as, or in a similar manner to, the accident in which plaintiff was injured?

If so, for each accident, state:

(a)   the date and time it occurred:

(b)   a description of how it occurred;

(c)   the name, or other means of identification, and address of the person to whom it occurred;

(d)   the location in which it occurred; and,

(e)   whether any safety precaution was taken as a result of it, and if so, a description of such safety precaution.

24. Was any repair or alteration made subsequent to the accident in the area where plaintiff was injured?

    If so, for each repair or alteration, state:

    (a)   a description of it:

    (b)   the date it was made;

    (c)   the name, address, and occupation of the person who made it; and,

    (d)   the reason it was made.

25. Was an investigation made by you, or in your behalf, as a result of the accident?

    If so, for each investigation, state:

    (a)   the date it was made;

    (b)   the name, address, and occupation of each person who made it; and,

    (c)   whether any report was made of it, and if so, the name and address of the person who has custody of the report.

26. If you will do so without a Motion to Produce, attach a copy of each investigation report to your answers to these interrogatories.

27. Did you or any employee make a report of the accident?

    If so, for each report, state:

    (a)   the name, address, and job title of the person who made it;

    (b)   the date and time it was made;

    (c)   the name and address of the person to whom it was made; and,

(d) whether written or oral, and, if written, the name and address of the person who has custody of it.

28. Did you receive a report of the accident from the plaintiff or any other person?

    If so, for each person, state:

    (a) his or her name and address;

    (b) the date and time he or she made the report;

    (c) the name, address, and job title of the person to whom he or she made the report; and,

    (d) whether he or she made a written or oral report, and, if written, the name and address of the person who has custody of the report.

29. If you will do so without a Motion to Produce, attach a copy of each written report concerning the accident to your answers to these interrogatories.

30. Do you contend that plaintiff was not authorized to be on that part of the premises where the accident occurred? If so, on what facts do you base such contention?

31. Do you contend that plaintiff was guilty of contributory negligence? If so, on what facts do you base such contention?

32. Do you contend that plaintiff assumed the risk of the accident? If so, on what facts do you base such contention?

33. Was there a policy of insurance that covered you on the date of the accident against the type of risk here involved?

    If so, for each policy, state:

    (a) the name and address of the insurer;

(b) the number of the policy;

(c) the effective date thereof;

(d) the nature of the coverage;

(e) the limits of liability; and,

(f) the name and address of the custodian of the policy.

34. Do you have, or know of the existence of, any photograph or diagrams relating to any matter concerning this accident?

If so, for each photograph or diagram, state:

(a) a description of what it depicts;

(b) the name, address, and occupation of the person who took or made it;

(c) the date, time, and place it was taken or made; and,

(d) the name and address of the person who has custody of it.

35. If you will do so without a Motion to Produce, attach a copy, at the expense of the plaintiff, of each photograph or diagram to your answers to these Interrogatories.

36. Were any statements obtained by you, or on your behalf, from any person concerning the accident?

If so, for each statement identify:

(a) the name, address, occupation, and name of employer of the person who made it;

(b) the name, address, and occupation of the person who obtained it;

(c) the date and time it was obtained; and,

(d)   whether written or oral, and if written, the name and address of the person who has custody of it.

37. If you will do so without a Motion to Produce, attach a copy of each written statement to your answers to these Interrogatories.

38. State the name, home address, and business address of the following persons:

(a)   all persons known to defendant or its representatives who witnessed the accident forming the basis of this claim;

(b)   all persons who came to the scene of the accident following the occurrence;

(c)   all persons who were within sight or hearing of the accident at the time it occurred but who did not actually witness it; and,

(d)   all persons having relevant knowledge concerning the happening of the accident and the cause therefor.

39. Have you or anyone acting on your behalf obtained a written or oral statement from the plaintiff? If so, for each and every such statement, set forth:

(a)   the name and address of the person who obtained the statement;

(b)   the date of the statement;

(c)   was it written or oral;

(d)   if oral, whether it was recorded or transcribed; and,

(e)   the name and address of the person who presently has custody of the statement or recording thereof.

40. Have you made any statement to any person concerning the accident? If so, for each and every such statement, set forth:

230

(a) the date of each statement;

(b) whether written or oral;

(c) if oral, whether recorded or transcribed;

(d) the name and address of the person who obtained each statement; and,

(e) the name and address of the person presently having custody of each statement or recording thereof.

41. Have you or anyone acting on your behalf obtained any written or oral statements as defined by state law from any person who has knowledge of the happening of the accident, whether as an actual witness or as a pre-accident or a post-accident witness? If so, for each and every statement, set forth:

(a) the name and address of the person from whom each statement was obtained;

(b) the date of each statement;

(c) whether each statement was written or oral;

(d) if oral, whether each statement was recorded or transcribed;

(e) the name and address of the person(s) who obtained each statement; and,

(f) the name and address of the person(s) who presently has custody of each statement or recording thereof.

42. State whether or not defendant or his representatives, other than his attorney, has possession of any written or typed and/or recorded memorandum that contains factual data obtained by them from interviews or discussions with any person who has knowledge of the happening of the accident. If so, for each and every such memorandum, set forth:

(a) The date of the memorandum;

(b) the name and address of the person who composed the memorandum; and,

(c) the name and address of the person who presently has custody of the memorandum.

43. State whether you, your representative, your attorney, or any other person to your knowledge caused to be made, or now has any, photographs, motion pictures, charts, diagrams, graphs, or recordings depicting or concerning the scene of the accident or the parties involved in the accident. If so, set forth the name and address of each and every person who presently has custody, and describe the contents of such photographs, motion pictures, charts, diagrams, graphs, and/or recordings.

44. At the time of the accident, was defendant covered by one or more insurance policies providing coverage for liability in excess of the applicable basic policy, including but not limited to, any personal or family coverage, excess coverage, "umbrella" policy, "catastrophe" policy, or any such additional coverage? If so, as to such policy, state the following:

(a) the name of the carrier issuing the policy and

(b) the amount of coverage provided.

45. Does defendant, its representatives or anyone acting in its behalf, other than its attorney, have in its possession a report concerning the plaintiff that was obtained from a credit bureau and/or insurance index system of claimants and/or a casualty, health, or life insurance company? If so, please state:

(a) from whom such report was obtained, setting forth the name of the organization and its last known address;

(b) the date which report was obtained; and,

(c) the name, last known address, and job title of the person and/or persons presently in possession of same.

46. Identify by name and address each and every person whom you expect to call as an expert witness at the trial of this claim. As to each witness, state:

   (a)   the subject matter on which he or she is expected to testify;

   (b)   the facts and opinions to which he or she is expected to testify;

   (c)   a summary of the grounds for each opinion;

   (d)   whether the facts and opinions listed in (b) above are contained in a written report, memorandum, or other transcript, and if they are, give the name and address of the present custodian of same and state, whether you will produce the same without the necessity of a Motion;

   (e)   if the opinion of any expert listed above is based in whole or part on any scientific rule or principal, set forth the said rule or principal;

   (f)   if the opinion of any expert listed above is based in whole or in part on any code, regulation, or standard, specifically set forth the section relied upon;

   (g)   if the opinion of any expert listed above is based in whole or in part upon any scientific or engineering textbook or other publication, identify said text or publication; and,

   (h)   if the expert has testified in court or by way of oral deposition within the past ten years, describe the court involved, set forth the caption of the case, the date of testimony, and the name and address of the attorney calling said expert as a witness.

47. With respect to each person you expect to call as an expert witness at the trial of this matter, state:

   (a)   his or her age, residence, and business address;

   (b)   the name and address of his or her present employer, or if self-employed, the name and address of the business and his or her occupation;

    (c)   the name and address of every person or firm who employed the expert for the last ten years and a detailed description of all duties at each place of employment. If the expert was self-employed, state specifically and in detail the description of his or her duties and responsibilities; and,

    (d)   his or her education background, specifying colleges attended, dates of attendance, degrees attained and in a detailed list of all writings prepared by the expert or in which the expert participated in any way whatsoever.

48. Did the defendant, its attorney, or anyone acting on its behalf receive any notices, reports, or complaints during a one-year period prior to the accident from any source or whatsoever concerning or relating to the condition of the area set forth above? If so, please state:

    (a)   the name and address of the author and

    (b)   the nature of each such notice, report, or complaint.

49. State whether or not, and in particular, how often periodic inspections and/or examinations were made of the area set forth above during a one-year period immediately preceding the date of the accident involved herein and since the date of the accident.

50. Describe the inspections made of the area referred to above just before and just after the accident, setting forth the names, addresses, and job classifications of each person or persons making such inspections.

51. Identify the location of any written or typed reports made of the inspections referred to in the preceding interrogatory.

52. State what physical cracks and/or holes and/or defects were discovered, if any, by the aforesaid inspection.

53. With regard to the defendant, please state the name, last known address, present whereabouts, if known, of the following persons:

 (a) President;

 (b) Vice President;

 (c) Treasurer;

 (d) Secretary;

 (e) Security Personnel; and,

 (f) Counter Person.

54. Please state the last known address and present whereabouts, if known, of all of defendant's employees who were on duty at the time of plaintiff's accident.

55. Identify and give the home and business addresses of all lay witnesses who you anticipate will testify at the trial of this matter, and state the subject on which he or she is to testify.

56. Identify and give the home and business addresses of all persons having knowledge of any discoverable matters.

57. If you have conducted any surveillance of plaintiff or any other person relevant to this litigation, state:

 (a) time and date of surveillance;

 (b) method used;

 (c) name, business address, telephone number, and employer of person taking this surveillance; and,

 (d) name, address, telephone number of the custodian of the medium used to record such surveillance.

58. identify with particularity all persons, animals, or vehicles involved in the occurrence, either directly or indirectly, and explain such involvement.

59. Explain in detail your version of how the occurrence happened, if you feel that it is not completely covered in your answers above.

YOUR ATTORNEY
Attorney for Plaintiff

Request for Production of Documents

YOUR ATTORNEY   ATTORNEY FOR PLAINTIFF
Identification Number 1234567
24 North Lawyer Row
My City, My State 98765-4321
(123) 555-5555

LEAH BILITY   COURT OF COMMON PLEAS

v.   CIVIL DIVISION

SUE PREAM COURT   DOCKET NUMBER: 3333333
and
ARTHUR DAVIT

REQUEST FOR PRODUCTION OF DOCUMENTS

Plaintiff hereby requests, pursuant to state law, that the defendants produce the documents I hereinafter request in accordance with the definitions and instructions contained herein within thirty (30) days after service of this request, at the offices of the undersigned and permit the undersigned to inspect and copy these documents.

1. All photographs, records, films, charts, sketches, graphs, and diagrams of the area involved in this accident or occurrence, the locale or surrounding area of this accident or occurrence, or any other matter or thing involved in this accident or occurrence taken and/or prepared.

2. All statements, memoranda, or writings (signed or unsigned) of any and all witnesses, including any and all statements, memoranda, or writings of plaintiff and/or defendants and/or all persons involved in this accident or occurrence. The statements referred to herein are defined by State Rule of Civil Procedure.

3. All transcripts and summaries of all interviews conducted by anyone on behalf of defendants of any potential witness or person who has any knowledge of the accident or its surrounding circumstances.

4. All interoffice memoranda between representatives of defendants or memoranda to defendants' file concerning the manner in which the accident occurred.

5. All interoffice memoranda between representatives of defendants or memoranda to defendants' file concerning the injuries you sustained.

6. A copy of any written accident report concerning this accident or occurrence, signed by or prepared by, defendants.

7. Any and all copies of reports, correspondence, memoranda, and writings rendered by any expert witness employed or consulted by defendants and/or anyone acting on defendants' behalf concerning this case.

8. The entire claims and investigation file or files of the defendants, defendants' counsel, or any other organization, excluding references to mental impressions, conclusions, or opinions representing the value or merit of the claim or defense or respecting strategy or tactics and privileged communication from counsel.

9. All property damage estimates rendered for any object belonging to you and/or defendants that was involved in this accident or occurrence.

10. Any and all documents containing the names and home and business addresses of all individuals contacted as potential witnesses.

11. Any and all press releases in the possession of defendants' counsel.

BY:_____

YOUR ATTORNEY
Attorney for Plaintiff

Motion to Compel Discovery

YOUR ATTORNEY   ATTORNEY FOR PLAINTIFF
Identification Number 1234567
24 North Lawyer Row
My City, My State 98765-4321
(123) 555-5555

IMA PLAINTIFF   COURT OF COMMON PLEAS

v.   CIVIL DIVISION

D. SCUVRY   DOCKET NUMBER: 35791113

MOTION TO COMPEL DISCOVERY

Plaintiff, by undersigned counsel, hereby moves the Court to enter an Order pursuant to PA. R. C. P. 4019 compelling defendant, D. Scuvry, to answer certain discovery propounded by plaintiff in this matter.

In support of this Motion, plaintiff avers as follows:

1. On November 3, 2004, plaintiff served Interrogatories and Requests for Production of Documents upon counsel for defendant by first class mail.
2. Pursuant to PA. R. C. P. 4006(a)(2), defendant's answers and objections to the said Interrogatories and Requests were due on or before December 3, 2004.
3. Plaintiff requires an Order of this Court pursuant to PA. R. C. P. 4019(a)(1)(i) compelling defendant to answer the said Interrogatories and to respond to the said Requests for Production of Documents.

WHEREFORE, plaintiff respectfully requests the Court to enter an Order compelling defendant to file full and complete answers to plaintiff's Interrogatories and documents responsive to Plaintiff's Request for Production or suffer appropriate sanctions to be imposed upon application to the Court.

IMA LAWYER, ESQUIRE
Attorney for Plaintiff

Order for Discovery

YOUR ATTORNEY
Identification Number 1234567   ATTORNEY FOR PLAINTIFF
24 North Lawyer Row
My City, My State 98765-4321
(123) 555-5555

IMA PLAINTIFF   COURT OF COMMON PLEAS

v.   CIVIL DIVISION

JERRY TRIAL   DOCKET NUMBER: 35791113

<u>ORDER</u>

AND NOW, this day of _____, 20____, upon consider-
ation of plaintiff's Motion to Compel Discovery, it is hereby ORDERED that the said
Motion is GRANTED. Defendant, Jerry Trial, shall answer plaintiff's Interrogatories and
respond to plaintiff's Request for Production of Documents within twenty (20) days of the
date of this Order or appropriate sanctions shall be imposed upon defendants following
application to the Court. All documents produced or withheld are to be numbered con-
secutively beginning with the number one.

BY THE COURT:

_____

Authorization to Release Records

You are hereby authorized and requested to furnish to _____ _____ or his representative, all my medical and drug records (including x-rays, if any), and reports, abstracts, and summaries thereof, accident and/or police reports, employment and earnings, histories and records, bills and statements, and all other information pertaining to me, to permit them to examine all originals and to make copies thereof.

_____   _____

DATE   NAME

                                                            _____

                                                            _____

                                                                           ADDRESS

Contingent Fee Agreement

I hereby appoint _____,
as my attorney to prosecute a claim for Personal Injuries against _____
_____,
relating to injuries that occurred on _____.
                                                    Date

      I hereby agree that the compensation for my attorney for services shall be determined as follows: that out of whatever sum is secured by my attorney from the above Defendant(s) by way of settlement or verdict, my attorney shall receive

      _____% thereof if my case is settled without filing a lawsuit, or

      _____% thereof if my case is settled after a lawsuit is filed, or

      _____% thereof if my case is settled after arbitration, or

      _____% thereof if my case must go to jury verdict.

The expenses, including the fees of witnesses, investigation, photographs, and other proper costs incurred in the preparation, trial, or settlement shall be deducted before payment of my attorney's fee, and all otherwise unpaid medical expenses shall be paid from the balance remaining after payment of my attorney's fee and expenses. SHOULD NO MONEY BE RECOVERED BY SUIT OR SETTLEMENT, MY ATTORNEY SHALL HAVE NO CLAIM AGAINST ME OF ANY KIND FOR SERVICES RENDERED.

      I hereby acknowledge acceptance of this Contingent Fee Agreement.

_____
NAME

                              _____

                                        ADDRESS

YOUR ATTORNEY
Identification Number 1234567
24 North Lawyer Row
My City, My State 98765-4321
(123) 555-5555

ATTORNEY FOR PLAINTIFFS

B. YONDA SCOPE
    and
MEL PRACTICE
    v.
CITY OF PHILADELPHIA

COURT OF COMMON PLEAS

CIVIL DIVISION

DOCKET NUMBER: 7654321

POINTS FOR CHARGE

DIRECTED VERDICT

1. Upon consideration of all of the evidence and the law applicable to this case, I hereby direct you to return a verdict in favor of plaintiffs, B. Yonda Scope and Mel Practice, and against defendant, City of Philadelphia.

<u>DUTY OF CARE</u>

2 Defendant's duty of protection and care to plaintiffs, on April 30, 1998, was the highest duty required by the law since the plaintiffs were invited visitors of the defendant at the time of this accident. Treadway v. Ebert Motor Company, 463 A. 2d 994, 998 (Pa. Super. 1981).

Defendant was under an affirmative duty on April 30, 1998, to protect the plaintiffs not only against danger which its employees knew about, but also against those which with reasonable care one or more of its employees might have discovered. Treadway v. Ebert Motor Company, 463 A. 2d 994, 998 (Pa. Super. 1981).

Plaintiffs entered the Philadelphia City Hall on April 30, 1998, with the City of Philadelphia's implied assurance of preparation and reasonable care for their protection and safety while they were there. Treadway v. Ebert Motor Company, 463 A. 2d 994, 998 (Pa. Super. 1981).

DUTY TO WARN

3. Defendant had an affirmative duty to warn the plaintiffs of any defects on the floor surface, which were either known to the City of Philadelphia or its employees, or which were discoverable by reasonable inspection. Greco v. 7-Up Bottling Co., 165 A. 2d 5 (Pa. 1960).

Defendant had an affirmative duty to warn the plaintiffs of any failure to maintain the school premises in a reasonably safe condition, and the plaintiffs were entitled to rely on the City's performance of this duty. Bersa v. Great Atlantic & Pacific Tea Company, 215 A. 2d 289, 292 (Pa. Super. 1965).

NEGLIGENCE

4. The legal term negligence, otherwise known as carelessness, is the absence of ordinary care which a reasonably prudent person would exercise in the circumstances here presented. Negligent conduct may consist either of an act or an omission to act when there is a duty to do so. In other words, negligence is the failure to do something which a reasonably careful person would do, or the doing of something which a reasonably careful person would not do, in light of all the surrounding circumstances established by the evidence in this case. It is for you to determine how a reasonably careful person would act in those circumstances. Pa. S.S.J.I. (Civ.) 3.01.

VICARIOUS LIABILITY

5. The defendant, City of Philadelphia, as an employer, is liable for any negligent acts or failures to act of its employees. Pa. S.S.J.I. (Civ.) 4.04. I instruct you that William Anderson and Donna Johnson are employees of the defendant and, as such, the defendant is legally responsible for any of their negligent acts or failures to act.

NOTICE

6. You must find that the defendant was negligent if you believe that the evidence has shown that the defendant, in the exercise of reasonable care, ought to have known of the existence of the water before the accident. Moultrey v. Great Atlantic & Pacific Tea Company, 422 A. 2d 593, 596 (Pa. Super. 1980).

Defendant is chargeable with constructive notice of a defective condition which exists for such a period of time that in the normal course of events, this condition would have come to its attention. Green v. Prise, 404 Pa. 71, 170 A. 2d 318 (1991).

PROOF OF NOTICE

7. The Plaintiffs can establish that defendant ought to have known of the existence of the water either by direct or circumstantial evidence. Moultrey v. Great Atlantic and Pacific Tea Company, 422 A.2d 593, 594 (Pa. Super. 1980).

CIRCUMSTANTIAL EVIDENCE

8. Circumstantial evidence consists of proof of facts, or circumstances, from which it is reasonable to infer the existence of another fact. You may consider circumstantial evidence and you should give it whatever weight you believe it deserves. Pa. S.S.J.I. (Civ.) 5.07.

PROOF

9. Plaintiffs need not exclude every reasonable possibility that could have caused the accident; it is not necessary that every fact or circumstance point to liability, but it is enough that there be sufficient facts for you to say that, by a preponderance of the evidence, liability is favored. Swartz v. General Electric Co., Pa. Super. 474 A.2d 1172 (1984).

PRECISION OF PROOF

10. The Plaintiffs are not required to prove the precise manner in which the water came to be on the floor, nor are they required to prove with mathematical exactness that the accident could only happen in one manner to the exclusion of all other possibilities. Finney v. G.C. Murphy Co., 178 A.2d 719 (Pa. 1902).

ASSUMPTION OF RISK

11. You may not find that the plaintiffs assumed the risk of their injuries unless you find that with appreciation and knowledge of an obvious danger, they purposely

elected to abandon a position of relative safety and chose to move to a place of obvious danger and by reason of the repositioning were injured. McIntyre v. Cusick, 372 A.2d 864, 866 (Pa. Super. 1977).

You may not find the plaintiffs assumed this risk unless you also find that they were subjectively aware of the facts which created the danger and that they appreciated the danger itself and the nature, character, and extent which made it unreasonable. Crance v. Sohanic, 496 2d 1230, 1232 (Pa. Super. 1985).

You may not find that the plaintiffs assumed the risk unless you also find that they fully understood the risks involved in walking over water and that they voluntarily chose to encounter these risks under circumstances manifesting a willingness to accept the risk. Fish v. Gosnell, 463 A.2d 1042, 1048 (Pa. Super. 1983).

Since the evidence has shown that the plaintiffs were not aware of the danger presented by the water, I instruct you to find that they did not assume the risk of their injuries.

CONFLICT OF TESTIMONY

12. You may find inconsistencies in the evidence. Even actual contradictions in the testimony of witnesses do not necessarily mean that any witness has been willfully false. Poor memory is not uncommon. Sometimes a witness forgets; sometimes he remembers incorrectly. It is also true that two persons witnessing an incident may see or hear it differently.

If different parts of the testimony of any witness or witnesses appear to be inconsistent, you the jury should try to reconcile the conflicting statements, whether of the same or different witnesses, and you should do so if it can be done fairly and satisfactorily.

If, however, you decide that there is a genuine and irreconcilable conflict of testimony, it is your function and duty to determine which, if any, of the contradictory statements you will believe. Pa. S.S.J.I. (Civ.) 5.04.

REAL PROPERTY EXCEPTION TO THE P.S.T.C.A.

13. You may return a verdict in favor of the plaintiffs and against the defendant if you find that the accident involves the care, custody or control of real property of the City of Philadelphia. 42 P. S. Section 8542 (b)(3). I instruct you to return such a finding

if you conclude that the defendant failed to provide sufficient matting protection to ensure safe entrance into the Philadelphia City Hall. Singer v. City of Philadelphia, 513 A.2d 1108, 1109-10(Pa. Cmwlth. 1986).

MONEY DAMAGES

14. If you find that the defendant is liable to plaintiffs, you must then find an amount of money damages which you believe will fairly and adequately compensate each of them for all physical and financial injuries they each sustained as a result of the accident. The amount which you award today must compensate them completely for damage sustained in the past, as well as damage they will sustain in the future. Pa. S.S.J.I. (Civ.) 6.00.

PERMANENT LOSS OF A BODILY FUNCTION

15. In order for the plaintiffs to be entitled to recover for their pain and suffering, you must find that they suffered a permanent loss of a bodily function. You may rely on their testimony and that of the doctors who testified in reaching this finding.

PAST PAIN AND SUFFERING

16. If you find that B. Yonda Scope has suffered a permanent loss of a bodily function, she is entitled to be fairly and adequately compensated for such physical pain, mental anguish, discomfort, inconvenience and distress as you find she has endured from the time of the accident until today. Pa. S.S.J.I. (Civ.) 6.01E.

FUTURE PAIN AND SUFFERING

17. If you find that she has suffered a permanent loss of a bodily function, B. Yonda Scope is further entitled to be fairly and adequately compensated for such physical pain, mental anguish, discomfort, inconvenience and distress as you believe she will endure in the future as a result of her injuries. Pa. S.S.J.I. (Civ.) 6.01F.

LOSS OF EARNINGS AND EARNING CAPACITY

18. B. Yonda Scope is entitled to be fairly and adequately compensated for the past, present and future loss of her earnings and earning capacity. This aspect of damages is awardable whether or not you find that she has suffered a permanent loss of a bodily function. 42 P. S. Section 8553 (c)(1).

MEDICAL BILLS

19. B. Yonda Scope is entitled to be fairly and adequately compensated for all outstanding costs of the medical diagnosis, treatment, and care required by the injuries suffered in this accident, and she is also entitled to compensation for all such future costs which may be incurred because of those injuries. Pa. S.S.J.I. (Civ.) 6.01A. You do not need to find that she has suffered a permanent loss of a bodily function in order for her to recover her past and future medical costs. Those costs are recoverable without regard to the permanency of the injury she suffered. 42 P.S. Section 8553 (c)(3). The only item of damages that depends upon a finding of permanency is for B. Yonda Scope's pain and suffering. Each of the other elements of damage is recoverable whether she suffered a permanent injury or not.

PROOF OF DAMAGES

20. The fact that the precise amount of damages which B. Yonda Scope has suffered or will suffer may be difficult to ascertain does not affect her right to recover those damages or your right to award them. Although you may not render a verdict based upon mere speculation or guesswork, the law allows B. Yonda Scope reasonable leeway in her method and proof of damages, so long as there is a reasonable basis in the evidence for you to estimate what her damages have been and likely will be. Starlings v. Ski Round Top Corporation, 493 F. Supp. 507 (M.D. Pa. 1980); Weinglass v. Gibson, 304 Pa. 203, 207 (1931).

Respectfully submitted,

_____

YOUR ATTORNEY
Attorney for Plaintiffs

Voir Dire Questions

YOUR ATTORNEY
Identification Number 1234567   ATTORNEY FOR PLAINTIFFS
24 North Lawyer Row
My City, My State 98765-4321
(123) 555-5555

RICK CHASER   COURT OF COMMON PLEAS
    and
N. TARA GATORESE   CIVIL DIVISION
    v.
CITY OF PHILADELPHIA   DOCKET NUMBER: 7654321

VOIR DIRE QUESTIONS

A.   Attorneys and Parties

1.   Does anyone on this jury panel know me?

2.   Do any of you know Lit. E. Gator, who represents the defendant, City of Philadelphia, or anyone from the Office of the City Solicitor?

3.   Does anyone on this panel know either of my clients, Rick Chaser and N. Tara Gatorese?

4.   Does anyone know these potential witnesses: Jerry Verdict, Lee Ding Questions, or C.U. Fall?

B.   Personal

5.   Can you each tell me your current marital status?

6.   Are any of you or your immediate families employed by a company engaged in the casualty or liability insurance business?

7.   Are any of you or your immediate families stockholders in any company which, in whole or in part, is engaged in the casualty or liability insurance company?

8.   Are any of you or your immediate families now employed, or have any of you or your immediate families ever been employed, as a claims adjuster or otherwise by a company or concern which, in whole or in part, was engaged in the casualty or liability insurance business?

9.   Are any of you or your immediate families now employed, or have any of you or your immediate families ever been employed, by the City of Philadelphia?

10. Can I ask each of you to tell me the type of work in which you and your spouse, if you are married, are at present involved and for how long?

11. Have any of you, or has any member of your family, ever been involved in an auto accident which resulted in the filing of any type of claim, either by or against you or some member of your family?

12. Have any of you ever been on a jury which tried an auto accident? When?

13. Have any of you ever sat on a jury panel in any kind of case? Type of case? When?

14. Most people know the facts must be proven beyond a reasonable doubt in criminal cases. Does everyone understand and accept that this is a civil case where facts are proven by a preponderance of the evidence which is not nearly as strict as a test as beyond a reasonable doubt, and requires much less evidence? In other words, does everyone understand that the test is not beyond a reasonable doubt, but rather "more likely than not"?

C.   Attitudes

15. Is there anyone on this panel who feels that a person injured by someone else's conduct should not sue for monetary compensation as a result of those injuries?

16. How many in this room feel that persons injured in an accident as a result of the negligence of another person should just bear his/her own losses and pain and suffering?

17. Has anyone here or any members of their families or any close acquaintance ever been sued? If so, did you feel that lawsuit against you was unjustified? Would the fact that you were sued make it difficult for you to sit as a fair and impartial juror in this case?

18. Is there anyone here who has any feelings for any reason against persons claiming money damages in personal injury cases?

19. Is there anyone among the panel who believes that there are too many personal injury lawsuits?

20. Is there anyone on this panel who, for religious or any other reason, does not believe in medicine, in doctors, or that a person may require professional medical treatment for physical pain and suffering?

D.   Damages

21. How many in this room have any personal convictions, fixed opinions, or religious beliefs that might make it difficult for you to award substantial compensation to these plaintiffs for the injuries they suffered, if the evidence during this trial supports such damages?

22. Do you agree that the size of the award you may make in this case should be in proportion to the seriousness of the injuries proven during the trial?

23. Have any of you ever been involved in, or is there now pending, either by you or against you, any litigation growing out of a civil action for negligence, and in particular, with regard to personal injuries?

24. Can each of you make a commitment to me that you will pay close attention to and fully consider and calculate the value of each element of damages on which His Honor the Judge instructs you at the end of this trial in reaching your verdict rather than just selecting an amount of money that feels as if it should be enough regardless of the evidence and the instructions, assuming the evidence will support a verdict for the plaintiffs?

25. Does anyone disagree with the concept that the City of Philadelphia has the same status as any other defendant and that it has duties and obligations which may render it legally responsible if it fails to fulfill those obligations?

26. Would anyone have difficulty returning a verdict against the City of Philadelphia if you felt that it had failed to fulfill the obligations imposed on it by law?

E.   General

27. Is there any reason whatsoever, why any member of this panel cannot sit and listen to the evidence in this case for several days, paying close and careful attention to it? Any reason, whether physical, or any other, why any of you cannot do that?

28. As you know, each party to a lawsuit is entitled to have his or her case tried by an unbiased and impartial jury, free from all prejudices or influences that would affect the decision. An attorney for any of the parties has a duty to his client to see to it that such a jury is selected, and this is my purpose in these questions. It is not my purpose to pry into your private life or to cause you embarrassment, but only to secure for my clients the fair trial to which they are entitled. I, therefore, ask you whether any of you know of any other matter, anything which I have not covered in my questions, which would for any reason influence you or prevent you from rendering a fair and impartial verdict in the case?

29. Is there any reason whatever, whether I have mentioned it or not, why any of you feel you cannot be fair and impartial jurors in this case?

30. Is there any member of the panel who would, for any reason whatsoever, prefer not to sit on this jury?

Respectfully submitted,

_____

IMA LAWYER
Attorney for Plaintiffs

Interrogatories-Execution

YOUR ATTORNEY   ATTORNEY FOR PLAINTIFF
Identification Number 12345
24 North Lawyer Row
My City, My State 98765-4321
(123) 555-5555

Anita Bank   COURT OF COMMON PLEAS

v.   CIVIL DIVISION

Hyden D. Cash   JULY TERM, 2005

                                        NO.: 0000

PLAINTIFF'S INTERROGATORIES IN AID OF EXECUTION
DIRECTED TO DEFENDANT

INSTRUCTIONS

A. You are required to file answers under oath to the following interrogatories within 30 days after service upon you, pursuant to Rule 3117 of the Pennsylvania Rules of Civil Procedure.

B. As used herein, the words "you" and "your" refer to the Defendant and Defendant's agents, representatives, attorneys, and all other persons acting or purporting to act on behalf of Defendant.

C. As used herein, "identify" or "identity", when used in reference to an individual person or entity, means to state his, her, or its name and address.

D. If a precise value, amount, or date cannot be supplied in responses to an Interrogatory, an approximate value, amount, or date should be provided.

INTERROGATORIES

1. Do you own any interest in real estate?

    If so, as to each such interest, state:

    (a) the location of the real estate;

    (b) the nature of your interest in the real estate;

    (c) the date you acquired such interest;

    (d) the amount which you paid to acquire such interest; and,

    (e) whether there are any mortgages on such real estate. If there are any such mortgages, as to each mortgage, state:

        (i) the identity of the mortgage;

        (ii) the amount of the original mortgage obligation; and,

        (iii) the outstanding obligations of the mortgage.

2. Have you conveyed any interest in any real estate to anyone within the last 12 months?

If so, as to each such conveyance, state:

    (a) the description of the real estate;

    (b) the interest which you conveyed;

    (c) the identity of the person to whom you conveyed that interest; and,

    (d) the consideration which you received.

3. Do you hold as mortgagee a mortgage in any real estate?

If so, as to each such mortgage state:

> (a) the description of the real estate;
>
> (b) the date on which you acquired the mortgage;
>
> (c) the original principal amount of the mortgage;
>
> (d) the outstanding balance due on the mortgage; and,
>
> (e) the identity of the mortgagor.

4. Do you own any automobiles, trucks, vessels, aircraft, or other vehicles?

If so, as to each such vehicle state:

> (a) the make, model, and year of the vehicle;
>
> (b) the identity of the registered owner of the vehicle;
>
> (c) the governmental agency registering the vehicle and the registration number; and,
>
> (d) the location of the vehicle.

5. Is anyone indebted to you in an amount in excess of $100.00?

If so, for each such indebtedness state:

> (a) the identity of the individual or entity which is indebted to you;
>
> (b) the amount of such indebtedness; and,
>
> (c) the date on which the indebtedness is due.

6. Do you have any savings, money market, or checking accounts, or certificates of deposit?

If so, as to each such account or certificate, state:

(a) the identity of the depository institution for the account or certificate of deposit;

(b) the title and registered owner or holder of the account or certificate of deposit; and,

(e) the current balance of the account or certificate of deposit.

7. Do you have or use any safe deposit box or other similar storage facility?

If so, as to each such facility state:

(a) the identity of the institution in which you rent, lease, or use such a facility;

(b) the box or other identifying number for such facility;

(c) the name under which such facility is rented, leased, or used; and,

(d) the contents of such facility.

8. Do you own or have any interest in any stocks, bonds, mutual funds, money market funds, or other securities or negotiable instruments?

If so, as to each such interest state:

(a) a full description of the stock, bond, security, or negotiable instrument;

(b) the par or face value of such stock, bond, security, or negotiable instrument;

(c) the registered and beneficial holders of the stock certificate, bond, security, or negotiable instrument;

(d) the dates on which interest or dividends are payable;

(e) the maturity date of any bond;

(f) the identity of the custodian of any and all documents evidencing the interest; and,

(g) the location of any and all such documents.

9. Do you own any jewelry, furniture, office equipment, precious metals or stones, television sets, radios, record players, antiques or collectibles, electrical appliances, power or hand tools, photographic equipment, works of art, furs, musical instruments, rare books or maps, collections of coins or stamps, silver or china, or other personality with an individual or collective value exceeding $250.00?

If so, as to each such item state:

(a) a full and complete description of such item and its present condition;

(b) the location of such item;

(c) whether or not such item is subject to any security interest; and,

(d) the identity of the holder of any such interest.

10. Are you a beneficiary of any trust fund?

If so, as to each trust fund state:

(a) the nature of the trust;

(b) the nature of your interest therein; and,

(c) the identity of each trustee.

11. Do you own any patents, inventions, trade names, trade secrets, trademarks, service marks, or copyrights?

If so, as to each such item state:

(a) a full and complete description of each item; and,

(b) the number of any other identifying features of such item.

12. Do you own any warehouse receipts, bills of lading, or other documents of title? If so, as to each such item, state:

(a) the identity of such item;

(b) the location of such item;

(c) whether or not such item is subject to any such security interest; and,

(d) the identity of the holder of any such security interest.

13. Are you the plaintiff in any lawsuit which is pending or in which a verdict of judgment has not been satisfied in whole or part?

14. Have you applied for a loan or mortgage within the last three years? If so, as to each such loan or mortgage application state:

(a) where you applied for such loan;

(b) whether or not you were granted such loan;

(c) the amount granted for such loan; and,

(d) what you did with the proceeds of such loan, if any.

15. In the last three years, have you acted as co-maker, guarantor, or endorser of any loan? If so, provide full details as to each such loan and your relationship thereto, including the amount of the loan.

16. Have you issued or furnished any financial statements within the last three years? If so, as to each such financial statement state:

(a) the identity of such financial statement and

(b) to whom such financial statement was issued.

17. Are you a party to a contract of any kind? If so, as to each such contract state:

    (a) the identity of such contract;

    (b) the nature of such contract; and,

    (c) the identity of the person or entity with whom you entered into the contract.

18. Does any governmental body owe you any money? If so, provide full and complete details thereof.

19. Have you made any claim under any policy of insurance within the last three years?

If so, as to each such claim state:

    (a) the name of the insurer;

    (b) the policy number;

    (c) the facts given rise to such claim; and

    (d) whether or not such claim has been paid.

20. Do you own or have interest in any partnerships or limited partnerships? If so, as to each such interest state:

    (a) a full and complete description of the partnership or limited partnership, including but not limited to, its name, purpose, assets, registered address, and the identity of each of its general partners;

    (b) the identity of the agreement or agreements governing the affairs of the partnership;

    (c) the nature and extent of the interest;

(d) the value of the interest, if any; and,

(e) the name under which the interest is owned or otherwise held by you.

21. Do you own or have any interest in any business, corporation, partnership, or joint venture other than those identified in responses to the foregoing interrogatories? If so, as to each, state:

(a) the identity of the business, corporation, partnership, or joint venture and

(b) a full and complete description of you interest in same.

22. Do you own or have interest in any asset or item of value individually or collectively worth in excess of $500.00 other than those identified in response to the foregoing interrogatories? If so, for each such asset or item state:

(a) a full and complete description of the asset or item;

(b) the nature of your interest in the assets or item; and,

(c) the value of the asset or item.

23. Are you unable to pay any of your debts or obligations? If so, provide full and complete details thereof.

_____

IMA LAWYER
Attorney for Plaintiff

Interrogatories-Attachment

YOUR ATTORNEY   ATTORNEY FOR PLAINTIFF
Identification Number 12345
24 North Lawyer Row
My City, My State 98765-4321
(123) 555-5555

Anita Bank   COURT OF COMMON PLEAS
     v.   CIVIL DIVISION
Hyden D. Cash   JULY TERM, 2002
                                                 NO.: 0000

INTERROGATORIES IN ATTACHMENT

TO: (Fill in the blank)

You must file with the Court answers to the following interrogatories within thirty (30) days after service upon you. Failure to do so may result in a default judgment being entered against you. A copy of said answers must be served on the undersigned. If your answer to any of the foregoing interrogatories is affirmative, specify the amount, value and/or nature of the subject property.

1. At the time you were served or at any subsequent time, did you owe the defendant(s) any money, were you liable to defendant(s) on any negotiable or other written instrument, or did defendant(s) claim that you owed any money or were liable to defendant(s) for any reason?

2. At the time you were served or at any subsequent time, was there in your possession, custody or control, or in the joint possession, custody or control of yourself or one or more other persons any property of any nature owned solely or in part by the defendant(s)?

3. At any time you were served or at any subsequent time, did you hold legal title to any property of any nature owned solely or in part by the defendant(s) or in which defendant(s) held or claimed interest?

4. At any time you were served or at any subsequent time, did you hold as a fiduciary any property in which defendant(s) had an interest?

5. At any time before or after you were served, did the defendant(s) transfer or deliver any property to you or any person or place pursuant to your direction or consent, and if so, what was the consideration therefor?

6. At the time you were served or at any subsequent time, did you pay, transfer, or deliver any money or property to the defendant(s) or to any person or place pursuant to the direction of defendant(s) against you?

7. At the time you were served or at any subsequent time, did you have or share any safe-deposit boxes, pledges, documents of time, securities, notes, coupons, receivable, or collateral in which there was an interest claimed by defendant(s)?

8. Identify every account (not previously noted), title in the name defendant(s) of in which you believe defendant(s) have an interest or whole or part, whether or not styled as a payroll account, individual retirement account, tax account, lottery account, partnership account, joint or tenants by entirety account, insurance account, trust or escrow account, attorney's account, or otherwise.

BY: _____

IMA LAWYER
Attorney for Plaintiff

This page intentionally left blank.

AO 89 (Rev. 5/85) Subpoena

United States District Court

—— DISTRICT OF ——

V.

SUBPOENA

CASE NUMBER:

TYPE OF CASE		SUBPOENA FOR	
☐ CIVIL ☐ CRIMINAL		☐ PERSON	☐ DOCUMENT(S) or OBJECT(S)

TO:

YOU ARE HEREBY COMMANDED to appear in the United States District Court at the place, date, and time specified below to testify in the above case.

PLACE	COURTROOM
	DATE AND TIME

YOU ARE ALSO COMMANDED to bring with you the following document(s) or object(s): *

☐ *See additional information on reverse*

This subpoena shall remain in effect until you are granted leave to depart by the court or by an officer acting on behalf of the court.

████ OR CLERK OF COURT	*Michael E. Kunz* MICHAEL E. KUNZ	DATE
(BY) DEPUTY CLERK		

This subpoena is issued upon application of the:	QUESTIONS MAY BE ADDRESSED TO:
☐ Plaintiff ☐ Defendant ☐ U.S. Attorney	ATTORNEY'S NAME, ADDRESS AND PHONE NUMBER

*If not applicable, enter "none".

AO 89 (Rev. 5/85) Subpoena

RETURN OF SERVICE(1)		
RECEIVED BY SERVER	DATE	PLACE
SERVED	DATE	PLACE
SERVED ON (NAME)		FEES AND MILEAGE TENDERED TO WITNESS(2) ☐ YES ☐ NO AMOUNT $_____
SERVED BY		TITLE

STATEMENT OF SERVICE FEES		
TRAVEL	SERVICES	TOTAL

DECLARATION OF SERVER (2)

I declare under penalty of perjury under the laws of the United States of America that the foregoing information contained in the Return of Service and Statement of Service Fees is true and correct.

Executed on_____   _____
Date   *Signature of Server*

                                            _____
                                               Address of Server

ADDITIONAL INFORMATION

---

(1) As to who may serve a subpoena and the manner of its service see Rule 17(d), Federal Rules of Criminal Procedure, or Rule 45(c), Federal Rules of Civil Procedure.

(2) "Fees and mileage need not be tendered to the deponent upon service of a subpoena issued on behalf of the United States or an officer or agency thereof (Rule 45(c), Federal Rules of Civil Procedure; Rule 17(d), Federal Rules of Criminal Procedure) or on behalf of certain indigent parties and criminal defendants who are unable to pay such costs (28 USC 1825, Rule 17(b) Federal Rules of Criminal Procedure)".

appendix b:
Checklists and Worksheets

Checklist 1:   Car Accident Checklist 266

Checklist 2:   Fall-Down Accident Checklist 270

Checklist 3:   Medical Treatment Worksheet 272

Checklist 4:   After the Accident Until Settlement Checklist 275

Checklist 5:   Lawsuit Checklist 277

Car Accident Checklist

Description of the Accident:

Description of the accident:

Date of accident:

Time of day:

Day of week:

Location:

Direction in which each car was traveling:

Parties Involved

Names, addresses, and phone numbers of driver of each car:

Names, addresses, and phone numbers of owner of each car:

Names, addresses, and phone numbers of passengers in each car:

Names, addresses, and phone numbers of all witnesses:

from doing daily activities. Remember, if you cannot perform daily activities in your home, you cannot be expected to be productive on the job.

The previous questions are reproduced in the Physical Residual Functional Capacities Questionnaire and can be found in Appendix A.

In the alternative, if the consultative examination concludes otherwise, the SSA may still deny the claims, basing its decision on the fact that you can still perform other work.

Strategy for Winning

In addition to asking the treating doctor questions that will assist the DDS in determining whether or not you meet or equal a listing, the questionnaires will also ask your doctor to render an opinion as to your ability to sit, stand, walk, lift, and bend. In addition, the doctor will be asked whether, with your disability, you would be likely to be absent from work. The answers to these questions are designed to demonstrate that with your limitations, at Step 5 of the sequential evaluation, you cannot be gainfully employed.

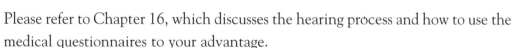

Please refer to Chapter 16, which discusses the hearing process and how to use the medical questionnaires to your advantage.

When to Obtain Medical Questionnaires

In terms of when to obtain medical questionnaires, it is the practice at my office to wait until at least the first denial before we ask the treating doctor to complete a questionnaire. We have adopted this policy not because we do not want to see that our clients get benefits sooner, but because at the initial application stage, there are several agencies involved in the claim. Specifically, the local Social Security district office acts as the fact gatherer collecting the information and the DDS is the evaluator of the information. Often there are time delays as information is being transferred back and forth. As a result, we sometimes do not know where to send the information.

Practical Point

You should never assume that simply because your doctor completes a questionnaire you will be awarded benefits. Provided the SSA has medical records that support the treating doctor's findings, the SSA may conclude that the claimant meets the listings.

LEGALLY SPEAKING

If you have the support of your doctor, and the SSA denies your claim, at the hearing stage you can argue before the judge that the SSA regulations state that the weight of a treating doctor should be considered over the finding of the consultative examination.

Submitting Questionnaires to Your Doctor

Assuming you have been denied benefits and have now filed for the first appeal, take the appropriate questionnaire to your treating doctor at your next appointment. During the visit, ask that he or she complete the form while you wait. Note that the form can be filled out by pen and the majority of the questions can be answered by checking boxes.

Once the report is completed, submit it to the SSA. However, where your claim is in the appeal process will determine where to submit your report. That is, if your claim is still being processed by the local Social Security office, send it there. However, if you have requested a hearing and have received an acknowledgment that your claim has been received by the Office of Disability, Adjudication, and Review (ODAR), you should send the report to that office.

- If you are at the Request for Reconsideration level, send the report directly to the DDS office that is evaluating the claim. You should also have a name of the person assigned to the claim. If the DDS is not handling the claim, send the report to the local Social Security office assigned to your claim.

Area Around the Accident

Number of lanes of each street:

One way or two way:

Condition of roadways:

Slope of each street:

Photographs of the scene:

Amount of traffic:

Traffic controls (lights, stop signs, etc.):

Vehicle Description

Speed of each vehicle at the time of impact and just before impact:

Length of any skid marks:

Use of brakes by each vehicle:

Use of horn by each vehicle:

Use of turn signals by each vehicle:

Point of impact on each car:

Movement of each car upon impact:

Final position of each vehicle:

License plate numbers of each vehicle:

Location of your car now:

Date the car was purchased:

Photographs of damage to each car:

Damage done to the vehicles:

Years, makes, and models:

Driver's license number:

Trip

Place where the trip began:

Destination:

Purpose of the trip:

Scheduled arrival time:

Conditions

Lighting conditions:

Weather:

Use of sunglasses:

Position of the sun:

Use of alcohol/drugs by any passenger or driver:

Use of car phones:

Use of radio/car stereo:

Use of windshield wipers:

Windows open or closed:

Use of defroster:

Use of glasses/contact lenses:

Driver smoking, eating, or drinking at the time of the accident:

Seat belt:

Stick shift or automatic transmission:

Last eye examination:

Name and address of eye doctor:

Injuries

Movement of your body at the moment of impact:

What part of your body came into contact with the vehicle:

Pain at the moment of impact:

Name of your insurance company: Policy number:

Coverages:

All auto insurance in your household:

Health insurance company: Policy number:

Coverages:

Fall-Down Accident Checklist

Description of Accident

Description of the accident:

Names, addresses, and phone numbers of all witnesses:

Date of the accident: Time of day: Day of week:

Location of the accident:

Condition of the accident area (e.g., sidewalk):

Photographs of the scene:

Place where the trip began:

Destination:

Purpose of the trip:

Scheduled arrival time:

Conditions Surrounding the Accident

Smoking, eating, or drinking at the time of the accident:

Last eye examination:

Name and address of eye doctor:

Use of headphones:

Lighting conditions:

Weather:

Position of the sun:

Use of sunglasses:

Use of alcohol/drugs:

Objects carried at time of accident:

Type and condition of shoes:

All conversation at the scene:

Police Involvement

Police district involved:

Name and badge number of officer:

Injury

What happened to your body as you fell:

What parts of your body came into contact with the ground:

How did you feel immediately after you fell:

Health insurance company: Policy number:

Coverages:

Medical Treatment Worksheet

Injury

Injuries as a result of the accident:

Type of pain (sharp or dull, constant or intermittent):

Hospital

Name and address of ambulance company:

Name and address of emergency room:

Mode of transportation to the emergency room:

Treatment at emergency room:

Medication:

Orthopedic appliances:

Arrival and departure times:

Mode of transportation home:

Condition for the rest of the day/night:

Ability to sleep:

Condition the next morning:

Continued Treatment

Name, address, phone number, and specialty of your family doctor:

Names, addresses, phone numbers, and specialty of all doctors/therapists seen for your injuries:

Mode of transportation:

Purpose of visits:

Referral source for each doctor:

Results of first doctor visit:

Results of subsequent visits:

Description of treatments/therapy:

Exercises:

Whirlpool:

Orthopedic appliances:

Dates of treatment for each doctor/therapist:

Medication:

Date of last medical treatment:

Continuing Effects

Pain when discharged:

Medical instructions upon discharge:

Pain since discharge:

Pain today:

Surgery:

Effect of accident on your normal daily activities:

Effect on household duties:

Effect on exercise/sports:

Effect on driving:

Effect on sleeping:

Effect on social activities:

Marital difficulties:

Emotional reaction to your injuries:

Your physical/emotional condition before the accident:

Prior/subsequent accidents:

Prior/subsequent injuries:

Prior/subsequent doctors:

Effect on Work

Next scheduled day of work after the accident:

Time missed because of the accident:

Reason for missing time:

Effect of accident on ability to work after return to your job:

Work schedule:

Average weekly wage:

Name, phone number, and address of supervisor:

After the Accident Until Settlement Checklist

Initial Steps

☐ Keep this book handy and read it.

☐ Be sure the Car Accident Worksheet or the Fall-Down Accident Worksheet, is filled out and stored for safe keeping.

☐ Go to the emergency room.

Background Work

☐ Consider hiring a private investigator to take statements and photographs.

☐ Contact witnesses and obtain favorable statements.

☐ Take photographs of the accident scene, property damage, and bruises and scars.

☐ Obtain the police report.

☐ Continue medical treatment and begin physical therapy.

☐ Keep a journal of your pain and suffering and daily activities.

☐ Get a copy of the property damage appraisal.

Legal Negotiations

☐ Negotiate settlement of the property damage claim.

☐ Consider whether to retain an attorney.

☐ Interview several personal injury lawyers.

☐   Negotiate a favorable contingent fee agreement.

☐   Send opening letters to the defendant and the insurance company.

☐   Take care of required insurance company forms and statements.

☐   Stay in close contact with any attorney your hire.

Help Your Lawyer

☐   Gather proof of lost earnings.

☐   Begin gathering your medical bills and reports.

☐   Keep all medical appointments.

☐   Send copies of all documents pertaining to the case to your lawyer.

☐   Make notes regarding your treatment and injuries.

☐   Research the statute of limitations deadline.

☐   Begin to gather information on settlements of similar cases.

☐   Gather final medical bills and reports after conclusion of treatment.

☐   Prepare a settlement demand letter.

☐   Contact insurance company to begin settlement negotiations.

☐   Settle the case.

☐   Sign a release.

☐   Get the settlement check.

Lawsuit Checklist

Research

☐   Consider the type of lawsuit and location where it should be filed.

☐   Make sure you are still within the statute of limitations deadline.

☐   Research complaint drafting.

☐   Carefully prepare the lawsuit papers.

Before the Proceedings Begin

☐   File the suit with the court.

☐   Promptly and properly serve the suit papers on the defendants.

☐   Make contact with the defendant's lawyer.

☐   Send interrogatories and request for production of documents to the defendant's lawyer.

☐   Complete gathering any proof of losses and damages that you will need to prove your case.

☐   File a discovery motion if answers to interrogatories and response to request for production of documents are not received promptly. (see form 9.)

Once the Process has Begun

☐   Take the defendant's deposition.

☐   Prepare for your deposition.

☐   Return to your doctor if your symptoms persist.

☑ Be sure to document loss of earning capacity, if any, by retaining a vocational expert and/or an economist.

☑ Obtain a disability statement if you are claiming lost earnings.

☑ Be sure your medical evidence has a statement causally linking the accident to your injuries.

☑ Be sure your medical evidence has a statement as to future surgeries and medical bills, if necessary.

☐ Prepare for any independent medical examinations.

☐ Respond promptly to any motions filed by the defendant's attorney.

☐ Prepare for any settlement or pre-trial conferences that are scheduled.

☐ Schedule videotape depositions of any doctors or expert witnesses.

☐ Prepare carefully for those depositions.

☐ Prepare your testimony.

☐ Prepare cross-examination of the defendant and defendant's fact witnesses.

☐ Subpoena your witnesses for trial.

☐ Prepare your witnesses for testimony.

☐ Prepare your opening and closing statements.

☐ Prepare your voir dire questions.

☐ Prepare your jury instructions.

☐ Prepare to cross-examine the defendant's expert witnesses.

☑ Familiarize yourself with the state and local or federal rules of evidence.

☑ Familiarize yourself with state and local or federal rules of civil procedure.

☐ Familiarize yourself with the rules of appellate procedure.

Index

A

administrative law judge, 76
advertisement, 47
alternate dispute resolution (ADR), 131, 132
ambulance chasers, 45, 183
Americans with Disabilities Act, 76
appeals, 174, 176
appraisals, 142
arbitration, 132, 137
   nonbinding, 131, 132
   panel, 106
argumentative, 170
asked and answered, 170
assault, 79
assumes a fact not in evidence, 171
assumption of risk, 167, 168
attorneys, 9, 14, 15, 32, 35, 36, 41, 86, 153, 183
   changing, 54, 55, 56
   costs, 53
   consultation, 14, 15, 48, 49
   dissatisfaction with, 53, 54
   fee agreement, 51, 52, 88
   finding , 45, 46, 47
   handling your case without, 17, 19
   law firms, 57, 58, 59
   referrals, 47
   reputation, 107
attractive nuisance, 67
auto accidents, 1, 2, 3, 6, 9, 10, 12–16, 20–25, 31, 32, 33, 34, 38–42, 45, 49, 50, 53, 57, 64, 65, 78, 79, 98, 99, 104, 108, 109, 110, 117, 138, 144, 170, 178

B

bar association, 46
battery, 79
beyond a reasonable doubt, 157
beyond the scope, 169
binding arbitration, 131, 132
burden of proof, 157, 173

C

catastrophic injury, 107
causation, 165
children, 63, 64, 65, 68, 69, 95, 160
civil procedure, 142

closing argument, 171, 172
comparative negligence, 42, 67, 167
complaint, 137, 182, 196, 199
contingency fee agreement, 51, 52, 71, 88, 241
credibility, 106, 107, 159, 179
cross-examination, 158, 159

D

damages, 79, 85, 88, 101, 102, 103, 104, 106, 162, 163, 164
    punitive, 79, 104
defamation, 80
defense medical examination (DME), 126, 146, 147, 148
demand letters, 100, 113, 114, 115, 116
    skipping, 116
depositions, 32, 41, 61, 122, 141, 142, 143, 144, 145
direct examination, 157, 158, 160
discovery, 40, 57, 60, 141, 142, 178, 238, 239
docket, 42
dog bite, 67, 69
    defenses, 68
    one free bite rule, 67

E

earning capacity, 162, 163, 164
electromyography, 106, 107
emergency room, 9, 10, 28, 114, 120, 158, 183
enhanced damages, 103
exchange of documents, 141
expert witnesses, 89, 90, 91, 146, 161

F

fall-down accident, 7, 40, 65, 66, 73, 74, 78, 99, 103, 166, 173

fault, 63
    admission of, 1
firms, 57, 58
first contact, 21
food poisoning, 72, 73
fraud, 181

G

good injuries, 99

H

health-care providers, 97, 108
hearsay, 43
herniated disc, 103, 105, 106, 107, 110, 111, 118
high-low arbitration, 131, 132

I

independent medical examination (IME), 141, 146
initial consultation, 48, 49
injuries
    aggravation, 105
    intentional injuries, 79
    pre-dated, 104
    psychological, 81
    severity, 107
insurance companies, 13, 14, 15, 18, 35, 56, 98, 115
    fraud, 181, 182
interrogatories, 40, 41, 141, 177, 178, 203, 219, 252, 260
invitees, 66

J

journals, 33
judgments
    collecting, 176, 177, 178

juries
  deliberations, 172, 173
  instructions, 172
  selecting, 152, 153, 154, 155
jury research, 111, 112
Jury Verdict Research, 111
Jury Verdict Review and Analysis, 46, 112

L

lawsuits, 9, 57, 133, 139
  choice of trials, 137, 138
  choice of venue, 138, 139
  handling your, 36, 37, 38, 39, 40
  keeping your case active, 57
  proving your case, 42
leading question, 168
legal journals, 46
legal malpractice, 69, 70, 71, 72
liability, 13, 15, 38, 53, 65, 66, 67, 80, 83
  products, 78, 79
  strict, 78
libel, 80
licensees, 66
listservs, 58, 59
loss of consortium, 164, 165
loss of earnings, 162, 163, 164

M

managed care, 98
mediation, 131, 132
medical bills, 14, 33, 102, 173
medical malpractice, 83, 86, 87, 90, 93, 95, 96
  determining whether you have a case, 83, 85
  helping your attorney, 94
  hiring an attorney, 86
  settling the claim, 93, 94
  valuing the claim, 92, 93
medical records, 33, 69, 85, 89, 106, 126, 142
medical testimony, 161
medical treatment, 33
motion for a new trial, 174
motion for judgment notwithstanding the verdict, 174
motion to compel discovery, 40, 142

N

negligence, 42, 63, 86, 90, 133
new client letter, 48
no-fault, 63, 73
nonbinding arbitration, 131, 132
nuisance value, 72, 92

O

objections, 168, 169, 170, 171
one free bite rule, 67
opening statements, 155, 156, 157
organizing information, 33, 35

P

padding, 52
pedestrians, 64
peremptory challenges, 154
photographs, 2, 4, 5, 7, 20, 21, 48, 60, 68, 114, 119, 142, 166, 172
physical therapy, 99
police reports, 20, 142
post trial motions, 174
post-traumatic stress disorder, 81
preponderance of the evidence, 157, 173
private investigation, 21
products liability, 78, 79

professional medical opinion, 105
property damage, 108, 142
psychological injuries, 81
punitive damages, 79, 95, 104, 109, 175

R

recorded statements, 23
recross-examination, 160, 167, 170
redirect, 160, 168, 170
referrals, 47
releases, 129
remittutur, 174
removal for cause, 155
repressed memories, 135, 136
request for production of documents, 40,
    141, 142, 236
rescue report, 20

S

scene of the accident, 2, 142
service of process, 39
settlement, 15, 18, 19, 33, 35, 36, 57, 60, 74,
    93, 108, 110, 113, 115, 121, 122, 123, 129,
    132
  conference, 122
  demand, 127
  demand letter, 100
  finalizing, 129, 130, 131
  online, 178, 179
  strategy, 123–128
sheriff sale, 177
slander, 80
slip-and-fall accidents, 1, 21, 55, 65, 66, 67,
    156, 173
small claims court, 36
Social Security, 74, 75
  benefits, 76
  hearings, 76, 77

soft tissue injury, 102
standard of care, 86
statutes of limitations, 16, 69, 71, 133, 134,
    135, 136
strict liability, 78
strike, 154
subpoena, 123
surgery, 103

T

testimony, 61, 69, 90, 126, 157
tort reform, 93, 95
treatment, 9, 33, 99, 106
trespasser, 66
trials, 67, 151, 152, 153, 154, 155, 156, 157,
    158, 159, 160, 161
  defense's case, 166

U

unauthorized practice of law, 19
unfair insurance practice statute, 182, 183
uninsured motorist coverage, 14

V

valuing an injury, 102, 104, 109, 111
venue, 138, 139
verdict finder, 111
verdicts, 173
voir dire, 152, 248

W

witnesses, 20, 89, 142
  expert, 89, 90, 91, 146, 161
workers' compensation, 73, 74

About the Author

Evan Aidman is the founder and principal of the Law Offices of Evan K. Aidman. Mr. Aidman received a Bachelor's Degree in psychology from the University of Florida where he was elected to the Phi Beta Kappa Scholastic Honor Society. He graduated from the University of Pennsylvania Law School, an Ivy League Institution, in 1983.

Mr. Aidman began his legal career as a law clerk for the Honorable Samuel M. Lehrer of the Philadelphia Court of Common Pleas. After five years as an associate in various law firms, Mr. Aidman hung out his own shingle. He has been practicing as a trial lawyer ever since.

Mr. Aidman is licensed to practice in the states of Pennsylvania and New Jersey. He won a $1.5 million verdict in 2003 for a wrongful death claim arising out of a bar room shooting. This case was covered by Philadelphia Daily News. The article is available on the firm's website, **www.LegalAidman.com**.

Mr. Aidman also moderates both a personal injury chat and a personal injury message board on this website. More that 1,000 individuals have contacted him in the last five years for legal help via email, chat, phone, instant message, or fax after visiting **www.LegalAidman.com**. Interested readers should check his chats and message board for more information.

The typical cases handled by the Law Offices of Evan K. Aidman involve:

◆ automobile accidents;
◆ fall-down accidents;
◆ accidents as work;
◆ medical malpractice;

- ◆ products liability (injuries caused by faulty equipment);
- ◆ food poisoning; and,
- ◆ legal malpractice.

The firm has an ever-broadening national network of trial lawyers, to whom referrals are made when the firm is not able to provide direct legal representation.

Mr. Aidman has served as an arbitrator of legal disputes on many occasions in the past twenty years. These arbitrations typically involve panels of three attorneys who sit in judgment of various types of disputes. He frequently serves as the chairman of such arbitration panels.

Mr. Aidman is a daily contributor to and participator in a trial lawyers' computer listserv. This listserv is a sounding board for top trial lawyers to share information in a dynamic format concerning the battlefront issues in personal injury litigation.

Mr. Aidman resides in Wynnewood, PA.